THE ADDISON-WESLEY NETWORKING BASICS SERIES

Connecting to the Internet

The Addison-Wesley Networking Basics Series

The Addison-Wesley Networking Basics Series is a set of concise, hands-on guides to today's key technologies and protocols in computer networking. Each book in the series covers a focused topic and explains the steps required to implement and work with specific technologies and tools in network programming, administration, and security. Providing practical, problem-solving information, these books are written by practicing professionals who have mastered complex network challenges.

Geoff Mulligan, *Removing the SPAM: Email Processing and Filtering,* 0-201-37957-0

John W. Stewart III, *BGP4: Inter-Domain Routing in the Internet,* 0-201-37951-1

Brian Tung, *Kerberos: A Network Authentication System,* 0-201-37924-4

Andrew F. Ward, *Connecting to the Internet: A Practical Guide about LAN-Internet Connectivity,* 0-201-37956-2

Visit the Series Web site for new title information:
http://www.awl.com/cseng/networkingbasics/

Connecting to the Internet

A Practical Guide about LAN–Internet Connectivity

WITHDRAWN

Andrew F. Ward UTSA LIBRARIES

Addison-Wesley
An imprint of Addison Wesley Longman, Inc.
Reading, Massachusetts • Harlow, England • Menlo Park, California
Berkeley, California • Don Mills, Ontario • Sydney • Bonn
Amsterdam • Tokyo • Mexico City

Many of the designations used by manufacturers and sellers to distinguish their products are claimed as trademarks. Where those designations appear in this book, and Addison Wesley Longman, Inc., was aware of a trademark claim, the designations have been printed in initial capital letters or in all capitals.

The author and publisher have taken care in the preparation of this book, but make no expressed or implied warranty of any kind and assume no responsibility for errors or omissions. No liability is assumed for incidental or consequential damages in connection with or arising out of the use of the information or programs contained herein.

The publisher offers discounts on this book when ordered in quantity for special sales. For more information, please contact:

AWL Direct Sales
Addison Wesley Longman, Inc.
One Jacob Way
Reading, Massachusetts 01867
(781) 944-3700

Visit AWL on the Web: www.awl.com/cseng/

Library of Congress Cataloging-in-Publication Data

Ward, Andrew F.
 Connecting to the Inernet : a practical guide about LAN-Internet connectivity / Andrew F. Ward.
   p. c.m.—(The Addison-Wesley networking basics series)
 Includes bibliographical references and index.
  ISBN 0-201-37956-2
  1. Internet (Computer network) 2. Local area networks (Computer networks) I. Title. II. Series.
 TK5105.875.I57W375 1999
 004.67'8—dc21   98–51310
                                                        CIP

ISBN 0-201-37956-2
Text printed on recycled paper.
1 2 3 4 5 6 7 8 9 10—CRW—02010099
First printing, February 1999

Contents

Preface—
Look before You Leap

As Internet usage continues to grow throughout the world, increasing numbers of network administrators face the task of connecting their local area networks (LANs) to the Internet. For these personnel, this project represents an entirely new challenge, and in some cases a daunting one. After all, there is much to consider when implementing a dedicated connection to the Internet.

In the past, only a small group of people possessed the skills and knowledge needed to build an Internet connection. Until recently, the Internet was not a huge network. Furthermore, until the 1990s, access was too expensive for small and midsize organizations. Lower access prices and an increase in the number of ISPs, however, have now led to a pervasive expansion of the Internet.

Today, network professionals need basic information about how to connect their LANs to the Internet. This book seeks to fill this information gap and explain the process of building and maintaining a dedicated connection from the LAN to the Internet. Unlike other networking projects, building a dedicated Internet connection poses a unique challenge because it requires functional expertise in a range of technical subjects, including:

- TCP/IP
- Internet services and functions
- Wide area networking
- Security
- Network architecture
- Testing and validation procedures

Moreover, constructing an Internet connection usually requires the administrator to involve other external parties, such as the Internet service provider (ISP), the telecommunications vendor, and sometimes a consultant (or two). Thus the process of connecting the LAN to the Internet requires both technical and project management expertise.

Many excellent books focus on specific aspects of Internet connectivity. In particular, the most popular subjects are TCP/IP and security. Excellent books can also be found on wide area networks (WANs) and Internet-specific topics such as Domain Name System (DNS). Yet, few books bring together the pertinent parts of these technical subjects in a manner that enables the reader to start building a connection without overloading him or her with unnecessary information. This book focuses on what is immediate and necessary to build such a connection.

This book really describes the process of connecting your LAN to the Internet. Its structure reflects the order in which you carry out tasks necessary to build an Internet connection. Each chapter discusses one particular element of the construction process, providing both conceptual information and useful tips on how to avoid common pitfalls in the construction process.

With the exception of Chapter 1, which provides additional information about TCP/IP and Internet services that is pertinent to building a connection, each chapter includes a checklist of key points to address when you build your connection. This book is your travel guide to putting your LAN on the Internet.

Audience

This book is intended for network and system administrators who are implementing an Internet connection for the first time, as well as managers who are overseeing the construction of such a connection. We have attempted to make the book international in scope so that the contents will prove useful to administrators throughout the world.

Prerequisites

Only one prerequisite exists for readers of this book—an understanding of the TCP/IP communications protocol. In particular, we assume the reader has a basic knowledge of the following:

- OSI Reference Model
- IP addressing

- Subnet masking
- Default gateways
- Domain Name System (DNS)

Acknowledgments

I never really understood why authors write acknowledgements until I wrote a book myself. Now I understand. Most books, including this one, are really a joint effort. Although the author may write the words, he or she depends on the support of many folks. This support includes sharing ideas, offering opinions, and encouraging the author's effort.

Without the help of many people, this book would not have been possible. In particular, I owe a world of thanks to Saskia (my spouse) for putting up with my crazy project, especially during weekends when we should have been doing fun things like backpacking. I also wish to thank my family and friends, who helped me keep my sense of humor and direction throughout the writing process.

Many thanks go out to my colleague and friend, Darryl Black, whom I blame entirely for this book. (I am joking, of course!) Without his involvement, technical skills, and encouragement over an occasional beer, I would not have completed this project. I also wish to acknowledge my colleagues at 3Com, from whom I have learned much over the years. Many thanks go to my managers, Scott Graham and Adam Wasylyshyn.

Of course, nothing would have been possible without the guidance of my editor, Mary Hart, and the Addison Wesley Longman team. In addition, I am indebted to the technical reviewers of this text, who shared their experiences, thoughts, and comments on Internet connectivity and made many suggestions about how to improve the book. They include Dustin Andrews, Howard Lee Harkness, Richard P. Jussaume, Brendan Kehoe, Dana Love, Alain Mayer, James McGovern, Ravi Prakash, Thomas H. Ptacek, Ian Redfern, Dan Ritter, and Vincent Stemen.

Andrew F. Ward

TCP/IP Internetworking and Internet Services

This chapter discusses the more advanced elements of TCP/IP internetworking as they pertain to setting up an Internet connection. This discussion assumes that you have a knowledge of TCP/IP and understand its fundamental structure. If not, now is a good time to visit the bookstore (again) and grab a introductory book on TCP/IP. The books written by W. Richard Stevens and Douglas E. Comer are considered some of the best on this subject.[1]

In particular, this chapter concentrates on the mechanics of data link and network layer communications within IP networks. It also provides information about the typical Internet services supported in today's local area networks (LANs). After reading this chapter, you should be able to answer the following questions:

- What are the important layers of the OSI Reference Model in TCP/IP?
- What are the components of packet-based communication?
- How do devices communicate within an IP network?
- What are the common Internet services and how do they operate?

Figure 1-1 helps explain the concepts in TCP/IP that are relevant to Internet connectivity. This basic diagram shows an Internet connection with a few workstations and a web server. We will focus on certain portions of the diagram when explaining how IP networks operate.

---

1. TCP/IP is actually a family of protocols based on IP. Although TCP is merely one of many protocols in the family, TCP/IP has become the standard name for the entire group. Sometimes pet names stick for life!

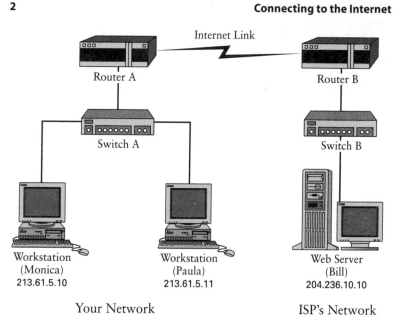

Figure 1-1 *Example Internet architecture*

1.1 Comparing TCP/IP to the OSI Reference Model

Nearly all TCP/IP protocols are defined at the network and transport layers of the **Open Systems Interconnect (OSI) Reference Model** shown in Table 1-1. These layers are where the action occurs in TCP/IP. You should memorize a few general concepts about TCP/IP in addition to certain basic information, such as addressing, masks, and so on.

- The network layer provides and controls routing. At this layer, the **Internet Protocol (IP)** provides addressing and routing functionality. The **Address Resolution Protocol (ARP), Reverse Address Resolution Protocol (RARP),** and **Internet Control Message Protocol (ICMP)** assist the packet delivery and routing processes. When you build an Internet connection, your first task is to enable your network devices to communicate with the devices in the Internet at the network layer.

- The transport layer provides and controls connections between network layer devices. It is responsible for delivery of data to and from the application program. The **Transmission Control Protocol (TCP)** provides guaranteed connections, while the **User Datagram Protocol (UDP)** provides a best-effort delivery service. TCP and UDP form the basis for most Internet service protocols, and you should understand how both function—especially when you deploy your security.

- TCP/IP does not provide any matching components for the upper layers of the OSI Reference Model. Instead, applications programs use Internet service protocols that are most often defined at the transport layer.

Table 1-1   TCP/IP and the OSI Reference Model

	Layer	TCP/IP Protocols	Function/Description
7	Application		TCP/IP doesn't define any services at this layer.
6	Presentation		TCP/IP doesn't define any services at this layer.
5	Session		TCP/IP uses the terms "port" and "socket" to refer to paths over which cooperating applications communicate. These paths come from the transport layer.
4	Transport	TCP, UDP	This layer guarantees that the receiver gets the data exactly as it was sent (TCP). It also provides best-effort service (UDP).
3	Network	IP, ICMP, ARP, RARP	This layer handles addressing and routing of data.
2	Data Link		TCP/IP doesn't define any services at this layer. It uses data link services made available from device drivers.
1	Physical		TCP/IP doesn't define any services at this layer.

1.2 Packet-Based Communication

The Internet is a large packet-based network. A **packet** is a small block of data exchanged between devices at the network layer.[2] Packet-based network technologies are **connectionless**, and delivery of packets is not guaranteed within such networks. Consequently, devices transmit packets without first establishing that the receiver is ready to accept them and stations do not acknowledge receipt of packets. Network protocols developed for connectionless environments usually include (at the transport layer) functions that enable devices to intercommunicate as if the network were connection-based. TCP provides this service in IP networks.

1.2.1 Media Access Control (MAC)

In packet-based networks, devices (called *stations, hosts,* or *nodes*) communicate at the data link layer by addressing one another's 48-bit **media access control (MAC) address**—not the network layer address. Each network interface card (NIC) in a workstation and server has a MAC address, as do the LAN interfaces on the routers. When devices communicate on a LAN, each must have a unique MAC address at the data link layer. Figure 1-2 shows such an example with MAC addresses.

Key points to remember about data link layer communications include the following:

- The MAC address is unique for each node. It is burned into a node's electronics and can be used to identify the manufacturer of the device. No two devices should have the same MAC address.
- Nodes may communicate only *directly* with other nodes on the same data link network. If a node needs to communicate with a node on a different data link network, it must use a device such as a router or bridge.

---

2. The terms **datagram** and **protocol data unit** (PDU) are sometimes used synonymously with *packet*. A datagram, however, refers to a packet that is transmitted without regard to sequencing or order. A protocol data unit refers to a packet that contains protocol-control information and data from an upper layer.

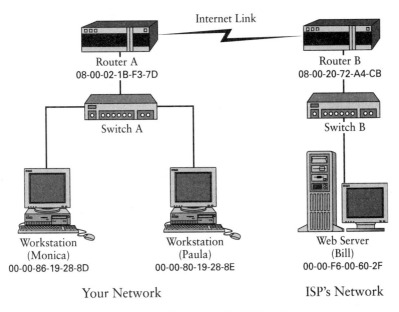

Figure 1-2 *Example Internet architecture with MAC addresses*

- TCP/IP does not define any functions at the data link layer. Rather, it employs the services of the data link layer software. For example, a NIC's device driver software provides data link functions.

In Figure 1-2, when the workstation Monica communicates with the web server Bill, Monica addresses the packets to router A's MAC (08-00-02-1B-F3-7D). Router A is then responsible for communicating with router B, while router B communicates with Bill. Similarly, when packets return from Bill, router A addresses the packets to Monica's MAC (00-00-86-19-28-8D). All of this communication occurs at the data link layer.

1.2.2 Frames

As noted earlier, a packet is a block of data defined at the network layer. It does not include any data link layer information necessary for transmission. To actually be transmitted at the data link layer, a packet must

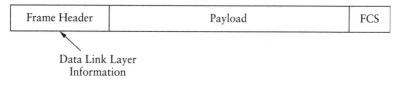

Figure 1-3 *Frame construction*

be placed within a **frame** that includes other information.[3] A frame begins with a **frame header** and ends with a **frame control sequence (FCS)**, which is also known as the **frame check sequence**. Figure 1-3 shows a basic frame with a packet as its payload.

The particular components and constructions of the frame header vary according to the network technology. For instance, several flavors of Ethernet, Token Ring, and FDDI frames exist. All frame headers have something in common, however—they lead with a **Data Link Control (DLC)** section containing the **destination MAC address (DA)** of the receiving station and **source MAC address (SA)** of the sending station.

1.2.3 Unicast, Broadcast, and Multicast Packets

In packet-based networks, packets can be addressed to the recipient(s) in three ways.

- **Unicast**—These packets are addressed to a single destination. For instance, if the workstation Monica communicates with the web server Bill, the packets exchanged between these hosts are unicast. Monica addresses the packets to Bill, and vice versa.
- **Broadcast**—These packets are addressed to all other nodes on a network. Broadcasting offers a way to communicate the same data to every node on a network at once. It is also used for querying purposes. Note that broadcasting results in all nodes on a network receiving the packets regardless of whether a particular node is interested in the contents.
- **Multicast**—These packets are addressed to a predefined group of nodes on a network, but not necessarily all of the nodes. Multicast

---

3. Often you will find the words *frame* and *packet* used synonymously, although frames are only at the data link layer and packets at the network layer and above.

is an efficient method of broadcasting packets only to those nodes that are interested in the contents.

Although the majority of the traffic through your Internet connection will be unicast, you may need to support broadcast or multicast-based protocols. It is important to understand these terms, because these packet types characterize the Internet services you will eventually support.

1.3 Communication in IP Networks

At this point we have enough background information to begin discussing how nodes communicate in an IP network. Let us start with an example. Figure 1-4 shows our hypothetical Internet connection. This diagram includes two IP LANs:

- The network labeled "Your Network" has an address of 213.61.5.0 with a mask of 255.255.255.0.
- The network labeled "ISP's Network" has an address of 204.236.10.0 with a mask of 255.255.255.0.

When nodes communicate on the same data link network, they frame the packets and send them to the recipient's MAC address. In Figure 1-4, the nodes Monica, Paula, and router A communicate directly at the data link layer using MAC addressing. Similarly, the nodes Bill and router B communicate directly using MAC addressing.

1.3.1 Address Resolution Protocol (ARP)

When nodes on the same network need to communicate, they must first resolve the network layer address into a data link layer address. Thus, to communicate on the same IP network, nodes must resolve IP addresses into MAC addresses.

In TCP/IP the **Address Resolution Protocol (ARP)** carries out this function. This protocol transforms an IP address into a 48-bit MAC address. The inverse process of resolving a MAC address into an IP address is called **Reverse Address Resolution Protocol (RARP)**.

In ARP, a router or node broadcasts a request asking for the MAC address of a specific IP host. When the specific node hears the ARP request, it responds with a packet containing information about its

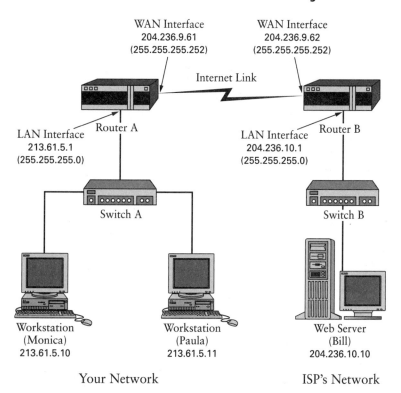

Figure 1-4 *Communication within an IP network*

own MAC and IP address. The requesting node then stores the results for future communication.

In our example, let's assume that the workstation Paula needs to communicate with the workstation Monica. If Paula does not know of Monica's MAC address, it broadcasts an ARP request to all nodes on the network asking for the MAC address of 213.61.5.10 (Monica). Both router A and Monica hear the broadcasted request, but only Monica responds by sending Paula a packet with the requested MAC address. Router A processes the requested information, but notes that the ARP asked for resolution of a IP address that did not match its own. It therefore drops the packet. Once the workstations know the others' MAC addresses, conversations can proceed at the data link layer using MAC addressing.

1.3.2 Routing

If devices on separate networks are to communicate, additional functions must be available to move the packets between networks. By definition, **routing** is the process of guiding a packet through a series of networks based on its network layer address. A network device that examines the network layer addresses (IP addresses) within a packet, and then forwards it towards the destination based on these values, is called a **router**. In IP networks, routers are also called **gateways**.

Each router maintains a **routing table**, which is also known as a **forwarding table**. The routing table lists all of the available networks learned by the router plus any other information added by an administrator. Table 1-2 shows a routing table with several entries.

Table 1-2 Routing Table

Destination	Mask	Gateway	Metric	Status	TTL	Source
0.0.0.0	0.0.0.0	218.156.96.5	1	—	—	Static
89.0.0.0	255.0.0.0	218.156.96.3	1	Up	160	RIP
129.213.0.0	255.255.0.0	218.156.96.3	1	Up	160	RIP
135.1.0.0	255.255.0.0	218.156.96.3	1	Up	160	RIP
139.87.0.0	255.255.0.0	218.156.96.3	1	Up	160	RIP
140.204.0.0	255.255.0.0	218.156.96.3	1	Up	160	RIP

The key elements of the routing table are as follows:

1. *Destination* is the host or network address to which a packet can be sent.
2. *Mask* is the 32-bit mask associated with a particular IP address entry in the routing table.
3. *Gateway* is the IP address of the neighboring router that can forward a packet toward the destination address.
4. *Metric* (sometimes called the *hop count*) is the number of routers between the host's network and the destination network.
5. *Time-to-Live (TTL)* is a value specifying how much longer (in seconds) a particular entry will remain valid in the routing table.

   6. *Source* indicates which routing protocol advertised the routing
   entry to the router.

   When a router receives a packet, it tries to match the destination IP
address against the entries in the routing table. First, the router attempts
to match the full 32-bit IP destination address with an entry in the
table. If this effort fails, it then tries to match the address with a network address. If a match is found, it forwards the packet to the gateway address associated with the network address.

   For example, if a packet destined for 129.213.10.10 reached the
router that had the routing table shown in Table 1-2, the router would
match the network address of 129.213.0.0 after applying the associated mask of 255.255.0.0 to the address 129.213.10.10. It would then
forward the packet to the gateway address of 218.156.96.3.[4]

   If the router cannot find a matching destination, it looks for a
default route. The default route is 0.0.0.0, with a typical mask of
0.0.0.0. The router sends any packet without a match to the gateway
listed for the default route. In Table 1-2, the default route has a source
of *static*. This source means that an administrator created the entry; it
was not learned.

   If no default route is available, the router drops the packet. If so
configured, it then sends a message to the sending station indicating
that it was unable to forward the packet because the "destination was
unreachable." This function is performed by the **Internet Control Message Protocol (ICMP)**.

   Figure 1-5 adds more detail to our example. Assume that the node
Monica (213.61.5.10) launches a web browser and enters the URL for
the web server at the ISP (204.236.10.10). The ensuing communication between the browser and the web server takes place as follows:

   1. The TCP/IP software on Monica sends packets destined for the
   web server (204.236.10.10) into the local LAN segment. The

---

4. The task of applying masks to IP addresses can be greatly aided by using a
network calculator. You can search the web and find many good ones using the
keyword "network calculator" or "subnet calculator." These tools help you
determine the network and host components of an IP address after applying a
particular mask.

TCP/IP driver on Monica notes that the destination address lies on a different IP network than Monica's network. It therefore sends the packets to its gateway address, which is the path out of the subnet. In this case, the gateway is router A (213.61.5.1). If Monica does not know the MAC address of router A, it must first use ARP to transform the IP address into a MAC address.

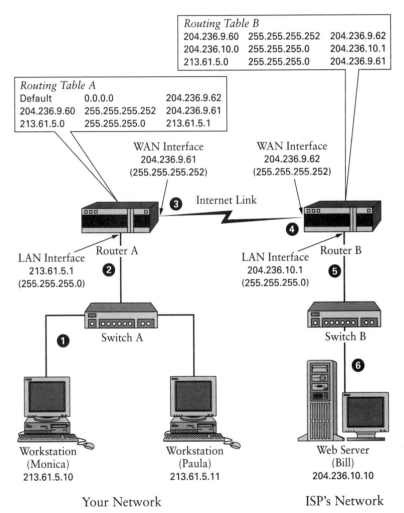

Figure 1-5 *Communication between IP networks*

2. Switch A receives the frames sent by Monica to router A. Switch A operates at the data link layer, bridging the frames to the segment leading to router A. Note that switch A does not examine the IP addresses, but rather forwards the frames based on the MAC address.

3. Router A receives the frames from Monica. It strips away the frame, leaving the IP packet. Next, the router inspects the packet's destination IP address (204.236.10.10) and consults its routing table for a match. In our example, it cannot find a match and therefore uses the default route, sending the packets to the associated gateway (204.236.9.62). Router A then places the packets within new frames and sends them to router B on the ISP's side of the WAN link.

4. When router B receives the frames from router A, it again examines the destination address of 204.236.10.10. It finds a match in its routing tables for the network address 204.236.10.0 and notes the gateway address is an attached subnet. If router B's ARP cache does not have a entry listing the MAC address of the web server (204.236.10.10), it first must use ARP to learn this information. Finally, router B places the packets into frames addressed to the web server's MAC.

5. Switch B receives the frames and bridges the packets to the segment with the web server. Once again, the switch does not examine the packet any deeper than the data link layer.

6. The web server receives the frames. Stripping away the frame, it processes the packets' contents.

1.3.3 Route Advertisement and Learning

Earlier, we noted that routers acquire the information in their routing tables through a learning process. In a LAN environment, administrators generally configure routers to exchange routing information with neighboring routers. In this setup, each router advertises the addresses of its directly attached networks and routes it has learned from other routers. On the other hand, it does not readvertise routes on the same ports from which they were learned. This approach prevents routes from being readvertised within the same network.

Table 1-3 IP Routing Protocols

Protocol	IP Protocol	Port
Border Gateway Protocol 4 (BGP4)	TCP	179
Inter-Gateway Routing Protocol (IGRP) Enhanced Inter-Gateway Routing Protocol (EIGRP)	9, 88	Not applicable
Open Shortest Path First (OSPF)	89	Not applicable
Routing Information Protocol (RIP)	UDP	520

Routers use a number of protocols to learn IP route information, including those shown in Table 1-3. Of these options, the most common protocol for the LAN environment is RIP.

For small to midsize LANs, RIP has evolved into the route-building protocol of choice. A RIP packet is a broadcast packet advertised by a router onto its attached networks. The RIP update is basically a copy of the routing table, less any information removed to prevent readvertising of routes.

When a neighboring router receives the RIP update, which can consist of many packets, it processes this information and enters it into its own routing table. After some time, the routing table on each router ceases to change, indicating that the network has reached a state of **convergence**.

RIP possesses its share of shortcomings (like everything else in networking). Its major drawbacks include the following:

- RIP is broadcast-based and uses precious bandwidth on LANs and WANs.
- In large networks, routing tables may never converge.
- RIP does not include mask information within the advertisements.

To cope with these issues, link state protocols emerged, such as OSPF, IGRP, and BGP. Basically, these newer routing protocols avoid the broadcast method and tell another router only when something changes. In general, link state protocols operate by using multicast packets that address only neighboring routers. These features increase the efficiency of the routing protocols by eliminating the broadcasts and speeding convergence.

Today, there really is no need to support a routing protocol at a basic Internet connection, for several reasons:

- Unless you have multiple links to one or more ISPs, a single route will exist from your network to the Internet—the default route. Consequently, the network does not need to learn about all routes in the Internet from the ISP. (The ISP probably won't advertise them to you anyhow!) Simply configure your default route to send all packets to the ISP's router.
- You do not need to advertise your routes to the ISP. The ISP knows who you are, and it knows what IP addresses you should be using. (It probably won't listen to your advertisements, though in some cases an ISP has learned "bad" routes from a customer.)
- You probably don't want to give away too much information about your networks. Although your ISP should be a secure outfit, some outsider may nevertheless be learning your routes and planning an attack.

Of course, some exceptions exist. In some cases, you may want to carry routing information through your Internet connection. Consider the following examples:

- Your ISP has a router on your site. This router, to which you have no access, will not forward packets into your network unless it learns your local routes.
- You have two Internet connections with one or more ISPs. In this case, you may need to play the BGP game and exchange routing information about your autonomous system with the ISP as peers. This case is beyond the scope of this book.

1.3.4 Internet Control Message Protocol (ICMP)

Common practice calls for a router to return error messages to a sending station if it cannot forward a packet to its destination address. ICMP provides this service in IP. Indeed, ICMP provides several functions— flow control, detection of unreachable destinations, redirection of routes, and checking of remote hosts. ICMP operates at the network layer, which makes sense considering its function is to control routing.

Although ICMP supports approximately 30 messages, you need to support only four of these when you construct your Internet con-

Table 1-4 Important ICMP Messages

Type	Message	Description
0	Echo reply	Responds to an echo request. "Hello, sending IP station, I am alive."
3	Destination unreachable	Informs the sending station that its packet could not be delivered to the destination. This packet can return about 15 codes indicating why the destination is unreachable.
7	Echo request	Verifies that another station is reachable through the network. "Hello, destination IP station, can you hear me?"
11	Time exceeded	Informs the sending station that the Time-to-Live field in the IP header portion of its packets has reached a value of 0.

nection. Table 1-4 lists these messages and describes their specific functions. The **Internet Assigned Numbers Authority (IANA)** web site provides a complete list of ICMP messages at http://www.iana.org/.

Two handy tools for debugging routing problems that use ICMP are the software programs ping and traceroute. The ping utility helps determine whether a destination address is reachable through the network. The traceroute utility will actually record the route that a packet takes *toward* its destination. Here we provide some examples of ping and traceroute. We will discuss the use of these utilities in more detail in later chapters.

```
tequila{drew}% ping -s www.awl.com
PING www.awl.com: 56 data bytes
64 bytes from www.awl.com (192.207.117.2): icmp_seq=0. time=125. ms
64 bytes from www.awl.com (192.207.117.2): icmp_seq=1. time=31. ms
64 bytes from www.awl.com (192.207.117.2): icmp_seq=2. time=13. ms
64 bytes from www.awl.com (192.207.117.2): icmp_seq=3. time=26. ms
----www.awl.com PING Statistics----
4 packets transmitted, 4 packets received, 0% packet loss
round-trip (ms) min/avg/max = 13/49/125
```

traceroute to www.awl.com (137.39.180.6), 30 hops max, 40 byte packets
```
1   218.156.12.5      2.858 ms     *           *
2   218.156.1.1       3.558 ms     2.725 ms    2.738 ms
3   137.39.207.17     55.015 ms    19.364 ms   8.346 ms
4   137.39.99.4       8.397 ms     8.5 ms      8.163 ms
5   137.39.180.6      10.37 ms     10.36 ms    10.456 ms
```

1.4 Internet Services

When you build an Internet connection, your sole mission is to enable users to access resources based on *services*. Everything you do builds toward this final goal. Internet services, by definition, are what applications employ in the TCP/IP protocol suite to do their work.

Some examples may help to clarify this abstract concept. For instance, when you launch a web browser and enter the **Uniform Resource Locator (URL)** of a site, the browser application communicates with the site using the **Hypertext Transfer Protocol (HTTP)** service. Similarly, when you run a **File Transfer Protocol (FTP)** software application, it employs the FTP service to accomplish its task. Your job, as a network administrator, is to construct a connection that provides services. Which services the connections supports is arbitrary—it's up to you and your colleagues.

Frequently services are called *protocols*. Indeed, most of the services—such as HTTP and FTP—include the word "protocol" in their name. In general, these service protocols use the features found in the transport layer protocols that you know so well—namely, TCP and UDP.

1.4.1 Emphasis on TCP and UDP

The bulk of Internet service protocols use either TCP or UDP as their underlying basis. Of these protocols, more use TCP than UDP because the former option offers guaranteed datagram delivery. Recall that the Internet is a connectionless network. By basing a protocol on TCP, you ensure that the data exchanged between hosts remains error-free and complete. The cost of this insurance comes in terms of performance. If performance is the driving requirement, then UDP is the best choice.

When a service protocol uses TCP or UDP, it distinguishes itself from other services through its port assignment.[5] The IANA web site lists the port assignments for TCP and UDP services. For instance, the HTTP service uses TCP port 80, while the **Domain Name System (DNS)** uses UDP port 53.

Both TCP and UDP packets are constructed in exactly the same way, so to support a service protocol you give access to packets that have source and destination ports in the TCP or UDP layer that match those assigned to the service. This strategy underlies the packet filtering used in most firewalls. (Later chapters provide is much more information about security.)

1.4.2 TCP Connections

When applications communicate using TCP, the entire conversation is called a **session**. The process of setting up this conversation is known as a **three-way handshake**. The handshake ensures that a connection exists with the destination station and that this station is ready to receive data. The flag bits in the TCP header help control the handshaking process. Figure 1-6 illustrates a TCP connection with a three-way handshake.

The handshake occurs as follows:

1. The initiating station sends a packet to the destination with the **synchronize sequence numbers (SYN)** bit set to 1 in the header flags. This packet also contains the **initial sequence number (ISN)** in the sequence field. The sending station increments this value in subsequent packets, thereby enabling the receiver to determine whether the packets arrived in order.

2. The destination replies to the SYN packet with one that has both the SYN and the **acknowledge (ACK)** bits set to 1 in the

---

5. When you use a network analyzer and read packets, the raw numbers in the packet will take the form of hexadecimal notation. Either you or the analyzer software must convert these data to decimal notation. By looking at the values in the source and destination port fields of a packet, you can derive what service protocol is being carried in the packet.

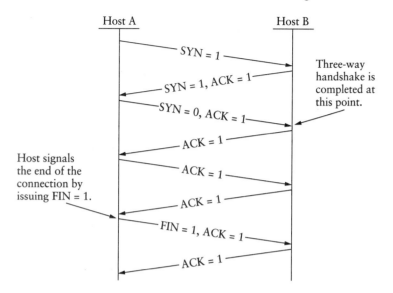

Figure 1-6 *TCP connection with three-way handshake*

header flags. The ACK bit signifies that the packet is now part of a connection between stations. Like the initial packet from the initiating station, the response packet contains an ISN value in its sequence field, enabling the initiating station to track packet order from the destination.

3. The initiating station sends a packet to the destination. The ACK bit is set to 1; because the sequence numbers are set, however, the SYN bit is reset to 0.

Throughout the remainder of the session, the ACK bit is set to 1. As a result, you can test a TCP packet to determine whether it is part of an *established* session. Much of Internet security depends on testing of packets to determine whether they are part of a permitted or established session. (The only packet that does not have the ACK bit set during the TCP conversation is the initial packet requesting the setup.) Many firewalls implement security policies by applying this test.

To close the session, a station sets the **finish (FIN)** bit to 1, producing another modified three-handshake that terminates the session.

Another way of shutting down the connection (rather abruptly) is for a station to set the reset bit to 1, which forces the initiator to reestablish the connection.

1.4.3 UDP Data Streams

Because UDP has no handshaking or acknowledgment, it is particularly well suited to situations where data needs to be quickly transferred. For example, the most common use of UDP is for DNS, which helps speed name resolution queries.

In addition, UDP is well suited for the transmission of voice and video, which involves **constant bit rate (CBR)** data. This is data that must flow at a steady rate with regular time intervals separating packets. With voice and video, however, small amounts of packet loss can be tolerated without too much degradation of service. UDP is the best choice for trying to mimic CBR data.

Applications such as RealPlayer use UDP to stream voice and video data to the receiving station. If you watch a RealPlayer session using a network analyzer, you'll witness a constant flow of incoming packets from the RealPlayer server to the client. The client does not issue a response to the server saying, "Hey, I got that last packet—it's okay to send the next!" UDP merely speeds things up by removing the error-checking function.

1.4.4 Request for Comments (RFC)

Many services are accepted into use by the Internet community through the **Request for Comments (RFC)** process managed by the **Internet Engineering Task Force (IETF)**. Thus, for many of the popular services, an RFC document elaborates the gory details of the service. This process can be especially helpful, especially when you are trying to discover more about unusual services. You can find many RFCs at the web site http://www.rfc-editor.org/.

1.5 Standard Internet Service Protocols

When configuring your Internet connection, you will need to choose which services to support. Table 1-5 lists the basic Internet services commonly deployed at Internet sites.

Table 1-5 Standard Internet Services

Category	Service	IP Protocol	Port
Domain Name System	DNS	UDP, TCP	53
File transfer	FTP	TCP	20, 21
Mail	SMTP	TCP	25
	IMAP4	TCP	143
	POP3, POP2	TCP	110,109
News	NNTP	TCP	119
Security/encryption	SSL	TCP	443
Terminal emulation	Telnet	TCP	23
Web	HTTP	TCP	80, 8080

As you can see from Table 1-5, most of these services are TCP-based. On the whole, the service protocols are therefore nothing more than standard TCP connections differentiated by port number. In some cases, however, the application of the service protocol has some strange permutations. The remainder of this section discusses some of the more important deviations from the "plain vanilla" TCP connection.

1.5.1 Domain Name System (DNS)

To support DNS, you need to enable both UDP and TCP ports 53. This approach is a bit unusual, as services use either TCP or UDP, but not both. What makes DNS confusing is the various permutations of client/server and server/server interactions that support **lookups** and **zone transfer** activities.

Table 1-6 shows the combinations of ports and protocols used for DNS activities. Remember, response packets invert the source and destination port values. If data loss occurs during a lookup, the requesting station should resend the request using TCP instead of UDP.

Table 1-6 DNS Activities

Activity	Source	Destination	Source Port	Destination Port
Lookup	Client	Server	>1023 (UDP)	53 (UDP)
Lookup	Server	Server	53 (UDP)	53 (UDP)
Zone transfer	Server	Server	>1023 (TCP)	53 (TCP)

Figure 1-7 illustrates some typical DNS traffic. In this diagram, an internal DNS server takes a lookup request from a client (step 1). This DNS server does not know the answer, so it sends a lookup request to an external DNS server in the Internet (step 2). The external server then responds to the internal server (step 3). Finally, the internal server responds to the client (step 4).

1.5.2 File Transfer Protocol (FTP)

Most Internet connections also support FTP, another standard service using TCP. FTP, however, has some twists that make it slightly more difficult to implement than other protocols. These twists arise because FTP comes in two flavors: standard and passive (PASV). It also makes simultaneous use of a control channel and a data channel, which presents complications.

Standard FTP: Standard FTP uses two channels. The control channel uses TCP port 21, and the data channel uses port TCP 20. The control channel is responsible for setting up the connection and overseeing the data transfer process. The data channel actually carries the data, as its name implies. Following is a blow-by-blow description of how standard FTP works:

1. The client establishes the control connection with the server per a normal three-way handshake process. Once established, the user logs in, provides a password, lists the file in directories, and performs other tasks. All of these commands are transferred using the control connection.

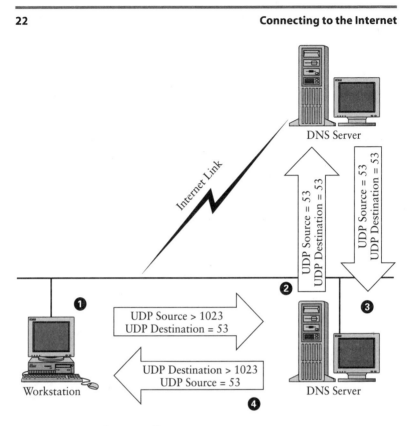

Figure 1-7 *Typical DNS traffic*

2. Once the client is ready to transfer data, it issues the PORT command to the server through the control channel.

3. The server acknowledges the PORT command and initiates another connection with the client using a three-way handshake. *This connection is initiated in the opposite direction— from the server to the client.* The source port used by the server is 20, and the destination port is typically the client's control port plus 1. For instance, if the client's control port is 1033, then the value used for the data port is 1034.

4. Once a data connection is established, the server and client can transfer data. When data transfer is complete, the two terminate their connection.

This process is unique because, in standard TCP connection setups, the client always initiates the connection with the server. Standard FTP becomes somewhat murky because the connection setup request for the data channel originates from the server back to the client! This challenge is especially interesting to handle when setting up packet filters for security. Figure 1-8 shows an example of standard FTP.

Passive FTP: Passive FTP (PASV), a variation of standard FTP, is used by many web browser software packages. If a user complains that FTP doesn't work from his or her browser, but a stand-alone FTP application does work, you should verify that the network properly supports passive FTP. Passive FTP works as follows:

1. The client first establishes the control connection with the server per a normal three-way handshake process. Once established, the user logs in, provides a password, lists the file in directories, and performs other tasks. All of these commands are transferred using the control connection.

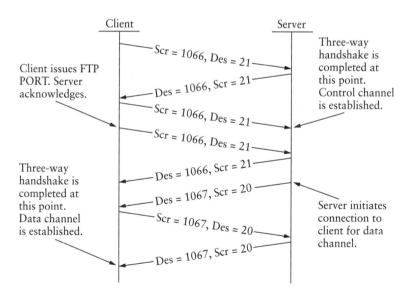

Figure 1-8 *Standard FTP*

2. Once the client is ready to transfer data, it issues the FTP PASV command to the server through the control channel.

3. The server acknowledges the PASV command and provides the client with a port number for the data channel. *The client initiates another connection with the server, using the destination port provided by the server and a source port equal to its control port plus 1.* For instance, if the client's control port is 1033, then the value used for the data port is 1034.

4. The server responds to the setup request and the data channel is established.

Figure 1-9 shows an example of passive FTP. In this diagram, the client randomly chooses ports 1066 and 1067 as the source ports. The server uses port 21 for the command channel, but randomly assigns port 3256 for the data channel. Notice that the client then initiates the setup request for the data channel to the server.

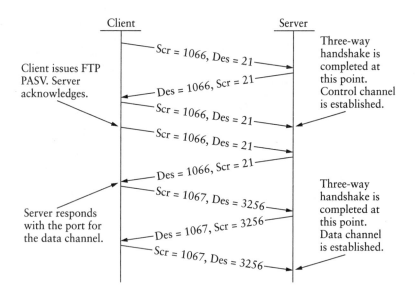

Figure 1-9 *Passive FTP*

1.5.3 Mail

The three mail protocols discussed in this section are the most prevalent ones used in today's Internet. Beware of mail, however. Although it is usually the primary reason for being connected to the Internet, it is a popular vehicle for hackers, reflecting the traditional weakness in UNIX mail engines. Many of these weaknesses are now being fixed with update mail packages.

Simple Mail Transfer Protocol (SMTP): Simple Mail Transfer Protocol (SMTP) is the postal carrier of the Internet. When mail servers exchange messages, they use the SMTP protocol. SMTP employs a standard TCP connection with destination port 25, although a newer variant called SMTP Secure (SMTPs) uses port 465. This approach closely mimics the implementation of SSL for HTTP over port 443.

You must support SMTP through your Internet connection if you plan to send mail to the Internet. Servers send mail using this protocol. Furthermore, many clients send mail with SMTP but read it with other protocols, such as POP3 and IMAP4. If your mail server resides outside of your network (as does the mail server maintained by your ISP), then you will need to support SMTP from the clients to the server. In contrast, if you maintain a mail server within your network, you will need to support SMTP only to and from the server. Other mail servers in the Internet must establish connections to your server to deliver mail.

Because the UNIX mail engine has been a traditionally complex beast, you should limit incoming SMTP connections only to your mail server(s). We'll talk about this issue later in the book. From a connection standpoint, however, SMTP is simply a straightforward TCP connection using port 25 on the destination server.

Post Office Protocol (POP): Post Office Protocol version 3 (POP3) is de facto mail protocol employed by ISPs for their customers. POP3 enables clients to download the contents of a mail message from a server. With respect to Internet connectivity, POP3 uses a TCP connection on port 110; the older version of this protocol, POP2, uses port 109.

Whether you need to support POP3 really depends on the location of your mail server. If it resides outside your network at your ISP, then you probably need to support this protocol, assuming that your mail clients use POP3.

Internet Message Access Protocol (IMAP): Internet Message Access Protocol version 4 (IMAP4) is emerging as a popular alternative to POP3. IMAP4 is a protocol used by clients to communicate with a mail server for the purpose of reading, manipulating, and sending mail. It uses a standard TCP connection on port 143.

Although IMAP4 is not as ubiquitous as its rival POP3, an increasing number of products now support it. The primary benefit of IMAP4 is the ability to read your mail off a server without downloading it first. Although more mail readers now support IMAP, you should nevertheless check with the mail administrator before enabling the service to make certain that this protocol is required. (Maybe this administrator is you.)

1.5.4 News (NNTP)

Network News Transfer Protocol (NNTP) supports the distribution, inquiry, retrieval, and posting of Usenet news articles over the Internet. It is designed for use between a news reader client, such as nn or GNUS, and a news server. It uses a standard TCP connection on port 119.

1.5.5 Terminal Emulation (Telnet)

Terminal Emulation over a Network (Telnet) is a service that allows you to access the command shell of another computer or network device. It operates via TCP port 23. Telnet comes as a standard software package with many operating systems. This very powerful tool is used extensively for network, server, and UNIX administration.

1.5.6 Web (HTTP)

Hypertext Transfer Protocol (HTTP) is the workhorse of the web. Like most Internet service protocols, HTTP uses a standard TCP connection on port 80. An increasing number of web servers, however, now use different ports. For example, some URLs require support for ports 81, 8000, 8002, and 8080. Although you need not support these ports automatically, you should watch out for possible deviations with HTTP. If a user cannot connect to a web site, check the semantics of the URL. Look for a URL that includes the port number. For instance, you might find a URL that reads http://www.beer-example.net:8000/.

1.5.7 Security/Encryption (SSL)

Secure Sockets Layer (SSL) is a security extension of HTTP. It was designed by Netscape Communications Corporation to provide secure communications on the Internet. SSL is used by the secure version of HTTP (HTTPS). This protocol encrypts the data within the HTTP packet to ensure that no one can listen to your network conversation.[6] Some web sites now implement SSL, especially now that e-commerce is evolving into a viable entity.

1.6. Non-TCP-Based and Non-UDP-Based Services

1.6.1 IP Protocols

Historically, most basic Internet connections needed to support only ICMP (protocol 1), TCP (protocol 6), and UDP (protocol 17). With further deployments of **virtual private networks (VPNs)** and the **Multimedia Backbone (MBone),** support for other IP protocols through your Internet connection is becoming more widespread. Although you should not automatically tackle these implementations, you should nevertheless understand how they differ from TCP- and UDP-based services. Then, when you must build your first VPN or MBone connection, you will have a basic idea of how to proceed.

The IANA web site maintains a current list of assigned IP protocol numbers. If you examine this list, you will notice that most of these IP protocols seem somewhat esoteric. To determine the service being carried in the packet, use a network analyzer to look at the value in the protocol field of the IP header. This value identifies the service. Following are some brief descriptions of the increasingly common services that do not use TCP or UDP.

---

6. Netscape Navigator includes a small key icon at the bottom-left corner of the screen. When your browser starts an encrypted communication with the server using SSL, this icon changes from a broken key to a solid one.

1.6.2 IP in IP Encapsulation

In the IP in IP encapsulation (protocol 4) scheme, IP packets are "tunneled" completely within another IP packet. The most prevalent application of IP tunneling is to enable two multicast networks to exchange data through the Internet, which normally supports only unicast traffic. Many ISPs elect to provide MBone service to their customers through dedicated tunnels using IP in IP encapsulation.

1.6.3 Generic Routing Encapsulation (GRE)

By definition, VPNs are tunnels. Most VPNs, however, do not use IP in IP encapsulation, but rather one of several protocols that enable non-IP packets to be encapsulated in the IP packet. The Internet standard protocol for tunnels is called the **Generic Routing Encapsulation (GRE)** protocol (protocol 47), and it is used by the **Point-To-Point Tunneling Protocol (PPTP)**.[7] A next-generation variant to PPTP, **Layer 2 Tunneling Protocol (L2TP)** (protocol 115), is also expected to become part of the tunneling standard in VPNs.

One concern that arises with tunneling relates to security. Because the actual data contents of a tunneled packet comprise another packet, unwanted packets can potentially ride undetected into your network.[8] To combat this potential security problem, you can deploy other mechanisms to validate whether a tunneled packet should be permitted through your network's Internet gateway. The most common security mechanism in a VPN is Secure IP (IPsec), which is covered in more detail in Chapter 4.

---

7. PPTP uses a combination of GRE (protocol 47) and TCP port 1723 for controlling the tunnel.
8. I like the analogy that tunneling is similar in concept to the *Alien* science fiction films. In these films, seemingly healthy people walk around their space ship incubating a baby alien in their bodies. Then, with all the gore and splendor of Hollywood, the baby aliens escape from the womb, killing their hosts in the process.

Selecting Your Internet Service Provider

One critical decision you will make when setting up your Internet connection is your choice of an Internet service provider (ISP). Good ISPs will treat you as a valued customer and really appreciate your business. Not-so-good ISPs may let you down at the worst moments. The cost and quality of ISPs vary widely, so shop wisely.

2.1 Chapter Overview

This chapter is divided into several major sections to help you analyze the offerings and qualifications of ISPs. After reading this chapter, you should be able to answer the following questions:

1. What are the different types of ISPs and the market focus of each type?
2. What are the basic access products and services you should expect from any ISP when you purchase an Internet connection?
3. What services should you expect from the ISP during installation and what post-sales support should you demand?
4. What extended and value-added services do ISPs offer in addition to the basic access products?
5. Why should capacity planning and oversubscription be factors in selecting your ISP?
6. Why must you verify that the ISP is building a network infrastructure to support your future access needs?

7. How do ISPs price their services and how should you negotiate contract issues?

The chapter ends with a checklist of items you should consider when reviewing the qualifications of ISPs.

2.2 Types of ISPs

ISPs are your conduits to the Internet. Indeed, the explosive growth in Internet access primarily reflects growth in the number of ISPs. In North America, Western Europe, and some industrialized Asian nations, the ISP population seems to have reached a saturation point. In other areas of the world, however, getting Internet access remains a long battle, usually because telecommunications service in those regions is unreliable.

If you want an Internet connection, you must deal with an ISP. Thus you will need to research the market and discover which ISPs serve the location where you will set up your connection. First, read the following two sections, which discuss the types of ISPs available. Then get your web browser fired up and ready to go. You now have a license to surf!

2.2.1 Network Service Providers

An ISP that maintains its own portion of Internet backbone is called a **network service provider (NSP)**. Typically, NSPs are large companies that maintain global networks and sell Internet service in many countries. They are also called *tier-one* ISPs.

Several characteristics distinguish NSPs from their ISP brethren:

1. NSPs sell connectivity to a range of customers, but normally only those with large, dedicated leased-line connections or those with high-bandwidth, on-demand phone service (such as ISDN).
2. NSPs provide connectivity to *tier-two* ISPs. These buying ISPs are called resellers or reselling providers (as discussed below).
3. NSPs maintain an Internet backbone that joins with the backbones of other NSPs at peering locations around the globe. Designated companies such as MCI WorldCom, Inc., maintain these peering sites.

4. NSPs generally do not provide dial-up Internet access to the home market, which consists of hordes of individual users. The dial-up market is the realm of reselling ISPs.

When you question prospective providers, NSPs in particular will often devote significant efforts to explain their backbone architecture and their plans for expansion to meet the demands of Internet users in the twenty-first century.

2.2.2 Internet Service Providers (Resellers)

Unlike NSPs, reselling ISPs have variable market segments. That is, they sell both to customers requiring dedicated leased-line connections and to customers requiring single dial-up connections. Features of reselling providers include the following:

1. The reselling providers have a greater share of the **small-office and home-office (SOHO)** market. Often, their solutions for inexpensive on-demand connections are well constructed.
2. Reselling providers sell dedicated leased-line connectivity for midrange capacities, usually providing line speeds ranging from 56K/64K to T1/E1. For the bulk of Internet connections, this speed is adequate. Only really huge outfits need greater capacity.
3. Sometimes reselling providers maintain their own regional networks. They may then choose to work with several NSPs to ensure that their network traffic always has a path to the Internet backbone.
4. Reselling providers tend to be regional players. This constraint simply means you cannot purchase Internet connectivity from a single vendor for your organization's five sites distributed throughout the world.

The pending consolidation in the Internet access market may have some effect on reselling ISPs. The number of "mom-and-pop" shops providing Internet access is expected to drop significantly during the next few years, meaning less choice for consumers. This trend really applies to reselling providers, although NSPs are certainly not immune from takeovers that lead to consolidation.

2.2.3 Which Type of ISP Is Right for You?

In the end, it really does not matter whether you purchase your Internet connectivity from an NSP or a reselling ISP, assuming that your provider meets your selection requirements. Although you might assume that the NSP is the way to go, the reselling provider can also be quite competitive. Because reselling players tend to be regionally oriented, they have a stake in the local business community. This characteristic may not apply to NSPs.

Before making your purchase decision, educate yourself about the ISPs available and the services they sell. The following general guidelines for selecting an ISP are largely subjective, but are based on the author's experiences in comparing ISPs providing similar Internet services:

1. Select an ISP that is committed to providing consistent and reliable service. It won't serve you well if the ISP provides lightning-fast packet routing with 43% uptime. You want 99.5% uptime. (Note that 100% uptime is unrealistic. Never believe an ISP's claims of 100% uptime—you'll be disappointed.)

2. Look for an ISP that emphasizes support and has procedures in place to notify you about systems work. Advanced notification implies that the ISP plans well and realizes the impact of its actions. On the same theme, find an ISP that informs you when things are not working, either via phone, e-mail, or pager.

3. Remember that price does not necessarily guarantee good or bad service. Try to contact other consumers who have dealt with your prospective provider and ask their opinions of the ISP's performance.

4. Take some time to delineate what you want to purchase. For instance, you may wish to purchase standard service that includes a news feed. Until you actually start prospecting the sites of ISPs, however, you may not have a good idea what you want to purchase.

5. If possible, try to meet with a sales representative of the ISP. Perhaps it's an old-fashioned idea, but an ISP is clearly serious

about winning your business if it is willing to spend some time with you in person.

2.3 Basic Access Products

Your first step in reviewing an ISP's qualifications should be an examination of the components of its basic Internet access product. This product can bear many names, but it should always address four areas:

- Internet services supported via the connection
- Leased-line capacities and technologies from which you can choose
- Access provisioning for the leased-line (WAN) circuit
- Equipment provisioning and recommendation

Most Internet access products appear to include the leased-line capacity in their brand names. For instance, service via a T1 circuit with a fixed monthly cost may be named "Fixed T1 InterAccess." The names usually provide a good indicator of what the service includes.

2.3.1 Internet Services Provided

When an ISP says it provides full Internet service, does it route every conceivable IP packet to your network regardless of the IP protocol? Alternatively, does the full service represent some smaller subset of this large picture? ISPs' literature often indicate the company offers access to Internet applications, including e-mail, the World Wide Web (WWW), FTP, Telnet, and network news. Although you need these staple services, you should make certain that the ISP will not filter traffic to your site based on IP protocol or protocol service.

For instance, imagine your disappointment if you want to establish a RealAudio connection, but your ISP does not support it. Make certain that you are purchasing a connection that fully supports a large range of services. *If anything, ask what an access service does not include.*

2.3.2 Connection Capacity (Bandwidth)

Next, you should determine the capacity of your connection. The ISP should give you a range of options. Your job is to guess the capacity that you will require. Some typical graduations in service capacities are shown here (notice the granularity of service in the range below 768 Kbps):

- 56 Kbps (64 Kbps International)
- 128 Kbps
- 256 Kbps
- 384 Kbps
- 512 Kbps
- 768 Kbps

- 1.54 Mbps (2.0 Mbps International)
- 3.0 Mbps
- 6.0 Mbps
- 9.0 Mbps
- 45 Mbps

Often the circuit capacity is called **bandwidth**. Although many people associate circuit capacity with speed, the two are closely linked but not entirely interchangeable. To be specific, **throughput** is the amount of data transferred over time in a circuit (measured in bytes per second), much like a volume flow rate of fluid in a pipe. **Latency** is the time required for a packet to travel within a network and can be compared to speed. (We'll discuss latency in more detail later in the book.) For the purposes of evaluating circuit capacities, you can assume that a larger circuit will carry more traffic without congestion than a circuit with smaller capacity.

The WAN technologies offered by the ISP will depend mostly on the services available from the telecommunication companies in your area. In North America, the following technologies are generally available:

- ISDN BRIs and Frame Relay for circuits between 56 Kbps and 128 Kbps
- Point-to-Point (PPP), Frame Relay, and Switched Multimegabit Data Service (SMDS) for circuits between 128 Kbps and 1.54 Mbps (DS1)
- Point-to-Point for circuits between 1.54 Mbps (DS1) and 45 Mbps (DS3)

As you stare at these listed capacities, you will likely ask, "How much capacity do I need?" This question is usually difficult to answer unless you have an Internet connection already and have used a network management tool to monitor its usage. The response, however, might surprise you.

You don't need as much as you may think. Following are some ballpark figures for connection capacities provided on the web site for GTE Internetworking, an ISP, found at http://www.bbnplanet.com/products/access.

- "If you are a small business with very few users who regularly send and receive e-mail and occasionally use the World Wide Web, a 56K leased line should meet your needs."

- "If your organization is medium-sized with heavy e-mail use or regular use of the Web, a T1 line with flexible pricing makes the most sense. T1 or faster also is recommended if your organization is planning on hosting a public web server at your site and you expect a significant amount site activity from the Internet."

- "Customers who are considering T3 are usually larger companies, organizations, regional Internet service providers, or companies specializing in on-line Internet services like search engines or interactive media services."

Of course, you should consult with your potential ISP to get its view on which circuit capacity you should purchase. Another ISP, DIGEX, offers a capacity-planning calculator to help you estimate the required size of your Internet connection; the calculator is found at http://www.digex.com/.

If you must support more than 100 users through an Internet connection, you should think about a T1/E1 circuit. With fewer than 100 users, you should consider lower-capacity connections, in the 512 and 256 Kbps range, if the price is reasonable. Chapter 8 discusses how to monitor and assess your Internet connection to ensure that you maintain sufficient capacity.

2.3.3 Access Provisioning (WAN Circuits)

An ISP's offering for Internet service often bundles the **provisioning** of the leased-line circuit into the product. The process of provisioning starts when the ISP (or, in rare cases, you) place an order with the telecommunications company to provide leased-line service between your site and the ISP's **point-of-presence (POP)**. The POP is the location where your leased line will connect to the ISP's network, as shown in Figure 2-1. Provisioning also includes the process of installing and testing the circuit.

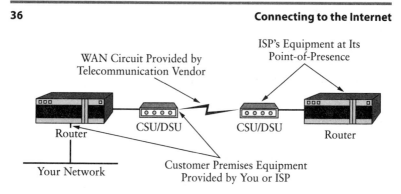

Figure 2-1 *Access provisioning*

Circuit provisioning can range from a smooth experience to one that tests your troubleshooting skills. ISPs select telecommunications vendors as their partners based on service and price reasons—in part because they can leverage large contracts with these vendors. More importantly, however, ISPs select their telecommunications partners for their ability to properly build and maintain circuits for the ISP.

One advantage of bundled provisioning is that it eliminates your need to ask the telecommunications company to obtain pricing, installation dates, and resolve related issues. The ISP simply arranges this process for you. On the other hand, ISPs usually charge extra for on-site activation of the circuit. If the ISP must put a technician on your site to make everything work, it will likely charge you for the service. Normally, though, phone support is sufficient and included in the activation phase of provisioning.

One concern with bundled provisioning is the ISP can charge a premium to the customer for a WAN circuit. You should therefore review the price quotation from the ISP and perhaps ask that the monthly access charges be listed as a line item. Ask your telecommunications provider to quote a price for the same circuit. You can then compare results. Typically, most customers opt for bundled provisioning because it requires less preparation work. Moreover, more reputable ISPs pass the monthly leased circuit fees directly to the customer without marking up the price.

You could also choose to provision the circuit yourself, so that you do not take the ISP's bundled service. Some ISPs actually charge the customer for this luxury! You should consider ordering your own circuit only if you have previous experience with WANs. Bear in mind, if you order the circuit you will be responsible for contacting the telecommunications provider when things go awry and for relaying information between the ISP and the provider. Usually it is better, however, for the ISP to own the circuit and thus assume full responsibility for its operation.

2.3.4 Equipment Selection and Provisioning

A major item that any Internet access product should address is equipment selection and provisioning. That is, it should state who provides the router and telecommunication equipment that connects your site via the leased line to the ISP's network—the **customer premises equipment (CPE)**. The general trend is to provide equipment according to one of the following models:

- The ISP owns, configures, and manages the equipment. You have no control (or access) to the CPE, even though it resides at your site.
- The ISP sells you preferred equipment. You own the equipment, but the ISP configures and manages it for you.
- You purchase, configure, and manage the CPE. The ISP has no control over this equipment.

If you are comfortable with configuring routers and telecommunications equipment, then the last option may work for you. Perhaps you may already have the equipment on hand.

The first two options are nice if you don't want the hassle of configuring equipment. In these cases, the ISP selects the equipment vendor to ensure compatibility with its POP equipment and the equipment at your site. In theory, this option has many benefits, but you should make certain you're comfortable with the ISP's choice of equipment vendors.

2.4 Installation and Setup Services

Once you understand the components of basic access service, you need to examine the ISP's service functions that will help establish your Internet presence. ISPs tend to offer many of the same standard services:

- Domain name registration
- Allocation of an IP address pool
- Mail record registration
- Activation support (installation)
- Post-sales support

Traditionally, the customer took charge of the first two items, with the ISP assuming responsibility for the remaining items. Now, however, although you could contact the regional registries of the Internet Assigned Numbers Authority (IANA) for IP addresses, and the InterNIC or top-level domain administrator for domain registration, the option preferred by these organizations is for the ISP to perform these tasks for you. The following sections describe each "service" in more detail.

2.4.1 Domain Name Registration

When you place your LAN on the Internet, you will want your presence to become known by a recognizable name. A subjective example would be www.greatbeer-example.org—a nonprofit agency, of course! (The more likely scenario is the marketing staff in your organization will spend much time and money deciding on this name.) Regardless of who develops the name, it must meet certain formatting standards. In addition, it cannot be already assigned to another organization.

Consequently, you should not be overly disappointed to discover that Coca-Cola Corporation has already nabbed the name coke.com. In a bit of good news, the **Internet Society (ISOC)** is considering adding new domains to DNS in addition to the standard identifiers of COM, NET, GOV, ORG, INT, MIL, and EDU, and country codes such as US, UK, IL, NL, and FR. Although it will be hard to shake the U.S.-centric slant in DNS naming, names are gradually becoming more international.

Most ISPs include the domain name registration service as part of the contract when you sign on as a customer. They will help you get the syntax correct for the country in which you will operate your connection. For instance, in Australia the structure of naming follows the U.S. model, with a .AU appended at the end—the Australian Navy, for example, would have a name such as navy.mil.au.

One word of advice—make certain that the contract you execute with the ISP clearly states who will register your name. Although the

InterNIC and the top-level domain administrators in various countries may prefer that the ISP register your name, it's an easy task to handle yourself. It is simply one less complication to avoid if you can.

2.4.2 Mail Exchange (MX) Records

The process of sending mail through the Internet and DNS are inextricably linked together. Essentially, a component in DNS called the **mail exchange (MX) record** helps Internet mail servers send messages to the proper receiving server. For instance, if you send a mail message to joe_sixpack@greatbeer-example.org, the sending mail server needs to know the name of the receiving server in the greatbeer-example.org domain. By querying DNS for the MX record of greatbeer-example. org, the sending server can learn the name of destination server—such as smtp.greatbeer-example.org.[1]

MX records are also used to provide fault tolerance and redundancy in mail systems. Most commonly, your ISP will represent a backup MX record for your site if your link to the Internet should falter. Your mail will then be delivered to the ISP's mail server for safekeeping until it can be transferred to your server upon restoration of your connection.

Of course, your ISP should help you with MX record administration upon activation and at any point in the future (while you remain its customer.) Normally, the process of MX record registration takes place when the ISP registers your DNS name. Don't leave this event to chance, however. You should explicitly ask if this service is included with the DNS registration.

2.4.3 Allocation of an IP Address Pool

By far, one of the prettier jewels you will wish to remove from your ISP's crown is a pool of IP addresses for use in your internal networks. Unless you plan to implement **network address translation (NAT)**, you

---

1. MX records become a bit trickier when your organization was previously known by a different DNS name. Thus, if you still want to receive mail at the old domain name, you must create a MX mail record that points the mail server of the old domain to your active mail server. It's all a game of names and proper registration in DNS.

should obtain a range of addresses sufficiently large to support your internal users.

Each host in your network needs to have a unique IP address to intercommunicate with the Internet. Because IP addresses are in demand, the ISP may be reluctant or unable to allocate large address ranges to you. Of course, you will want a continuous range of addresses to simplify your administration of the addresses. A few key points about address lending will make your life easier:

1. Never forget that the ISP merely loans you address space for the duration of the contract. This consideration may lock you in to dealing with one ISP for an extended period or force you to implement other IP address solutions such as NAT and **Dynamic Host Configuration Protocol (DHCP)**.

2. Keep in mind that the only devices requiring an official IP address are those that converse with other hosts in the Internet or route packets through the Internet. For instance, if you maintain a lab network whose devices don't need Internet access, do not assign official IP addresses to those devices. Instead, use addresses from the range of private addresses defined by the IANA and prevent your Internet router from learning those subnets. The IANA web site provides a list of recommended IP private addresses.

3. If you have special requirements for IP addressing, verify that the ISP can support your request before signing a contract with it. It would really be disappointing to discover after activating your connection that your ISP could not honor your address space request.

2.4.4 Activation Support (Installation)

If you are new to implementing WAN circuits, the process of activating your Internet connection could pose some new obstacles. Consequently, ISPs usually offer activation services in which they coach you over the telephone. Some ISPs even offer on-site activation services—albeit for an extra fee. Chapter 3 covers the process of WAN circuit provisioning in more depth.

Before activation can occur, you should have in place the CPE that will enable your LANs to connect to the ISP's POP (regardless of who purchases and owns this equipment). The nice thing about having the ISP provide and maintain this equipment is the ISP will preconfigure as much of it as possible before shipping the CPE to you.

The activation event consists of enabling routing on both ends of the WAN circuit and then testing the equipment to ensure that packets are being routed between the ISP's network and yours. Usually, the ping and traceroute programs are used to test connectivity between devices. Thus, in addition to the routers, you should plan on having a workstation in your network that supports these utilities.

In a clean activation, everything will work without a hitch. Your network and the ISP's network will intercommunicate with ease. Of course, the world isn't perfect, so be ready to troubleshoot. The installation team at the ISP will be ready to help you get things rolling—it's their job. Later chapters give specific tips on how to troubleshoot the startup process.[2]

2.4.5 Post-Sales Support

It is impossible to overemphasize the importance of post-sales support. Most ISPs are adept at performing the setup and establishing a connection to their networks. Consider the activation to be equivalent to a wedding. The real test of your relationship with the ISP, however, comes later through the lifetime of the contract. Is your ISP there for you when you need it most?

In some respects, it is difficult to gauge the strengths and weaknesses of an ISP's support. How do you know how good an ISP is in this field unless you become its customer? Can you trust its sales pitch and marketing literature on the topic?

---

2. In the case where the ISP will be managing the premises equipment, it will often need access to the CPE via analog phone lines and modems. Modem access to the premises equipment enables the ISP to troubleshoot and fix configuration issues when your Internet connection fails. Be prepared to provide some analog phone lines to the premises equipment. The ISP can arrange to install those lines along with the leased-line circuit.

The following list describes some things to look for when rating an ISP's post-sales support services. Also, don't be scared to ask tough questions if you suspect these services may not meet your standards.

1. Does the ISP provide support 24 hours per day, 7 days per week (24 × 7)? Avoid companies that don't meet this standard. For those that do, ascertain the following: What exactly does 24 × 7 mean to the ISP? Where is the support staff located? Who exactly is available for support? You want to make certain the ISP really can provide such support, rather than merely saying it to win customers.

2. What service-level guarantees does the ISP provide? When the ISP says it offers Internet access with 99.9% uptime, ask the company how it measures uptime. Is uptime measured on your circuit or across the ISP's entire network? In addition, ask how the ISP will compensate you if it fails to meet its service-level guarantee. Common contracts include clauses that state the ISP will credit you for a day's worth of Internet service should it miss its service guarantee by some stated value.

3. Does the ISP provide early notification of system work? Very few ISPs give you an advance warning when they will be servicing systems that affect your connection; this information may be extremely valuable to you, however, especially if your organization depends heavily on the Internet connection. Advance notification allows you to plan for outages and inform your user community.

4. How does the ISP handle down connection and circuit situations? Ask the ISP how it plans to communicate a down connection. Better yet, ask how the ISP will contact you to address a problem. In addition, find out about the escalation procedure for problems. You don't want 1,000 users pounding on your door asking when the Internet connection will be online when you can't even get a status report from the ISP!

5. What additional services does the ISP provide that distinguishes its post-sales support from that of other ISPs? For example, does it offer guest access to a host in the ISP's network that

supports Telnet, FTP, ping, traceroute, mail, and other useful programs? Having the ability to test connectivity back to your site is extremely helpful.

The bottom line is the ISP should regard you as a valued customer, with the features of its post-sales service reflecting this viewpoint. Don't ask for roses every Friday, but do expect consistent performance and quick resolution of problems when they do occur.

2.5 Extended Services

ISPs are moving far beyond providing standard access services. Five years ago, users were absolutely ecstatic if the ISP gave them standard access with no hitches. The advent of "extended" services has changed this perception, however. Offers such as web hosting, security advising, virtual private networks, remote access, faxing, MBone, news, and knowledge services (consulting) permit ISPs to offer much more to their customers.

Many of these services are not included in the standard access services. Although these options are fast becoming core services for many organizations, most ISPs consider them to be "value-added" services—meaning they charge money for these services in addition to the charge for the standard connection. When dealing with an ISP, make certain it clearly itemizes in its price proposals the costs for extended services. You may find that your particular ISP does not charge extra for news service or MBone.

2.5.1 Web Hosting

Web hosting is hot, hot, hot! In its basic implementation, web hosting is a service in which the ISP maintains the server equipment and server software for your web site. The server resides in the ISP's server farm, presumably closer to the Internet backbone than the server in your private LAN. The ISP rents disk space on this server to you. You are granted access to the server and control the contents of the web site. Seldom do ISPs advise you on site content. Instead, they will often refer you to a partner or **value-added reseller** (**VAR**) that can help you develop your site.

Of course, many permutations of this basic concept exist. For instance, some organizations prefer not to share a server with another organization and opt to use dedicated servers for their sites. Some ISPs will assume operational control and maintenance of equipment you purchase. You simply locate the equipment at the ISP's server farm.

Web hosting provides several advantages:

- Your organization does not need to hire staff capable of operating and maintaining a web server.
- A web server in the ISP's server farm offers greater fault tolerance and uptime than one in your network.
- The overall cost of web hosting is probably less expensive than operating your own server, as the ISP can realize greater economies of scale.
- Locating your web server at an ISP reduces the traffic on your Internet connection. If your web site is a very active one, this decrease in bandwidth usage can be significant.[3]

If your web site is a critical component of your organization's Internet presence, then web hosting can make a lot of sense. Some site developers may not like the idea of giving up control over their web server because of security issues, but others see tremendous benefits in web hosting.

One word of caution before you permit your ISP to take over web hosting—make certain that it is up to the task. If possible, visit the site where the servers will reside. Also, ask about the qualifications of the support staff who will administer the servers. In short, make the ISP prove that it knows how to manage a large collection of servers.

2.5.2 Security

Security is another extended service that many ISPs offer their customers. In its basic form, the ISP will audit your site and determine its vulnerability to unauthorized access via the Internet connection (read:

---

3. These days it is very common for web servers to cache the contents of frequently accessed web pages. Keeping a temporary copy of a web page on the local server reduces Internet traffic. Web caching is used on international data circuits to reduce overall traffic.

attacks). Based on the audit results, the ISP will advise you on steps to take to tighten the security holes. In a more complex form of security, the ISP may install, manage, and monitor a firewall design that protects your network from unwanted intrusions.

Security is undoubtedly a major concern of most organizations with an Internet connection. Keeping abreast of all possible forms of attack and then modifying your site's security to prevent such attacks is a full-time job. Having the ISP aid you in establishing and honing your site's Internet security might prove a very good investment. After all, an unauthorized attack could be very costly, especially if it kept your network off the Internet for an extended period or resulted in the theft of sensitive information. Because security is such an important and deep topic, Chapter 4 will be devoted to this issue.

2.5.3 Virtual Private Networks

VPNs represent an interesting addition to the lineup of extended services that ISPs now offer their customers. In short, VPNs provide another means of connecting remote sites to your site through the Internet without purchasing dedicated leased-line circuits.

Although VPNs are a new commodity for most users, the firewall software manufacturers have offered mature products for several years. Currently, the IETF is working with various vendors to develop VPN-specific protocols for encrypting data. It appears now that Secure IP (IPsec) will emerge as the standard.

Key points to consider about VPNs include the following:

- VPNs are expected to replace the leased lines to branch offices in the coming years.
- Non-IP protocols can be carried by VPNs through IP tunneling protocols.
- **Quality of service (QoS)** is a major issue for VPNs at the moment. Most ISPs cannot provide committed information rates between Internet hosts if the VPN is not entirely within their own network.[4]

---

4. QoS issues are not limited to VPNs. Other services such as voice-over-IP also require QoS guarantees.

VPNs are also called **extranets** and, surprisingly, private networks. Don't get mired down with the nomenclature, however. Instead, spend some time becoming more familiar with VPNs' benefits and drawbacks. Chapter 4 further discusses VPNs from a security standpoint.

2.5.4 Remote Access

If you ever had to support a marauding band of marketing managers and telecommuters, you know just how difficult it can be to provide fault-tolerant remote access. In the past five years, remote access has moved from being a perk enjoyed by executives to a basic deliverable service for an organization's employees. The costs associated with it are staggering, but ISPs stand ready to join you in this battle.

Depending on your needs, it might make sense to support your mobile users via your ISP. In this scenario, the ISP maintains and manages the remote access equipment infrastructure. Your users call to the ISP's equipment, pass an authentication test, and then gain access to the Internet and optimally into your private network to retrieve e-mail and perform other tasks.

Under this setup, you manage the authentication proceedings and your ISP manages the connection infrastructure. In reality, ISPs have provided remote access for years. The primary difference here is that users are also granted access into your internal network through a firewall. Because this approach can involve some complex security issues, ideally you should understand the whole process and system before signing up.

2.5.5 Faxing

Some ISPs now offer fax services. The ISP's network actually carries your fax traffic, which is normally routed over the public phone network. You send the fax through your Internet connection to the ISP. The ISP then transports the fax through its network to a POP located near the receiving system. At the POP, the call is placed and the document is actually faxed to the receiver.

The benefit is the ISP can provide less expensive long-distance service for faxing than your telecommunications provider can. Also, members of your mobile work force can gain greater faxing capabilities by simply connecting to the ISP's network as remote access users. Systems have also been devised to receive faxes.

2.5.6 Multicasting and MBone

A few ISPs have entered into the business of providing multicast and MBone services. Basically, IP multicast supports the distribution of multimedia data over the Internet, such as real-time audio, video, and other data. By definition, multicasting sends the data to multiple hosts at the same time, but not all hosts—only those that subscribe to the multicast feed. In this way, the service is analogous to cable TV. You subscribe to receive broadcasts from particular channels, but do not receive broadcasts from the other channels.

Companies such as UUNET Technologies already offer multicasting services. In the words of UUNET, "our multicast service—UUCast—is a low-cost alternative to current streaming configurations. Based on multicast Internet protocols, UUCast enables you to broadcast a single stream of content to thousands of customers simultaneously. Each end-user receives a high-quality, real-time simulcast at a much lower cost to you." Other popular streaming configurations are RealAudio, RealVideo, and CU-seeme.

2.5.7 News Feed

Before the advent of HTTP and the web, people exchanged information in article format using the USENET news service. News remains a very popular means of Internet publishing, especially with respect to trade, scientific, and engineering information. A fairly robust following of news devotees also employ it for pursuing their personal interests and hobbies.

In the past, news feeds were considered an additional purchase. Today, the cost of the news feed is typically covered by the basic Internet service fee. Because news traffic can easily consume the available bandwidth on an Internet link, however, it typically remains inactivated until the customer requests the feed.

Because so many newsgroups exist, you should ask the ISP to configure your news feed between the ISP's news server and your server to support only those newsgroups you wish to receive. If you are not careful, you can easily clog your news server with tons on unwanted articles. (Consider yourself forewarned—the disk space consumed by news is staggering!) Some IPS now offer news reader services where they maintain the news server, and your clients read from the server.

2.5.8 Knowledge Services (Consulting)

Because of their greater experience in building and maintaining their own networks, ISPs are generally qualified to help you design, build, and manage your own network. Most ISPs have expended a significant effort to either develop their own consulting services or partner with other organizations that can augment the ISP's services.

Gauging the strength of an ISP's consulting service is essentially a best-guess event. You won't really know how good it is until you enlist their service. Even then, because consulting remains such a personalized commodity, your experience with an ISP's consultants might differ completely from another organization's experience. To try to avoid unpleasant surprises, obtain some references from the ISP and actually check them.

2.6 Capacity Scaling and Oversubscription

When assessing an ISP, verify that your connection's capacity can be increased to higher bandwidths in the future. Once an organization gets the taste for the Internet, its usage of the connection will only increase. Ask the ISP for a recommendation about scaling your connection to higher bandwidths in the future, and make certain this plan makes sense.

One thing to keep in mind when you talk about capacity planning is the **oversubscription** rate. When an ISP sells you a connection to its network, it assumes that you will use only a portion of the leased circuit capacity at your site. You may have moments of peak traffic, but on balance your utilization of the WAN circuit will be lower than its rated capacity. Capitalizing on this fact, ISPs tend to oversell their available capacity to the Internet, creating oversubscription (illustrated in Figure 2-2).

It's not uncommon for ISPs to oversubscribe their capacity by a factor of 4. Thus, when you purchase a T1, for example, you should ask whether you are allowed full use of the circuit. Some ISPs will sell you a connection, but stipulate limitations on your use of the circuit

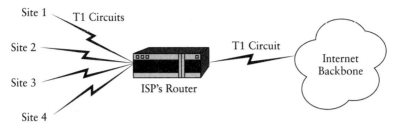

Figure 2-2 *Oversubscription*

because of oversubscription problems. Interrogate your ISP about its oversubsription rate.

2.7 Network Infrastructure

Most ISPs are spending incredible sums to upgrade their networks. The primary thrust of these upgrades is to boost the networks' overall carrying capacity. This trend will likely continue for some time with the burgeoning use of the Internet.

When quizzing a potential ISP, ask some tough questions about its network architecture. Ask to see a map of it and projections for its growth. Some ISPs have their maps posted on their web pages. Be wary of those that refuse to show you their architecture—they may have something to hide. An ISP that's working hard to upgrade its network will want to advertise this fact to its prospective customers.

If you are considering purchasing your service from a reselling provider, ask the following questions about its network:

- How is capacity being purchased from NSPs to service the customer base? Make certain that the ISP is not oversubscribing its service.
- How is the network design fault-tolerant? Study how the ISP has connected to one or more NSPs. If one or more of these connections fail, will the ISP still be able to connect to an NSP? Also, examine the fault tolerance of the ISP's network.
- What carrying capacity is being designed from the POPs to the provider's network? Again, you are looking for oversubscription problems. Is the ISP selling multiple high-capacity circuits from a

POP, but attempting to connect these to its network using a circuit with insufficient capacity?

- Who are the NSPs for the ISP? Take a look at the backbones of those providers.

If you are considering purchasing your connection from an NSP, you should ask similar but slightly different questions:

- How many **Internet exchange points (IXPs)** does the ISP's backbone use to connect with the peering partners (that is, other ISPs and agencies)? The more IXPs an ISP uses, the more robust its backbone will be. Who are the peering partners?
- What is the backbone carrying capacity and infrastructure? For instance, has the ISP upgraded its backbone to OC-12 (622 Mbps) over SONET? Find out where the company is heading with its backbone infrastructure.
- What carrying capacity is being designed from the POPs to the provider's network? Watch out for oversubscription problems.

2.8 Pricing

Pricing is always an important consideration when selecting an ISP. The relevance of price in the decision-making process is a matter each customer must establish. Sometimes the higher-priced provider may provide better service than others do. Do not assume a more expensive provider is automatically better, however—do your homework on the topics previously discussed in this chapter.

This section provides some tips to keep you on track when you start discussing money. It can be difficult to compare the offerings of ISPs based on price unless you clearly understand the pricing structures for their products. When you compare prices, try to examine the bottom line. There are a thousand ways to price things, but in the end you still need to pay the ISP each month. Pay attention to startup costs, monthly costs, and yearly costs. Doing so will keep you focused.

2.8.1 Fixed versus Usage-Based Pricing

ISPs price their access services using a fixed fee or a usage-based fee schedule. In some cases, they provide two methods of pricing for essentially the same service. This approach is especially common when dealing with higher-capacity leased-line circuits, such as E1s and T1s.

Under a fixed fee schedule, you pay a set amount for the Internet service, whether you use it all day and all night, or not at all. Fixed pricing is sometimes the only option available for lower-bandwidth circuits such as ISDN or 56/64 Kbps Frame Relay.

With a usage-based fee schedule, the monthly price is based upon the average sustained usage during the month. The ISP monitors the utilization level on your leased circuit at fixed intervals (usually 5 minutes) throughout the month. At the end of the month, it calculates the average utilization based on these measurements.

Table 2-1 provides an actual example of a usage-based price quotation for T1 service from a large ISP. For comparison, the fixed fee schedule for the same service is $2,495 per month for a one-year term. It should be obvious that the fixed price schedule would be more economical if you expected your site to sustain an average utilization greater than 384 Kbps.

Service fees do not include the cost for the leased circuit. You must add the leased circuit cost to your monthly fee to determine your true monthly cost.

2.8.2 Obtaining Quotations

Ask each prospective ISP for a written price quotation. They should be happy to send such information, often transmitting these rates very quickly via e-mail or fax. Some web sites even have online forms that you can complete and submit to obtain a quotation.

Table 2-1 Usage-Based Pricing Example

T1 Usage Level	Monthly Rate
0 to 128 Kbps	$1,295
128 Kbps to 256 Kbps	$1,895
256 Kbps to 384 Kbps	$2,495
384 Kbps to 512 Kbps	$2,750
Over 512 Kbps	$3,000

When requesting a quotation for service, remember the following points:

- Stipulate which services you wish to purchase. For example, you might say, "Please price the Internet access service, plus a news feed, using a 256 Kbps connection with usage-based pricing." You may wish to stipulate other criteria as well, such as service level required.
- Request that the quotation be broken out into the following components: startup, monthly, and yearly costs. These costs may need to be further presented in two components: service and leased circuit costs.
- Make certain prices for extended services are listed as line items in addition to the basic Internet access service.
- Ask for a discount. In the worst case scenario, you will not be offered one. If you do receive such an offer, get it in writing.
- Ask if multiyear pricing is available. You will often get a better deal if you purchase Internet service via a multiyear contract.

Table 2-2 presents a fictitious price quotation, with the price components being highlighted.

Normally the price quotation will be delivered with an expiration date. If you can't make a decision before that date, you must obtain a

Table 2-2 Fictitious Quotation		
Item	Monthly Fee	Yearly Cost
Startup Costs		
Activation Charges		$ 2,000
Leased Circuit Installation		$ 1,300
Premises Equipment (Router and CSU/DSU)		$ 2,500
Totals:		$ 5,800
Recurring Costs		
Super-duper T1 Internet Access (Fixed)	$2,495	$29,940
Leased Circuit Fees	$ 827	$ 9,924
Total:	$3,322	$39,864

new quotation. Also, most quotations are accompanied by the contract terms and conditions. That brings us to the next topic—contract terms.

2.8.3 Contract Terms

When you actually decide which ISP will have the honor of serving your site, you execute a signed contract with that company for the service. As with all service contracts, you should read the fine print. If you work in a litigious country (like the United States), then you might even want a lawyer to read it as well. At minimum, the contract should include the following items:

- Description of services to be provided
- Service-level guarantees
- Pricing (by attaching the quotation)

In addition, look closely for termination and conversion clauses. Know the ISP's expectations should you cease being its customer before the contract expires. The following terms are not uncommon:

- Conversion clauses—in which you must elect to switch from usage-based to fixed pricing before a certain date or else be locked into usage-based pricing after your original contract expires.
- Early termination penalties—which make you reimburse the ISP some percentage of what it would have earned had you remained its customer.
- End of contract clauses—which switch you from fixed to usage-based pricing at the end of a contract.

2.8.4 Negotiating

ISPs want your business. You want an Internet connection. Both of you want what the other has to offer. Do you think you might negotiate to get a better deal for your organization? Perhaps so. We have provided a few recommendations when negotiating with ISPs. After reading them, you are on your own.

- Be open and state that the ISP is in a competitive situation with other ISPs (if it is the truth). This scenario can sometimes lead to a competitive price discount. It also gives the salesperson some ammunition when pleading your case to a sales manager.

- When talking about price, expect an ISP's offer for price discounts to increase based on the length of the contract. Two- or three-year contracts offer the best price reductions.

2.9 Checklist—Selecting the ISP

The following checklist offers a guideline to selecting an ISP. It is really a list of things to consider as you review the qualifications of each provider.

Basic Service Requirements

Services Provided

❑ Does "full" service completely support standard Internet service protocols (that is, e-mail, WWW, FTP, Telnet)?
❑ Which service protocols are not included?

Connection Capacities and Technologies

❑ How much bandwidth do you need?
❑ Which connection rates are available?
❑ Which WAN technologies are available?
   ❑ ISDN
   ❑ ADSL
   ❑ SMDS
   ❑ Frame Relay
   ❑ PPP
   ❑ Other

Access Provisioning (WAN Circuits)

❑ Will the ISP coordinate circuit installation with the telecommunications vendor?
❑ Where is the nearest POP?
❑ Which activation services are available?
   ❑ Telephone
   ❑ On-site

Equipment Selection and Provisioning

❑ Does the ISP offer premises equipment for you to purchase or rent?
❑ Does the ISP offer to manage your on-site equipment?
   ❑ If so, is an analog line required?
❑ Will the ISP configure this equipment?
❑ Do you wish to purchase and configure your own premises equipment?
   ❑ If so, are there compatibility issues with the ISP's POP equipment?

Installation and Support Considerations

Domain Name Registration and MX Mail Records

❑ Will the ISP assist you in registering your chosen domain name?
❑ Will the ISP register your MX mail records?

IP Address Pool Allocation

❑ Will the ISP grant you a block of IP addresses that meets your needs?
❑ Will you implement Network Address Translation (NAT) instead?
❑ Will you use DHCP so as to use a smaller pool of addresses more efficiently?

Activation Support (Installation)

❑ When activating the connection, what will the ISP require you to have running?
❑ Do you need a TCP/IP workstation with the ping and traceroute utilities?
❑ Is premises equipment operational and tested?

Post-Sales Support

❑ Is 24 × 7 support available and properly staffed?
❑ What service-level guarantees are available?
❑ Is early notification of work is provided?
❑ What are the escalation procedures of the ISP?

❑ How are you notified of a problem?
❑ What additional services does the ISP provide to distinguish it from other companies?

Availability of Additional Services

Extended Services

❑ Web hosting services
❑ Security auditing and solutions
❑ Virtual Private Network solutions
❑ Remote access solutions
❑ Faxing services
❑ Multicast and MBone
❑ News feed
❑ Consulting services

Growth of the ISP's Infrastructure

ISP's Network Infrastructure

❑ Can you get a map of the provider's networks?
❑ How far has the ISP oversubscribed its connections to the Internet backbone?
❑ How is the ISP upgrading its network to meet future needs?
❑ How fault-tolerant is the ISP's network?
❑ Is the carrying capacity from the POP sufficient?
❑ Who are the ISP's NSPs or peering partners?
❑ How many IXPs does the provider use to connect to peering partners (if applicable)?

Pricing and Contract Issues

Pricing

❑ Is there fixed pricing?
❑ Is there usage-based pricing?
❑ Have you received written quotations?
❑ Are quotations provided with itemized costs?
    ❑ Startup costs listed
    ❑ Recurring costs listed

❏ Are there competitive discounts available?
❏ Are there multiyear discounts available?
❏ Are the extended services listed as line items?

Contractual Issues

❏ Does the contract stipulate prices, services to be provided, and service-level guarantees?
❏ Have you examined termination clauses?
❏ Do you need a lawyer or someone else to review the contract?

Provisioning Your
Wide Area Network

Provisioning the wide area network is a task that requires some education and preparation. The concepts, terms, and lingo used in the WAN are quite different from those associated with the LAN. Provisioning the WAN circuit for your Internet connection normally involves one or more parties, including the ISP and the telecommunications provider. You should learn as much as possible about the provisioning process beforehand to ensure that it goes smoothly, even if the ISP will do the actual circuit ordering.

3.1 Chapter Overview

This chapter covers the process of building the WAN circuit for your Internet connection. Because the details of your particular connection will depend on the services provided by your telecommunications vendor, it will not explain WAN provisioning using cookbook-like recipes. Instead, by using your knowledge of the fundamental concepts of the technologies employed by telecommunication vendors, you will be able to adapt your knowledge to the details of your situation.

This chapter attempts to address more than just the North American market. Most of the telecommunications companies and agencies now build their infrastructures based on **International Telecommunications Union (ITU)** standards. This was not always the case, however. Even today, differences between the standards deployed in North America and those in Europe and Japan persist.

The various sections of this chapter discuss general telecommunications concepts, communications technologies, and networking equipment required for the WAN. After reading this chapter, you should be able to answer the following questions:

1. Which circuit capacities (bandwidths) are available in North America and internationally?
2. Which communications technologies are commonly used for WAN circuits, and in particular for Internet access?
3. How do telecommunications vendors present the circuit for use in your facility?
4. How do telecommunications providers condition the signals in the circuit?
5. What premises equipment do you need to connect the WAN circuit to your network equipment?

A WAN provisioning checklist, which you might find useful in preparing for the circuit installation, appears at the end of the chapter.

The provisioning process will be greatly simplified if you partner with a reputable and knowledgeable ISP. If you take bundled provisioning with your service (the recommended approach), the ISP should address most of the technical issues directly with the telecommunications vendor. Nevertheless, it is in your best interest to be as knowledgeable as possible about the entire process.

3.2 Circuit Capacity (Bandwidth)

The circuit capacities available will vary according to the telecommunications system implemented by the vendors or government in your country. In effect, three systems define the infrastructures for digital signaling:

- North American
- European
- Japanese

These three distinct systems developed during a period when no international body defined global communications standards. As a result, the telecommunications equipment vendors in North America,

Japan, and Europe forged their own standards in conjunction with their local governments.

The advent of the ITU changed this scattershot approach. The ITU develops new communications standards intended to ensure global interoperability between telecommunications infrastructures. For instance, modem communications standards are now accomplished through the ITU. The legacy of these previous systems remains, however.

Tables 3-1, 3-2, and 3-3 give the digital signal hierarchy for the North American, European, and Japanese systems, respectively. As you review these tables, keep the following points in mind:

- The *transmission rate* is the theoretical maximum for the circuit. The actual transmission rate will be less because of in-band circuit management functions.
- The *carrier* designation is the traditional name for the circuit. The *digital signal* designation is the new (and hopefully universal) method for circuit naming. The designators can be used interchangeably, though most people still use the original carrier designators (such as T-1, E-1, and so on).
- The common denominator in all systems is the *digital signal zero (DS-0)*.[1] It denotes a single 64 Kbps channel. *It is a global standard.*
- Carrier circuits combine multiple DS-0 channels into a single circuit. The number of such channels in a carrier depends on the system. Thus a DS-1 in Europe contains a different number of DS-0 channels than does a DS-1 in North America.

For the most part, the three systems are remarkably similar. The major differences involve the carrier names and the quantity of DS-0 channels provided by the carriers. In practice, the most commonly provisioned circuits are DS-1 and DS-3. The DS-2 specification exists, but

---

1. Originally, digital carrier circuits were intended to transmit digitized voice signals. The minimum circuit needed for transmitting voice signals is 64 Kbps. Thus carrier circuits contain multiple DS-0 channels. The three regional systems differ in the quantity of DS-0 channels per carrier circuit.

few equipment manufacturers sell electronics that enable telecommunications carriers to build DS-2 circuits. Consequently, few telecommunication vendors sell DS-2 circuits. Instead, most ISPs sell dual DS-1 connections for sites that need more capacity than a single DS-1 can offer, but do not need a DS-3.

With the introduction of fiber-optic transmission media a decade or so ago, the telecommunications equipment vendors were able to

Table 3-1   North American Digital Signal Hierarchy

Transmission Rate (Mbps)	T-Carrier (T-n)	Digital Signal (DS-n)	Number of DS-0 Channels	Number of DS-1 Channels
0.064		DS-0	1	
1.544	T-1	DS-1	24	1
6.31	T-2	DS-2	96	4
44.74	T-3	DS-3	672	28

Table 3-2   European Digital Signal Hierarchy

Transmission Rate (Mbps)	E-Carrier (E-n)	Digital Signal (DS-n)	Number of DS-0 Channels	Number of DS-1 Channels
0.064		DS-0	1	
2.048	E-1	DS-1	32	1
8.448	E-2	DS-2	128	4
34.368	E-3	DS-3	512	16

Table 3-3   Japanese Digital Signal Hierarchy

Transmission Rate (Mbps)	T-Carrier (T-n)	Digital Signal (DS-n)	Number of DS-0 Channels	Number of DS-1 Channels
0.064		DS-0	1	
1.544	T-1	DS-1	24	1
6.312	T-2	DS-2	96	4
32.064	T-3	DS-3	480	20

Table 3-4 Optical Signal Hierarchy

Transmission Rate (Mbps)	Optical Rate (Mbps)	SONET (OC-n)	SDH (STM-n)	DS-1 Channels[2]
44.74	51.84	OC-1		28
155	155	OC-3	STM-1	84
622	622	OC-12	STM-4	336
1,244	1,244	OC-24	STM-8	672
2,488	2,488	OC-48	STM-16	1,344
4,976	4,976	OC-96	STM-32	2,688
9,953	9,953	OC-192	STM-64	5,376

increase their transmission rates significantly. The availability of fiber led to the development of the transport technology called **synchronous optical network (SONET)** in North America and **synchronous digital hierarchy (SDH)** in Europe and elsewhere. In essence, SONET and SDH are synonomous.

In SONET, the transmission rates are called optical carriers (OC-n). In SDH, the transmission rates are referred to as synchronous transfer mode (STM-n). Table 3-4 shows the optical signal hierarchy. Notice that the actual data transmission rate for the OC-1 differs from the optical rate, reflecting the overhead due to asynchronous-to-synchronous mapping.

Because SONET and SDH are highly fault-tolerant technologies, telecommunications companies (telecoms) have switched from using copper wiring to fiber when connecting the central office to the customer site. In metropolitan areas, a telecom often chooses to deploy fiber to a customer site and then multiplex the connection to lower-capacity circuits, especially for customers who lease a number of circuits from the telecom. For example, telecoms can now provide an OC-3 circuit to a customer site and then multiplex it into individual DS-3 circuits or even DS-1 circuits.

---

2. The DS-1 circuit used in this column is the North American and Japanese version, with 24 DS-0 channels.

3.2.1 DS-1 Circuits (E-1 and T-1)

The vast majority of installed data circuits for Internet connections use a DS-1 circuit. In the North American and Japanese systems, DS-1 is commonly called T-1, and it has a rated capacity of roughly 1.544 Mbps. In the European, DS-1 is called E-1, and its rated capacity is 2.048 Mpbs. DS-1 is the staple WAN circuit for several reasons:

- DS-1 can be fractionalized into lower-capacity circuits by disabling a portion of the DS-0 channels in it.
- DS-1 circuits can be deployed easily using conditioned copper. In many locations, copper wiring is the only infrastructure deployed by the telecommunications company. (The other option is fiber-optic cable.)

If you purchase an Internet connection with a rated capacity greater than 128 Kbps and less than the capacity of DS-1, expect to have it provisioned using a DS-1 circuit.[3] The telecom will install a DS-1 circuit, but activate only portion of the DS-0 channels. For example, a 512 Kbps circuit in the United States uses a DS-1 circuit with 24 DS-0 channels. Only the first eight DS-0 channels are used, however (8 × 64 Kbps = 512 Kbps). Table 3-5 lists the number of DS-0 channels required to create the most common fractionalized DS-1 circuits.

Table 3-5 Fractional DS-1 Capacities

Capacity (Kbps)	Activated DS-0 Channels
128	2
256	4
384	6
512	8
768	12
1,024	16

---

3. In areas where ISDN circuits are cheap, the ISP may offer an alternative solution using inverse-multiplexed **basic rate interface (BRI)** circuits.

From an economic standpoint, it doesn't make sense to lease fractionalized circuits larger than 768 Kbps. Basically, the cost of leasing a very large fractionalized DS-1 circuit is equivalent to that of leasing the entire DS-1 circuit.

Although the rated capacities of DS-1 and fractionalized DS-1 circuit may seem low compared with those found in today's LANs, even these circuits may cost a fair amount of money to lease per month. In the United States, a DS-1 circuit provisioned entirely within the telecom's network costs approximately $800 per month to lease.

3.2.2 Dual DS-1 Circuits

Life becomes a bit more interesting when you need more than a DS-1 circuit but less than a DS-3 connection. ISPs sell dual DS-1 solutions for these situations. In a dual DS-1 setup, your premises router connects to the ISP's router using two individual DS-1 circuits. The routers are configured to load-balance the traffic. This solution offers the benefits of some inherent fault tolerance. If one circuit fails, the other will be available to carry the connection.

Several permutations of this concept exist. In one approach, you present two DS-1 circuits to the router. This option often requires that you use the same router equipment as the ISP and configure the load balancing in some manner. Common approaches are to deploy Multilink PPP specifications or Cisco's Express Forwarding multilink option, both of which are router-specific. The number of DS-1 circuits can usually be scaled up to six on most routers. Figure 3-1 shows the concept of a dual DS-1 connection.

In another approach, the two DS-1 circuits are bonded together at the channel service unit/data service unit (CSU/DSU) and presented to the router as a single WAN circuit. The process of sending data

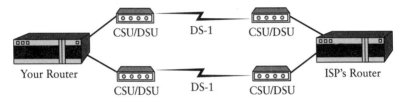

Figure 3-1 *Dual DS-1 connection*

through several pipes simultaneously and presenting a single interface to a router is called **inverse-multiplexing (IMUX)**. It requires additional hardware and may not be available from all ISPs.

Inverse-multiplexing inside a router uses extra serial ports and can increase the CPU workload. On the other hand, combining DS-1 circuits via a CSU/DSU IMUX solution is a more scalable option. Most IMUX solutions can combine as many as eight DS-1 circuits and present the aggregated bandwidth as a single circuit to the router.

3.2.3 DS-3 Circuits (T-3 and E-3)

When you need more capacity than a dual DS-1 connection, or IMUX solution, can provide, DS-3, or fractionalized DS-3, will be your choice. DS-3 is the North American and Japanese T-3 and E-3 is the European name. The respective capacities are 45 Mbps, 32 Mbps, and 34 Mbps.

Similar to a DS-1 circuit, the DS-3 connection can be multiplexed into individual DS-1 circuits. For instance, a T-3 circuit can be used as 28 individual T-1 circuits. The same logic applies within the European system, wherein an E-3 circuit can be fractionalized and 16 E-1 circuits used within it. In essence, fractionalized DS-3 allows you to increment the circuit capacity by factors of DS-1.

The monthly lease price for a full DS-1 circuit is roughly the same as that for a fractional DS-1 circuit containing 8 to 10 active DS-0 channels (giving a capacity of approximately 768 Kbps). A similar breakpoint exists with the DS-3 circuit. Depending on the price structure employed by the telecommunications vendor, the price breakpoint for a DS-3 circuit is approximately 10 DS-1 circuits. Thus, if you are currently leasing 10 individual DS-1 circuits, then it probably makes sense to consider leasing a full DS-3 circuit and fractionalizing it into DS-1 connections.

Many ISPs do not offer fractionalized DS-3, but rather deploy a full (nonfractional) DS-3 circuit and then limit the customer to partial use. In these cases, the Internet connection represents a full DS-3 circuit to the ISP, and the ISP limits the circuit capacity using a CSU/DSU to ensure that the customer does not exceed a predetermined limit. For example, the ISP may set a 6 Mbps limit on a DS-3 circuit. In other cases the ISP will only sell usage-based DS-3 service.

D-3 circuits are generally reserved for ISPs and very large Internet access customers. When an upstream ISP provides service to the downstream company, it typically uses one or more DS-3 circuits. Many ISPs that maintain a portion of the Internet backbone use DS-3 circuits in their networks.

3.3 Components of WAN Circuits

Knowing the components that constitute telecommunications circuits will help you understand the jargon used by your ISP and telecommunications vendors. The best way to present this terminology is via illustrations. Presented here is a hit parade of terms:

- Central office (CO)
- Interexchange
- Interoffice channel
- Local loop
- Point-of-presence (POP)
- Span
- Tail circuit

By far, the most commonly encountered terms are the **local loop** and **central office (CO)**. The local loop is the physical circuit between the customer's site and the telecommunications provider's nearest facility, otherwise called the central office.

Figure 3-2 shows a hypothetical WAN circuit between your router and the ISP's router in its POP. This example illustrates a complex case, such as an international circuit. It depicts a WAN circuit built by three telecommunications vendors—your local telecom, a long-distance telecom, and the ISP's local telecom. The three circuits (1, 2, and 3), when hooked together, create a WAN circuit between the sites.

In Figure 3-2, circuits 1 and 3 are the **tail circuits** between the customer's site and the **interexchange** facility. The local telecommunications provider connects a circuit to the long-distance provider's circuit at the interexchange. The interexchange is also called the long-distance provider's **point-of-presence (POP)**.[4]

Circuit 2 is the long-distance provider's circuit between the POPs. Commonly, it is called the **interoffice channel (IOC)**, especially when the overall circuit between the endpoints contains tail circuits. Local telecoms also use the term "IOC" to distinguish the portions of a circuit

---

4. Often, a single facility will function as a POP for multiple long-distance providers. In the author's experience, the interexchange is a common location for provisioning errors to occur.

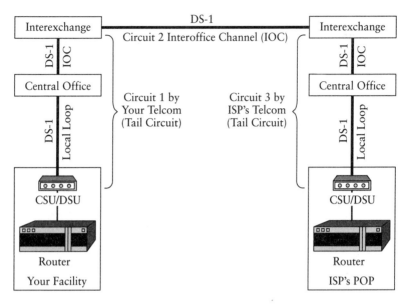

Figure 3-2 *Circuit components*

between their own facilities. For example, the piece of the tail circuit between the central office and the interexchange comprises an IOC.

Luckily, most WAN circuits for Internet access require only a single telecommunications provider. This telecom provisions the circuit from end to end. Figure 3-3 depicts a circuit built entirely within a single telecom's infrastructure. Notice the absence of tail circuits or interexchanges in this diagram.

Before leaving the topic of WAN circuit components, we should discuss circuit ownership and identification. Unless you tell your ISP that you will order and provision the WAN circuit to their POP, *the ISP owns the circuit*. This ownership implies that the ISP pays the monthly fees for the circuit directly to the telecom. In turn, your monthly payment to the ISP includes a component for the leased-line cost.

This arrangement can create complications if you encounter problems with the circuit. The ISP is responsible for working with the telecom in resolving problems. If you discover a problem with your circuit and call the telecom directly, it may refuse to deal with you—from the telecom's viewpoint, the ISP is the customer! This situation can be incredibly frustrating, especially if your ISP fails to aggressively tackle WAN-related problems.

The best course in this situation is probably to obtain the circuit IDs for your circuits before you experience a problem. All WAN troubleshooting starts by identifying the circuit. In addition, you should ask to be made a site contact with the telecom. As an official contact, you will have the authority to open trouble tickets and take other steps to resolve WAN-related problems. On the balance, however, reputable ISPs will be aggressive in resolving WAN issues, making this recommendation unnecessary. Although some ISPs may object to this arrangement, remember one thing—you're the customer! The ISP owns the circuit and assumes 100% responsibility for fixing WAN problems.

3.4 Circuit Technologies

When a telecom builds a WAN circuit between your site and the ISP's POP, it creates a physical path for transmitting digital signals between the circuit's endpoints. In addition, the circuit must be able to support the particular technology that will use the infrastructure. A number of

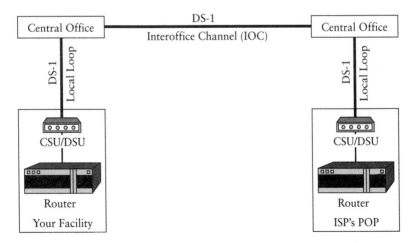

Figure 3-3 *Locally provisioned point-to-point circuit*

technologies are popular for use in WANs, and thus Internet access circuits:

- Point-to-point
- Frame Relay
- Switched Multimegabit Digital Service (SMDS)
- Integrated Service Digital Network (ISDN)
- Asynchronous Digital Subscriber Line (ADSL)

In many ways, a WAN circuit technology is analogous to a LAN technology such as Ethernet or Token Ring. Essentially, these LAN technologies define how a physical infrastructure supports intercommunication between devices attached to it. Similarly, WAN technologies define how endpoints access the network and exchange information.

3.4.1 Point-to-Point

Point-to-point circuits are a common, but relatively expensive method of building WAN circuits. Historically, such circuits were the only types available until the invention of packet switched technologies such as X.25, Frame Relay, and SMDS.

As its name implies, a point-to-point circuit enables only two endpoints to intercommunicate. In this type of circuit, the telecom's equipment simply conditions and repeats the digital signal transmitted between the end stations. Typically, point-to-point circuits support only serial communications. Figures 3-2 and 3-3 illustrated point-to-point links.

Although a point-to-point circuit can support a variety of communication protocols, the **Point-to-Point Protocol (PPP)** is becoming the standard communications protocol implemented on this circuit type. PPP provides a method for transporting multiprotocol datagrams over point-to-point links. As a consequence, protocols such as IP, IPX, and AppleTalk can be carried over a PPP link.

In provisioning Internet connections, a point-to-point link has become a popular option for several reasons:

- The circuit's capacity is completely dedicated to your use.
- The circuit is more secure because it is not shared with other customers of the telecom.

- Packet latency in a point-to-point circuit is less than that observed in a packet-switched network.[5]
- Configuring a router to use PPP over a point-to-point circuit is not complicated.

The major drawback of the point-to-point circuit is its cost. Because it is a dedicated connection, the telecom charges more for it.

ISPs typically use a point-to-point circuit to support access at the DS-1 (T-1/E-1), fractional DS-3, and full DS-3 (T-3/E-3) capacity levels. At least in the United States, ISPs rarely provision fractional DS-1 circuits for PPP access. Instead, customers can elect usage-based pricing on a full DS-1 circuit or choose another technology such as Frame Relay or ISDN.

3.4.2 Frame Relay

Frame Relay is a packet-switching technology commonly employed in WAN connections. Unlike a point-to-point circuit, which contains only two endpoints, a Frame Relay network consists of many nodes sharing the same physical network. For this reason, Frame Relay is known as a point-to-multipoint technology.

Over the last five years, telecommunications providers in North America have made huge investments in this technology. Many ISPs also have Frame Relay offerings, not just because it is readily sold by telecommunications providers, but because the technology permits ISPs to aggregate the bandwidth of many customers into a single circuit. In effect, an ISP can oversell available bandwidth and make a profit. In addition, ISPs can offer lower-priced circuits to their customers.[6]

---

5. Packet latency is the travel time of a packet between its source and destination, usually measured in milliseconds (ms). In a point-to-point circuit, latency is generally about 10 ms per 1,000 circuit miles.

6. A Frame Relay circuit from an ISP should cost less than an equivalently sized point-to-point circuit, because you must share bandwidth with other customers and do not have full use of the available bandwidth, as you would with a point-to-point circuit.

Some advantages of using Frame Relay service are as follows:

- It tends to be less expensive than equivalent point-to-point circuits.
- The availability of a maximum burst rate permits your data rate to burst as needed.
- It is widely available at fractional DS-1 rates.

The major disadvantage of Frame Relay is the added latency in the network imposed by packet switching.[7] For local circuits, this consideration should be negligble. Long-distance Frame Relay circuits, on the other hand, tend to exhibit higher latencies when compared with similar point-to-point circuits.

Typical capacities for Frame Relay encompass the fractional DS-1 circuits, such as 128, 256, 384, 512, 768, and 1,024 Kbps. The maximum available capacities for Frame Relay circuits are 1,544 Kbps (T-1) and 2,048 Kbps (E-1).

Figure 3-4 shows a Frame Relay configuration between an ISP and two customers. The ISP uses a DS-1 circuit into the Frame Relay network, while the customers use 256 and 512 Kbps circuits.

Because Frame Relay is a packet-switched network technology, each packet must contain information about its source and destination address in the network. This arrangement resembles LAN technologies' use of media access control (MAC) addresses at the data link layer to identify the source and destination stations.

In Frame Relay, the packet header contains a **data link connection identifier (DLCI)** field, which plays a similar role as the MAC. Frame Relay switches in the telecom's network read the DLCI value and switch the packet toward its destination. Frame relay networks are typically represented as amorphous blobs or clouds in diagrams and pictures. This is because a switching network does not necessarily guarantee a consistent route between the sending and receiving stations. In reality, though, the path is usually consistent unless there is a switch failure in the network.

---

7. In long-distance Frame Relay circuits, latency is approximately 20 ms per 1,000 circuit miles.

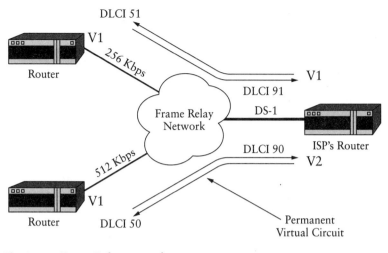

Figure 3-4 *Frame Relay network*

The path between the sending and receiving station is called a virtual circuit. For all practical purposes, the DLCI value represents a virtual circuit identifier. There are two flavors of virtual circuits in Frame Relay.

1. In a **switched virtual circuit** (**SVC**) setup, your virtual circuit to another frame relay device is built on demand and then destroyed when no longer needed, just like your home phone service.

2. In a **permanent virtual circuit** (**PVC**) setup, you configure your virtual circuit to permanently connect to a specific DLCI. The circuit is always available and connected. The PVC is the most common deployment of Frame Relay and the type used to build Internet connections.

Note that it is possible to create multiple PVCs using the same physical port. When you set up a PVC you create a virtual port on your router. The nomenclature of the virtual port varies from vendor to vendor. In Figure 3-4, the ISP has two virtual ports configured on the DS-1 WAN port, V1 and V2. Similarly, the customers have each a single virtual port for the PVC to the ISP's router.

One *major* difference between Frame Relay and point-to-point circuits is the available circuit capacity. In a point-to-point circuit, the circuit capacity is yours to squander, but this is not true in the shared Frame Relay network. Guaranteeing available bandwidth in shared networks falls under **quality of service (QoS)**—the new buzzword.

There are two benchmarks for comparing circuit capacities in frame relay:

1. The **committed information rate (CIR)** is the guaranteed capacity offered by the telecommunications provider on your virtual circuit. The telecom absolutely ensures that data rates reaching this value will be supported.
2. The **port speed** is the absolute maximum data rate accepted by the telecom on your circuit. The port speed will exceed the CIR. Data rates between the CIR and the port speed are guaranteed on a best-effort basis by the telecom.

If you plan to install a Frame Relay circuit, you should verify both the port speed and CIR values on the circuit. Typically, the port speed is twice the CIR—for instance, a 128 Kbps CIR circuit will normally have a port speed of 256 Kbps. The CIR is effectively the circuit's maximum capacity. In many cases, this value will determine your leased-line costs.

When you implement a Frame Relay device, the telecom or ISP might ask you to activate the **local management interface (LMI)** features on your virtual port. LMI is a protocol used in frame relay to manage circuit health and other related issues. Four LMI standards exist:

- Consortium LMI
- Annex-D LMI (IEEE, ANSI)
- NTT LMI
- ITU LMI

Ask your ISP or telecom if LMI is implemented on the circuit; if it is, then ask what type is used. Sometimes a telecom will implement LMI during the provisioning process to ensure that each portion of a circuit is operational, but then turn it off when the circuit is completely built and tested.

3.4.3 SMDS

Switched Multimegabit Data Service (SMDS), also known as **cell relay**, is another WAN technology that ISPs can use to connect their customers to the Internet. At the moment, deployment of SMDS remains limited, compared with point-to-point and Frame Relay technologies.

Bellcore developed SMDS as a metropolitan area network (MAN) technology conforming to IEEE 802.6 standards. It was designed to interconnect offices (and the LANs in those offices) across sites in a metropolitan area, such as a city.

Access occurs through DS-0, DS-1, DS-3, or SONET circuits (though most often via DS-1 or DS-3). Because SMDS consumes a fair amount of overhead, a T-1 connection provides a capacity of only 1.17 Mbps and a T-3 connection provides only 34 Mbps. Table 3-6 lists the typical access speeds supported by SMDS.

Notice that these access rates match the LAN speeds commonly encountered several years ago—probably at the time SDMS was formulated. The exception is 25 Mbps ATM, which has not gained much popularity. With the addition of DS-0 service to the technology, however, SMDS can now compete with Frame Relay for fractional DS-1 service.

SMDS is a connectionless WAN technology, like Frame Relay, but uses fixed-length cells. Because it is connectionless, it employs cell addressing to determine the source and destination of the cell in the network. SMDS addresses are of two types: individual addresses, for unicast traffic, and group addresses, for multicast traffic. Table 3-7 shows some example addresses.

Table 3-6 SMDS Access Rates

Access Class	Access Speed (Mbps)	Same Speed as
1	4	Token Ring
2	10	Ethernet
3	16	Token Ring
4	25	ATM
5	44.736	T-3

Table 3-7 SMDS Address Examples

SMDS Address	Type
C14085551212FFFF	Individual address
E14085551234FFFF	Group address

Access to the SMDS network is accomplished through the subscriber network interface (SNI). The SNI at the telecom's switch allows only cells from your assigned address to enter and leave the network through your site connection. Thus, for a connectionless technology, SMDS provides a high degree of security and privacy. An imposter attempting to send or receive cells using your address will fail.

To connect a router to an SMDS network, your system must support three levels of the **SMDS Interface Protocol (SIP)**. Your router provides the SIP-3 protocol, which encapsulates the user data into proper protocol data units. This conversion protocol allows SMDS to be deployed on other technologies, such as ATM. SIP-1 and SIP-2 are provided by a third-party CSU/DSU.

Because SMDS has not been widely deployed by telecoms, most ISPs do not offer it. It does offer several advantages, however:

- Billing is usage-based instead of by allocated circuit capacity (you pay for what you use).
- SMDS ensures fair allocation of bandwidth.
- The technology can use ATM adaption layers 3 and 4 (unspecified bit rate) and thus supports data networking.
- SMDS offers better circuit security than Frame Relay.

The concerns with SMDS are as follows:

- Its latency is uncertain (causing possible protocol time-outs, though delays are specified to be kept to less than 20 ms).
- SMDS is unsuitable for many digitized voice and video services (because of the unknown latency).
- It is difficult to troubleshoot connectionless services.

To implement an SMDS connection, you must have specific CSU/DSU and router equipment that supports SIP. Furthermore, you'll need to work with the telecom and implement the correct individual and group addresses on your equipment. In short, if your ISP offers an SMDS service, it probably makes sense to become more familiar with the technology by reading additional texts on the subject and asking a lot of questions.

3.4.4 ISDN

Integrated Services Digital Network (ISDN) is a global telecommunications standard. It has been successfully deployed in Europe for years, and is now finding greater implementation in North America and elsewhere. ISDN excels in its ability to handle both voice and data on demand. Crudely put, ISDN is a digital phone line. When your network equipment needs a WAN connection, it calls another device, thereby creating a circuit. When the call is finished, the circuit terminates and you no longer pay any usage charges.

ISDN circuits include two components:

- The **bearer (B) channel** carries the digitized voice or data. It is a 64 Kbps circuit-switched channel, which means that the entire circuit is connected to a single destination (as in a telephone call). Because the B channel is also full duplex, it can receive and send data at the same time.
- The **delta (D) channel** carries signaling information and sometimes data. It can have a capacity of either 16 Kbps or 64 Kbps.

ISDN comes in two basic flavors—the **basic rate interface (BRI)** and the **primary rate interface (PRI)**.

- BRI is the standard ISDN service deployed by telecom providers to homes and offices. It consists of two bearer channels and a single delta channel (hence its designation as 2B+D service).[8] BRI can therefore offer a capacity of 128 Kbps (2×64 Kbps). Sometimes the D channel is used to carry data as well, though this option is only now being offered within vendors' products.

---

8. In ITU parlance, two standards for ISDN BRI exist—the 2B+D "S" interface and the 2B+D "U" interface. The "U" interface is the common one and requires only a single wiring pair, such as the type normally found in a home. ISDN BRI equipment can work at five cable kilometers from the central office. In North America, this distance translates to about three cable miles from the central office.

- PRI actually consists of a T-1 or E-1 circuit, depending on which digital signaling system the country uses. In North America, PRI comprises the 23B+D standard built on a T-1 carrier, where the D channel is actually 64 Kbps (a DS-0 connection). In Europe, PRI consists of the 30B+D standard, where again the D channel is 64 Kbps. The European PRI is built using an E-1 carrier.

In addition, a variant of the ISDN called CAPI 2.0 is used in Germany. Another variant is employed in France, but its differences from the major standard are minor.

Figure 3-5 shows a typical ISDN configuration connecting customers to an ISP's router. In this diagram, the customer uses an ISDN BRI, which provides up to 128 Kbps service to the ISP. The ISP uses a PRI to service the incoming calls from the BRIs. It can effectively service 23 B channels simultaneously (in North America). In this figure, the customers configure their routers to dial the number of the ISP's PRI. In practice, only ISPs purchase PRIs from the telecommunications provider, while the customer uses one or more BRIs.

ISDN's attraction derives from its flexibility and potentially lower costs than an equivalent 128 Kbps circuit using a point-to-point construction. Because it is an on-demand service, the customer pays per-minute usage fees in addition to a monthly service fee. Typically, these costs are lower than the lease costs for a 128 Kbps point-to-point circuit.

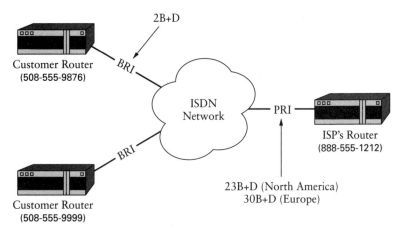

Figure 3-5 *ISDN network*

Costs may not always be lower with ISDN, however, especially if the circuit is used extensively throughout the entire day. Also, if the ISP's PRI necessitates a long-distance call, then additional charges apply. Billing for ISDN is similar to that for a regular phone line, and often billing plans are available that provide various amounts of free dialing during the month. Yet even with all of these potential cost increases, ISDN remains an attractive service to small organizations that need decent connection rates to the ISP, but only on a periodic basis.

One concern with ISDN relates to the circuit setup time. As an on-demand service, ISDN must create a new circuit before any data can be transferred. In most cases, the setup time is less than a second; in some cases, however, it may take several seconds to establish the circuit. Most application programs can handle such a delay. Once the circuit is established, it behaves like a point-to-point circuit, albeit with higher latency.[9]

3.4.5 ADSL

Asymmetric Digital Subscriber Line (ADSL) is a new-generation digital phone service that can provide data transmission rates approaching 8 Mbps in the downstream direction from the CO and 1.5 Mbps in the upstream direction. ADSL belongs to the xDSL family, which represents a collection of similar DSL technologies. Other members of this family include Rate Adaptive DSL (R-ADSL), High Bit-Rate DSL (HDSL), Single-Line DSL (SDSL), and Very High Bit-Rate DSL (VDSL).

DSL was originally developed to provide video-on-demand. The explosive growth in the Internet access market has since expanded this objective to include Internet/intranet access to online services. In effect, xDSL technologies deliver broadband communications over copper infrastructures.[10] As a result, they can simultaneously provide video-on-demand, TV signal delivery, interactive entertainment, and voice transmission. Among the DSL technologies, ADSL appears most likely to be deployed by telecommunications companies for high-speed Internet

---

9. An ISDN circuit has a latency of about 40 ms, whereas point-to-point circuits have latency of 4 to 8.
10. Broadband refers to the method of creating data channels by allocating frequency ranges within a transmission medium such as cable.

access. It provides much higher downstream data rates, which matches traditional Internet usage from the customer site.

As with ISDN, delivery of the digital signal to the customer's premise via ADSL uses the standard two-wire copper infrastructure found throughout the world. The distance limitation from the CO to the customer premises is 18,000 feet (slightly greater than 5 kilometers). For the fastest speeds, the wiring limitation is 12,000 feet (3.5 kilometers).

ADSL provides dedicated bandwidth to the customer that is not shared with other customers (such as with cable modems), much like ISDN. That's where the similarity ends, however. Key distinctions of ADSL as an access service include the following:

- Voice and data transmission is split on the wire. Analog voice service is carried under 4KHz, while data is carried above 4KHz. The analog service is also called plain old telephone service (POTS).
- DSL carries its own power on the line. If a power failure occurs, DSL data transmission ceases, but analog voice service still operates.
- DSL provides dedicated access circuits (as with point-to-point technology) at much higher data rates than ISDN (8 Mbps/1.5 Mbps versus 128 Kbps).

Figure 3-6 shows the premise wiring architecture. Use of ADSL requies that you obtain several new pieces of premise equipment, including the following:

- **Splitter**—This device separates the incoming ADSL signal from the telecom into a POTS segment and a digital service segment. It works by using filters that separate the low-frequency voice service (below 4KHz) from the higher-frequency DSL service (above 4KHz).
- **ADSL Transmission Unit (ATU)**—This device converts the DSL signal for the terminal equipment (described below). Conceptually, this operation is comparable to the function of a CSU/DSU. The customer's device is called an ATU-R, while the device in the telecom's CO is known as an ATU-C.

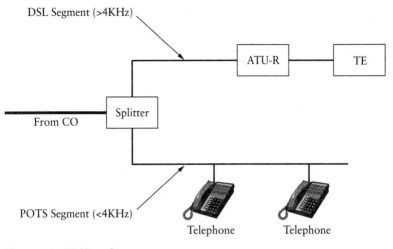

Figure 3-6 *ADSL architecture*

- **Terminal Equipment (TE)**—The terminal equipment is the end system using the ADSL service, such as a PC or television.

Many observers expect that network equipment manufacturers will eventually produce combined devices that incorporate both the splitter and the ATU into a single product. Furthermore, the availability of ADSL interface cards for routers should increase over the next few years.

For premise wiring, it is advisable to run separate Category 5 cabling for the DSL segment from the splitter to the ATU-R within the facility. Although DSL can be run on a single wire pair within a two-wire pair sheath, its signal may interfere with POTS signaling in the adjacent pair. This concern is especially apparent with older wiring.

The major drawback of ADSL at the moment is its limited deployment by telecommunications providers. To date the greatest deployment of this technology has occurred in North American, European, and Asian-Pacific regions (in that order). Much of this deployment has taken the form of market trials.

Adoption of ADSL was initially slowed by a disagreement between the standards bodies regarding the two possible modulation schemes—

carrierless amplitude/phase (CAP) modulation and discrete multitone (DMT) modulation. In February 1998, the ITU adopted the DMT scheme, thus eliminating (hopefully) this constraint to full implementation. (In general, corporations do not like purchasing products based on yet-to-be ratified standards. Similar rancor arose with modem standards in the past.)

Most industry analysts agree that the telecommunications companies will increase their ADSL deployment in the next several years to meet the high demand for high-speed Internet access from both homes and corporations. You should ask your prospective ISP if it now offers ADSL service.

To obtain more information about ADSL, you can visit the web site of the ADSL forum at http://www.adsl.com/. Another good overview of xDSL is found in the white paper by Robyn Aber, entitled "xDSL Local Loop Access Technology—Delivering Broadband over Copper Wires," found on 3Com's web site at http://www.3com.com/xdsl/white_papers.html.

3.5 Delivering the Circuit

In this section, we will examine how the telecommunications provider delivers the circuit to your site. In telecom-speak, the physical infrastructure upon which your circuit is built is called the facility or outside plant. In all cases, the telecom will need to connect its local office to your site via some infrastructure—usually copper wiring or fiber-optic cable.

3.5.1 Facilities

The bulk of outside plants have been constructed with copper wiring. Within the last decade, many telecommunications providers have deployed fiber-optic cabling as well, albeit largely in metropolitan areas. Outlying areas and rural communities tend to receive their telecommunications services over copper infrastructures.

Copper Wiring: Copper wiring can be used to deliver circuits to your site ranging from DS-0 (64 Kbps) to DS-3 (34/45 Mbps) capacity. Two configurations of copper wiring are used, with the type selected depending on the circuit technology to be carried:

- Single-pair (two-wire) configurations can carry DS-0 or POTS analog circuits. The POTS circuit is the standard wiring linking homes to the central office. Digital services that can be carried over a single pair include the ISDN BRI and ADSL.
- Two-pair (four-wire) conditioned copper can carry DS-1 through DS-3 circuits. This physical path is called a span. Conditioned copper refers to the repeaters that regenerate and condition the digital signal between your site and the central office. Depending on the distance between the two locations, the span may include several repeaters. Technologies carried on conditioned copper include ISDN PRI, point-to-point, Frame Relay, and SMDS.

Fiber-Optic Cable: Fiber-optic cable is now the preferred material for outside plant construction. Fiber has several distinct advantages over copper wiring:

- Imperviousness to electromagnetic disturbances, such as lightning and proximity to high voltages
- Exceedingly high data-carrying capacity thanks to the technologies employing fiber transports (that is, SONET, SDH)
- Enhanced repairing capabilities
- Fault tolerance thanks to the technologies employing fiber transports (that is, SONET, SDH)

The major drawback to fiber is its expense. Typically, the SONET equipment in the central offices and at the customers' sites proves quite costly. For the most part, telecoms that provide circuits using fiber infrastructures install their termination equipment at your site, which you cannot touch or manage.

Virtually all digital services can be carried to your site via fiber-optic cabling. Currently, the standard approach calls for provisioning a SONET node on your site and then multiplexing the signaling to lower capacity circuits. For instance, in North America an OC-3 connection can be multiplexed into three DS-3 circuits. Each DS-3 circuit can be further broken down into 28 DS-1 connections.

3.5.2 Premise Demarcation

Regardless of the physical plant used to deliver the circuit to your site, the telecom will need to provide some termination point where you connect your equipment, known as the **demarcation**. Every piece of equipment up to the demarcation is the responsibility of the telecom. Beyond that, the equipment is called customer premises equipment (CPE).

RJ48C: In North America at least, most DS-1 (including fractional DS-1) circuits terminate at the demarcation using an RJ48C connector. The RJ48C connector is nearly identical to the RJ45 connector used in LAN wiring for Ethernet, Fast Ethernet, and Token Ring. For all practical purposes, it is identical to the RJ45 jack used for 10baseT Ethernet wiring.

When either you or the ISP orders the circuit, you should insist that it terminate in your facility on an RJ48C block near your CPE. We recommend that you use only a certified Category 5, twisted-pair cable for connecting your equipment to the RJ48C demarcation. Make certain that your cable has all eight wires in a straight-through configuration. If possible, purchase cabling with different colors than those of your standard in-house LAN cabling. In busy data closets, connecting the premise equipment to the demarcation using yellow, red, orange, purple, blue, and green cables facilitates cable tracing.

Coaxial: In Europe, most DS-1 circuits terminate at the demarcation with a coaxial pole, otherwise known as a BNC connector. In North America, DS-3 circuits terminate with a coaxial pole. You connect your equipment to the demarcation using a coaxial cable.

This type of connector and cable is widely used by cable television companies in North America. Specifically, this cable comprises RG-59/U with an impedance of 75 ohms. Similarly, in Europe the coaxial cable must have impedance of 75 ohms and meet the CCITT standard G.703 for interface wiring to an E-1 digital network. Take care not to use the coaxial cable for 10base2 Ethernet, also known as Thin-Wire Ethernet.

3.6 Circuit Conditioning

In provisioning of DS-1-level carriers, the European system holds definite advantages over the North American system. In the European E-1 carrier, channels 31 and 32 are reserved for controlling the communications in the first 30 channels. The full 64 Kbps channel capacity of the 30 DS-0 circuits remains available for use. Effectively, an E-1 connection has 1.92 Mbps capacity (30 × 64 Kbps). Your premise equipment needs little configuration to support the signaling in channels 31 and 32.

In the North American system, the circuit control occurs within each DS-0 circuit, thus "robbing" each channel of some carrying capacity. Making matters worse, you can choose from several types of signal control when implementing a T-1 connection with the North American system. This section explains these configurations, and what they will mean when you build your WAN circuit.

3.6.1 North American T-1

When you provision a DS-1 circuit within the North American system, you must select framing and line coding formats. In essence, framing determines how electronic signaling on a T-1 connection is divided into 24 DS-0 channels, plus how the communication on the T-1 circuit is controlled. Line coding determines how successive bits with the same value are separated from one another. Instead of going into the gory details of T-1 framing and line coding, Table 3-8 simply presents the configuration options.

Sometimes the telecom will ask you how you want to frame and line-code your T-1; in other cases, it may not give you an choice because it supports only one configuration. We recommend line coding and framing on a T-1 connection in the form of B8ZS ESF, the standard configuration for T-1 circuits in North America. This approach will enable you to realize the full 1.544 Mbps capacity in the T-1 channel.

The alternative to B8ZS is **alternate mark inversion (AMI)**. AMI uses robbed-bit signaling, which provides significantly less available

Table 3-8 T-1 Line Coding and Framing

Element	Options	Recommendation
Framing	D4, ESF	ESF
Line coding	AMI, B8ZS	B8ZS

bandwidth per T-1 circuit than does B8ZS. You should question your ISP or telecommunications provider if it intends to use a configuration with AMI and D4. In particular, this issue affects many smaller telecom carriers in North America with older infrastructures and equipment.

3.6.2 European E-1

In the European E-1 system, signaling and control are accomplished via dedicated DS-0 channels 30 and 31. Framing and line coding takes place on the data-carrying channels as well. Line coding is high-density bipolar 3 (HDP3). Framing is CCITT G.703, which is similar to T-1's ESF. When you configure an E-1 circuit, the wiring interface and the signaling will therefore conform to the CCITT standard G.703.

3.6.3 North American T-3

Configuring the North American T-3 carrier is a bit easier than the T-1 carrier. Effectively, you have no choices as to framing and line coding. The T-3 carrier sets these standard values. The only choices you need to make with a T-3 circuit involve whether you will use the full carrier capacity or fractionalize the carrier into 28 T-1 channels:

- Using the full T-3 connection as a single 45 Mbps circuit creates a *clear channel.*
- Dividing the T-3 connection into 28 T-1 channels is called *fractionalizing.* It is accomplished using M13 or C-bit parity multiplexing.

3.7 Premise Equipment Configuration and Connections

In this section, we consider the typical premises equipment needed to connect your router to the WAN circuit.

3.7.1 CSU/DSUs

For DS-1 circuits using Frame Relay, point-to-point, and SMDS, a hybrid device called a CSU/DSU must be placed between the telecommunications provider's network and your router. The CSU/DSU is really two devices rolled into one box:

- The **channel service unit** (CSU) performs control and protective functions on the T-carrier or E-carrier. Specifically, the CSU provides the line coding and framing for your end of the circuit.
- The **data service unit** (DSU) converts the digital data from a router into voltages and encoding for the T-carrier or E-carrier. Usually the DSU connects to your router via a serial V.35 interface. Other types of serial connections between the DSU and your router can include RS-232, RS-449, and X.21.

Because some fundamental differences exist between the E-1 and T-1 carriers, the CSU/DSUs for E-1 and T-1 circuits are separate products.

3.7.2 T-1 Circuits

For T-1 or fractional T-1 circuits, you set various parameters on the CSU/DSU to match the T-carrier provided by the telecommunications provider. Table 3-9 outlines these parameters.

In addition to the elements mentioned in Table 3-9, you must make channel selections. Channel selection in a T-1 carrier determines the effective capacity of the circuit. On the CSU, you must indicate which channels you will use. Table 3-10 gives the common number of channels employed to create various circuit capacities (assuming B8ZS line coding).

Table 3-9 CSU/DSU Configuration Options

Element	Options	Recommendation
Line coding	AMI, B8ZS	B8ZS
Framing	ESF, D4	ESF
Loop power	Wet, dry, or span	Wet
Clocking	Span, internal	Internal
Line buildout	0dB, 7.5dB, 15dB	0dB

Table 3-10 Common Channel Selections

Capacity (Kbps)	Channels
64	1
128	2
256	4
384	6
512	8
768	12
1,536	24

Remember that each DS-0 channel provides a capacity of 64 Kbps (B8ZS) or 56 Kbps (AMI). Thus, by activating the correct number of channels on your CSU, you can configure the device for your circuit. The channels must be contiguous, meaning that they must be selected in ascending order. For instance, you cannot create a 256 Kbps circuit by activating channels 1, 2, 3, and 6. You would need to activate channels 1 through 4.

3.7.3 E-1 Circuits

When configuring the CSU/DSU for the E-1 carrier, you need to address only a few options:

- If you plan to use the entire 2.048 Mbps as a single circuit, then select *unstructured* framing. If you will use fractionalized E-1, then select *structured* framing. Sometimes structured framing is called CRC4, as it employs error-checking functions.
- The clock source needs to be designated as either internal or the network (span).
- The line impedance must be set to 75 ohms if your connector is a BNC type or 120 ohms if the connector is a DA15 type.

Of course, if you are configuring a structured (fractionalized) E-1 you must also select the active DS-0 channels. Most newer CSU/DSUs provide software configuration menus that will guide you through the device setup process. They also indicate the default settings for most parameters.

If you plan to use the full E-1 capacity, you should inquire about whether the network equipment manufacturer offers a G.703 module. This type of module enables you to connect your router directly to the E-1 circuit. With these devices, however, you cannot employ an unstructured E-1 connection.

3.7.4 T-3 Circuits

Configuring a CSU/DSU for a T-3 carrier is a bit different than configuring one for a T-1 carrier. Fewer choices exist, because T-3 uses standardized framing and line coding. Instead of explaining the details of T-3 circuitry, we will simply point out key things you need to know when setting up a T-3 circuit:

- You must obtain a CSU/DSU that is specifically geared toward handling T-3 circuits.
- When you ask the telecommunication providers to provision a T-3 carrier, stipulate whether you want it multiplexed into 28 T-1 channels or kept as a clear channel circuit. For T-3 and fractional T-3 circuits, ask for clear channel.
- Your CSU/DSU will have the capability of presenting the T-3 connection to your router as a single circuit or as some fractionalized component of the T-3.

Normally, you connect the CSU/DSU to your router using a high-speed serial interface (HSSI) cable, which resembles a SCSI cable. Your router must have a HSSI module that accepts such high-speed connections.

3.7.5 ISDN Network Termination

Connecting your router to ISDN service differs from connecting to a Frame Relay, point-to-point, or SMDS network. The main issue relates to whether your ISDN connection is a BRI or PRI.

NT-1 (BRI): Telephone companies in North America and Europe deliver ISDN BRI circuits to their customers using different **network termination (NT)** equipment. This equipment resides between your equipment and the telecom's network. Sometimes the network termination is built into a module on your router; at other times you must purchase it as a separate device (like a CSU/DSU). Two types of NT equipment exist:

- The "U" interface is the typical network termination in North America. It converts the standard two-wire ISDN circuit to a four-wire circuit, enabling you to hook up additional devices, such as a phone and router.
- The "S" interface is the common termination in Europe and elsewhere. You can attach various ISDN devices to this four-wire circuit.

In Europe, the telephone companies present the customer with a four-wire ISDN circuit. In North America, the customer must convert the two-wire circuit into a usable four-wire circuit via a device called the NT-1.

Most network equipment manufacturers provide ISDN BRI interface modules for their routers, with some including the NT-1 device in the module itself. When you provision your router equipment, you should verify that the interface matches that of the telecom provider. In all cases, connect your equipment to the telecom's demarcation using a standard Category 5, straight-through cable with all wire pairs available.

For ISDN, you will need the following equipment:

- If your ISDN BRI is located within a European system, you need a BRI device with an "S" interface. The telephone company has already provided the NT-1 unit.
- If your ISDN BRI resides within a North American system, you need a BRI device with a "U" interface, which means that it includes an NT-1 unit. If your BRI device has an "S" interface, you must provide an external NT-1 device, placing it in the path between the telecom's demarcation and your BRI equipment.

Finally, to make matters even more confusing, the telephone companies in North America use two kinds of NT-1 devices that are differentiated by their encoding schemes. The two data encoding schemes are as follows:

- 2B1Q (two bits mapped into one quaternary symbol)
- Alternate mark inversion (AMI)

The 2B1Q scheme is the dominant method in use today. The AMI scheme is older and rarely used.

PRI: The ISDN PRI can be directly connected to the customer premises equipment without going through a network terminal device. In North America, the PRI is implemented using a standard T-1 circuit that uses B8ZS to provide clear channel 64 Kbps per DS-0 channel. In Europe, the PRI is often delivered by means of an E-1 carrier.

Today, most networking equipment can handle direct PRI connections, often via built-in CSU functions that manage the T-1 or E-1 carrier. Although you can connect directly from the demarcation to the network, it might make better sense to place a CSU between the demarcation and your equipment. Should a lightning strike or some other destructive electronic event occur, you want to make certain that your equipment is safe.

ISDN Terminal Equipment Configuration: When you have an ISDN circuit installed to your facility, you need to know several important pieces of information before configuring your ISDN terminal equipment. That is, you must know the **service profile identifier (SPID)**, **directory number (DN)**, and CO switch type. Typically, the ISP or telecommunications provider will give this information to you.

- A SPID identifies each B channel in an ISDN circuit. It often appears as a telephone number with 0000 or 0101 appended to the end. Typically, you configure your ISDN equipment with these values to enable it to communicate with the ISDN switch in the central office. Failure to configure the SPIDs exactly as indicated by the telecom will result in a nonfunctioning ISDN circuit.
- The DN is the "phone number" of the ISDN equipment. Usually you are assigned one DN per each B channel. This value appears as a normal phone number. When your ISDN equipment dials the ISP's equipment, it dials the ISP's DN. In Figure 3-5, the DN of the ISP is 888-555-1212.

- When you configure your ISDN equipment, you set the CO switch type parameter to match the switch deployed in the telecom's central office.

3.8 Checklist–WAN Provisioning

Circuit Technologies

Point-to-point

❑ Is the baud rate of the router port set to match the circuit capacity?
❑ Is the serial port of the router set for PPP?

Frame Relay

❑ What is the DLCI for the PVC to the ISP?
❑ What are the CIR and port speed on the circuit?
❑ Is LMI enabled on the Frame Relay network, and if so what type?
❑ Is the baud rate of the router port set to match the circuit capacity?
❑ Is the router port set for Frame Relay?

SMDS

❑ What is the individual address for your SNI?
❑ What is the group address for your SNI?
❑ Does your CSU/DSU support SIP-2 and SIP-1?
❑ Does your router support SIP-3
❑ Is the baud rate of the router port set to match the circuit capacity?
❑ Is the router port set for SMDS?
❑ Have you configured virtual ports on your router?

ISDN

❑ Does your ISP offer ISDN service?
❑ Is this service a viable option for your needs?

ADSL

❑ Does your ISP offer ADSL service?
❑ Is this service a viable option for your needs?

Delivering the Circuit

Demarcation

❏ Have you asked the telecom how it will terminate your circuit (that is, RJ48C, coaxial)?

❏ Have you purchased the proper cabling to connect your equipment (CSU/DSU) to the demarcation?

Circuit Conditioning

Circuit Conditioning

❏ Will the T-1 circuit use D4 or ESF framing?

❏ Will the T-1 circuit use AMI or B8ZS line coding?

❏ Will the E-1 circuit require setting the framing to G.703?

❏ Will the E-1 circuit require setting the line coding to HDP3?

Premise Equipment Configuration and Connections

Premise Equipment Configuration and Connections

❏ Have you set the T-1 CSU/DSU line coding?

❏ Have you set the T-1 CSU/DSU framing?

❏ Have you set the T-1 CSU/DSU loop powering?

❏ Have you set the T-1 CSU/DSU clock?

❏ Have you set the T-1 CSU/DSU LBO?

❏ Have you set the E-1 CSU/DSU framing (structure or unstructured)?

❏ Have you set the E-1 CSU/DSU clock source?

❏ Have you set the E-1 CSU/DSU line impedance?

❏ Have you set the T-3 CSU/DSU timeslots?

❏ If using an ISDN BRI, do you need a "U" or "S" interface?

❏ If using an ISDN BRI in North America, does your BRI equipment include an NT-1 device, or must you provide it?

❏ If using an ISDN BRI in North America, is the telecom providing the circuit using 2B1Q or AMI encoding?

❏ If using an ISDN circuit, have you obtained the SPIDs for the B channels?

❏ If using an ISDN circuit, have you obtained the DNs for your terminal equipment?

❏ If using an ISDN circuit, have you obtained the CO switch type?

Planning Your Security

There's no doubt about it—Internet security is a very hot topic these days. This chapter provides an introduction to the concepts of Internet security. *Implementing security at your Internet connection is a mandatory step.*

Many products on the market will enable you to implement security. Most of these products are called firewalls. They range from basic packet filters to advanced network access control systems. Your job is to use the information presented in this chapter to find a security product that meets your needs and budget.

Bear in mind that Internet security is an ongoing concern. Once you build your Internet connection, you will continually need to reassess and adjust your security policy. Two excellent books to help you continue your security education are *Firewalls and Internet Security: Repelling the Wily Hacker,* by William R. Cheswick and Steven M. Bellovin, and *Building Internet Firewalls,* by D. Brent Chapman and Elizabeth D. Zwicky.

4.1 Chapter Overview

This chapter discusses various components of security. The initial sections begin by explaining concepts; the later sections address more advanced topics. After reading this chapter, you should be able to answer the following questions:

1. What do interior, exterior, default stance, and direction mean with respect to security policies?

2. What are the common network access control methods available to screen IP traffic and provide security?

3. What are the typical features found in firewall products sold today?

4. What are some typical network architectures used when implementing firewalls and packet filters?

5. What policies should you deploy for the most common Internet services?

6. What is security auditing, how is it deployed, and why is it important?

7. How do you stay current with new threats and news in the security community?

The chapter ends with a checklist of things to ponder as you build your connection's security.

4.2 The Real Need for Security

Never believe that your site is immune from an Internet attack because your organization is small, your connection has low bandwidth, or the information contained in your network is not sensitive. In truth, your network runs some chance of being hacked simply by virtue of being connected to the Internet. The skills and patience of determined crackers are legendary.[1] As more people become connected to the Internet, the likelihood only grows that a few bad elements will try to spoil the party for the others.

It does not seem to make much difference whether your site is a large, multinational company or a small office. Well-known organizations are nice, large targets. Crackers simply like to hack, however, and if they can access your wardrobe, they will look through your underwear drawer regardless of your identity. (Pardon the comparison.) Being small does not help in the case of automated searches that scan for vulnerable sites. Crackers like to use small sites as springboards for attacks on larger sites, a strategy that helps them hide their tracks.

---

1. Some folks within the security community prefer the term *cracker,* which denotes an evil hacker.

Important terms to know regarding attacks include the following:

- **Intrusion** (or *hack*). A blanket term describing an event in which an unauthorized party gains access to your network, its components, and resources. Intrusion events run the gamut from relatively benign to really destructive.
- **Denial-of-service (DoS).** An actual attack in which your Internet connection or some other system in your network is rendered unusable or destroyed. These attacks are deliberately intended to break systems.
- **Information theft.** A serious hack in which some piece of valuable information is gleaned from your network or its systems. This type of maneuver is the domain of industrial and governmental espionage.

Is an anonymous army of crackers out there planning to steal your secrets and break your infrastructure? Possibly, but in most cases most hacks are perpetrated by ex-employees who know something about the targeted systems. The bottom line is that the risks are real, so you should implement a reasonable security policy to protect your network and operate with the assumption your network can be attacked. If you take such precautions, chances are your network (and your employment) will survive.

4.3 World View, Default Stance, and Direction

4.3.1 World View

When you begin to think of security, you must define where your network ends and the Internet begins. This point defines your "world view" for security. Although it may sound obvious, you should begin thinking of your networks as **interior** objects and everything outside the Internet router as **exterior** objects. Your mission is to protect your interior networks from the exterior networks. Your router serves as the gateway between these two worlds. Figure 4-1 shows such a security world view, depicting the interior and exterior networks.

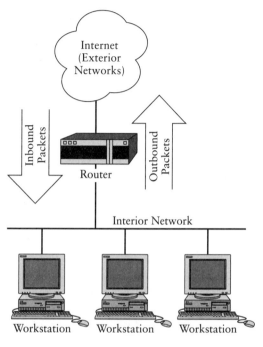

Figure 4-1 *Security world view*

4.3.2 Default Stance

After you define where the interior and exterior networks meet, you must establish a **default stance,** or the philosophy that defines your security policies. Effectively, only one stance exists: All packets are denied except those expressly permitted, with the denied packets being dropped.

This stance requires that you set up policies for each service supported through your Internet connection. If the service is not included in the policy, then it is not supported. This policy ensures that you always know what traffic *should* be flowing through the connection. Unfortunately, it also means that every time a user wants a new service, he or she must ask you to enable it.

4.3.3 Default Action

The implementation of the default stance is guaranteed by the **default action.** If your packet filter or firewall has checked all of the defined policies and it still does not know what to do with a packet, the default action specifies whether to forward it (permit) or toss it out (deny). *Denying a packet through your filter should always be your default action.*

4.3.4 Direction

Finally, the concept of direction is important in security. Packets to the Internet are *outbound*. Packets to hosts in your interior network are *inbound*. Figure 4-1 includes arrows indicating these directions.

4.4 Access Control Technologies

The primary method of protecting your site is to deploy one or more access control systems between your interior networks and the Internet. The technologies used by these systems fall into the following categories:

- Packet filters
- Circuit proxies
- Application gateways
- Stateful inspection
- Network address translation (NAT)

The first three technologies describe system architectures that can be deployed independently in your network. The last two items are techniques that are applied with one of the three system architectures. In particular, stateful inspection and network address translation are commonly used in packet-filtering architectures.

4.4.1 Packet Filtering

The most basic way to implement your security policy is via **packet filtering**. Frequently, routers perform packet filtering, which is included as a standard software feature. Various workstations can also serve as routers, especially those with UNIX or Windows NT operating systems. Packet-filtering software packages are available for these systems as well.

Unlike a router, which makes a forwarding decision based on information in the IP header, a packet filter looks further into the packet, examining the network and transport layer headers before deciding what action to take. Table 4-1 shows the common elements used for packet filtering.

Table 4-1   Common Packet-Filtering Fields

Header Type	Field
IP	Source address
	Destination address
	Protocol (for example, 1=ICMP, 6=TCP, 17=UDP)
	Options
TCP/UDP	Source port
	Destination port
	ACK flag

In particular, the ACK flag is used extensively to test inbound TCP packets. As described in Chapter 1, the first packet in a TCP connection setup (also known as a three-way handshake) has the ACK flag unset; subsequent packets have the ACK flag set. Thus the packet filter can test inbound TCP packets to determine whether they are part of an established TCP connection.

Some packet filters apply filtering rules only to the first packets in a TCP session. The idea behind this approach is that any packet with the ACK flag set is part of a permitted session and therefore doesn't need reexamination.

Additional pieces of information that the router or workstation knows but that are not included within the TCP/IP headers are the interface on which the packet was received and the interface to which it will be sent. Most routers can filter in either the inbound or outbound direction on a per-port basis. When the scope of these pieces of information is considered, it becomes apparent that a packet filtering router can perform some amazing feats in screening your Internet traffic.

Typical Implementation: Normally, packets are filtered on the inbound direction as they enter the packet-filtering device (for example, a router). This tactic prevents the filtering device from unnecessarily processing packets that it later drops. Also, it protects the filtering device from coming under attack itself. Most routers support filtering in the inbound, outbound, and eitherbound directions on a per-port basis.

A traditional packet filter works by sequentially applying rules that allow or dissallow packets to be forwarded based on the header contents. It compares these header values with those in a list of rules. The rules are enforced sequentially, starting with the first rule in the list and ending with the last rule. If the header contents match a particular rule, then the filter executes the action stipulated by the rule. The last rule in the list is the default action, which determines what should be done with a packet that doesn't match any previous rule. As noted earlier, *this last rule should always drop the packet to enforce your default stance.*

Before writing your filter policies, you should brush up on the Internet services that your system will support. This critical step can sometimes require much research on your part. Before you support any Internet service, however, you want to undertand how it works. Ask the following questions:

1. What IP protocol does the service use? Most services are TCP- and UDP-based. Look out for services that use other IP protocols such as ICMP, IP-Tunnel, and PPTP.
2. If the service is TCP- or UDP-based, what port or range of ports does it use?
3. Does the service require inbound connections? For instance, will you have servers available to the outside world?
4. Do you need to restrict the service between specific IP hosts, or do multiple hosts need the service?

Let's look at an example of packet filtering. Figure 4-2 shows an Internet connection where the interior hosts need to access hosts in the Internet using DNS, HTTP, and Telnet. The filter policies on the router must be configured to allow the outbound packets for these services. Additionally, the connection must accept replies from the servers to the interior hosts. All other incoming and outgoing packets will be dropped.

Table 4-2 shows a generic filter policy for this router. The notation 0.0.0.0/0 indicates any IP network or host. The "/24" is the mask notation for 255.255.255.0. *Pay careful attention to masks within your rules, as misconfigured ones can lead to major security holes.* Notice the last rule, which specifies the default action for the filter policy.

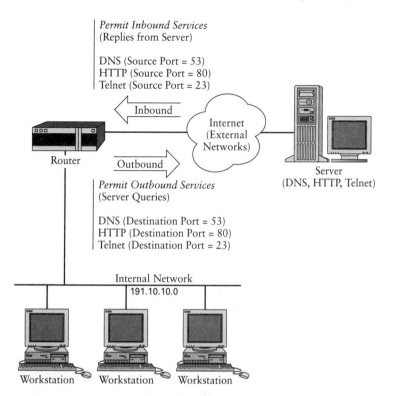

Figure 4-2 *Packet-filtering example*

Table 4-2 Filter Policy

No.	Action	From	To	Protocol	Dest. Port	Source Port	ACK
1	Permit	191.10.10.0/24	0.0.0.0/0	UDP	53	>1023	
2	Permit	191.10.10.0/24	0.0.0.0/0	TCP	80	>1023	
3	Permit	191.10.10.0/24	0.0.0.0/0	TCP	23	>1023	
4	Permit	0.0.0.0/0	191.10.10.0/24	UDP	>1023	53	
5	Permit	0.0.0.0/0	191.10.10.0/24	TCP	>1023	80	Established
7	Permit	0.0.0.0/0	191.10.10.0/24	TCP	>1023	23	Established
8	Deny	0.0.0.0/0	0.0.0.0/0				

Reading from the top down, we can see that the first three rules (1–3) allow traffic to leave the interior network (191.10.10.0/24) and go to any other network or host (0.0.0.0/0) as long as the protocol, destination, and source port match those shown. These rules support the outbound traffic for DNS, HTTP, and Telnet.

The next three rules (4–7) support inbound traffic for DNS, HTTP, and Telnet, respectively. Look closely at the source and destination ports. Because the source ports are well-known values, we can cautiously assume that these packets originate from the server. To ensure further security, we can check the ACK flag of each packet. Packets with the ACK flag set are assumed to be part of established TCP connections.

Finally, rule 8 enforces the default stance. It denies all packets from any host to any other host.

Although this example demonstrates filtering using English-like lingo, some "no frills" packet filters may require you to write rules using packet offsets and hexidecimal values for the port numbers. Get your decimal-to-hexidecimal calculator ready! Complicating matters even further, the offset may start at the beginning of the packet, the beginning of the IP header, or the beginning of the TCP or UDP header, depending on the implementation.

Pros and Cons of Packet Filtering: The majority of security products use packet filtering as the basic method for deploying security. Major advantages of packet filters (versus circuit proxies and application gateways, which are covered later) include the following:

1. Packet filtering is the simplest method of filtering and therefore least expensive. Most routers include filtering functions by default—you can filter for free!

2. Unlike some implementations of circuit proxies and application gateways, packet filters don't require any changes to the clients. In essence, they operate without the knowledge of the user community, except when they block a service.

3. Packet filtering is the fastest method of screening traffic because it scans only the TCP/IP header, not the packet payload.

Of course, packet filtering also has some limitations. Most security experts agree that this technology alone offers insufficient protection for an Internet connection, for the following reasons:

1. Some Internet services are difficult to screen safely using the contents of the TCP/IP header—in particular, services such as DNS, FTP, and those using random port assignments based on **remote procedure calls (RPCs).**

2. Packet filtering relies heavily on IP addresses, which offers no defense against forged addresses. Recall that the TCP/IP header does not indicate the router port at which the packet was received. Only when port information is coupled with IP addresses can IP address spoofing be detected.

3. Packet filtering relies heavily on port numbers, which also offers no defense against forgeries. The source port of a packet cannot be relied upon for security, because an attacker can set the source port to an arbitrary value and spoof a permitted service.

4. UDP packets are difficult to filter. UDP is considered less secure because it is easier to spoof than TCP. TCP requires that the cracker predict the server response, whereas UDP does not.

5. Many attacks are very difficult to screen using generic packet filtering.

6. Packet filters are easy to misconfigure.

7. Some packet filters can be extremely difficult to implement because they require you to write the rules using hexadecimal values and offsets.

8. The existence of too many rules can adversely affect a router's performance. Typical rule lists can become quite large, making testing more prone to mistakes. Also, the improper ordering of rule execution can slow a router. Always try to place the most commonly employed rules at the top of the list so they will be executed first.

4.4.2 Circuit Proxies

Another method of filtering traffic between the interior and exterior networks is a **circuit proxy.** It is somewhat of a hybrid between ordinary packet filtering and application gateways (discussed later in this chapter).

We can draw a distinction between a circuit proxy from a packet filter based on the fact that a circuit proxy intercepts outbound traffic between interior and exterior hosts. It screens the packets and then forwards them with *the circuit proxy's own source IP address* on behalf of the interior hosts. To an exterior host, the device making the requests is the proxy server. Responses are therefore directed back to the proxy, which in turn sends the packet to the interior host. In this way, the proxy server shields the external hosts from knowing the true IP address of the interior host. Figure 4-3 illustrates circuit proxying.

Typical Implementation—SOCKS: The most common method of implementing a circuit proxy is to set up SOCKS software on a server and interior clients. It's a bit difficult to explain succinctly what SOCKS entails, but suffice it to say that SOCKS is a client/server architecture

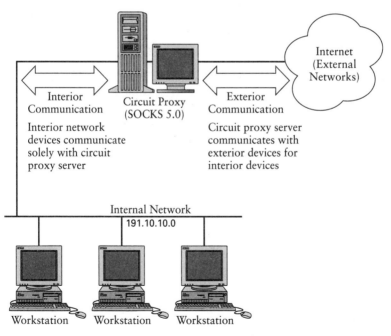

Figure 4-3 *Circuit proxying*

for circuit proxies. Originally developed by David Koblas, SOCKS is now under the stewardship of NEC. If you visit NEC's web site on SOCKS (http://www.socks.nec.com/), you'll find a detailed description of the product. An increasing number of companies are joining the SOCKS bandwagon, including Microsoft (with its Proxy Server software) and various firewall vendors.

Pros and Cons of Circuit Proxying: When compared with packet filtering, circuit proxying offers some advantages:

1. Circuit proxies hide interior IP addresses from exterior devices. It is extremely difficult for the bad guys in the Internet to glean interior address information from packets that originate from a proxy server.
2. Because proxies communicate on behalf of the interior client, the exterior hosts are given only one point of attack—the proxy server.
3. Because circuit proxies do not examine the data payload, they work more rapidly than application gateways.

Disadvantages of circuit proxies include the following:

1. Circuit proxies operate more slowly than packet filters.
2. Clients must address all Internet-bound packets to the circuit proxy. Circuit proxies require you to install new or recompiled runtime libraries at the client; application gateways and packet filters do not.
3. Circuit proxies use packet filtering, and thus have the same general disadvanges as generic packet filters.
4. Circuit proxying products are effective for screening only TCP and UDP connections. Most other IP packet types don't use port numbers.

4.4.3 Application Gateways

Unlike packet filters and circuit proxies, application gateways inspect the contents of the data payload within the packets. As result, the transaction between the client and the exterior host can be scrutinized for malicious or dangerous activity. Also, application gateways can authenticate users and log activity.

An application gateway works similarly to a circuit proxy, in that it sits between the interior and exterior hosts. It converses with exterior hosts on behalf of the interior hosts, and vice versa. This approach differs somewhat from circuit proxying, where the device intercepts outbound packets and changes the source IP address. Basically, the application gateway acts as a relay between the interior and exterior hosts to ensure that neither converses directly with the other.

Generally, application gateways support only a limited group of services, including HTTP (web), FTP, Telnet, SNMP, and SMTP (mail). The gateway usually comprises a server of some sort. This server may then be named according to the service it proxies. For instance, an application gateway for HTTP is called an HTTP proxy.

Although their use does not require modification of runtime libraries at the client like circuit proxying, application gateways may necessitate modifications to the application programs that will communicate through the proxy. For instance, if you set up an HTTP proxy, you must modify the settings in your browser software to enable communication through the proxy server. Some newer versions of proxy server software do not require such client software reconfiguration. Check with the software manufacturer to determine whether client modifications are necessary.

Pros and Cons of Application Gateways: Advantages of application gateways include the following:

1. A great feature of application gateways is their ability to authenticate a packet's validity based on its data. This capability significantly increases the effectiveness of the security mechanism. For this reason, application gateways are considered the most secure means of implementing security for certain Internet services, such as HTTP, FTP, and Telnet.

2. Because application gateways inspect packet contents, they can potentially protect against viruses. Today, many viruses are spread as e-mail attachments. Screening the packet content is ultimately the best security.

3. Newer application gateways do not require modification to the client, unlike circuit proxying.

Disadvantages of application gateways include these considerations:

1. Because application gateways inspect the packet payloads, they work more slowly than packet filtering and circuit proxying. Consequently, you may have to deal with a user community moaning over their inability to display web pages at lightning speed.

2. Some application gateways require the user to modify how the application accesses the service. Although this issue is not the same inconvenience as implementing new runtime libraries with circuit proxying, it is nevertheless a consideration when trying to implement effective, yet transparent security.

3. Application gateways are service-specific. To accommodate a new service, you may have to purchase an new proxy package. Today, proxy software is readily available for the most popular Internet services.

4.4.4 Stateful Inspection

Within the last few years, a hybrid of the packet filter and the application gateway has emerged called **stateful inspection.** Invented and patented by CheckPoint Technologies, it is the network access control mechanism used by most firewall products today. In fact, some router manufacturers now include "firewall" services in their software that goes beyond traditional packet filters and screen IP traffic using stateful inspection.

Stateful inspection maintains a cache of state information on existing sessions. It first intercepts packets at the network layer (like a packet filter), then examines additional information within the entire packet (like an application gateway) before making a security decision. In particular, a network access control system using stateful inspection looks for information within the packets that indicates the state of communication between hosts. In most cases, this information can be gleaned only by looking deep into a packet's payload and examining all protocol layers (for example, the application layer).

For example, intercepting and analyzing the PASV command in an FTP session enables a system to anticipate the FTP client's data channel connection attempt. In another example, a stateful inspection system can track a UDP communication like it was an established TCP-based session. By reviewing the entire packet contents, a stateful inspection system can build a table of active "conversations" between hosts and then monitor these communications to ensure they meet a defined security policy.

Typical Implementation: As mentioned, stateful inspection is typically used within firewall products as the preferred network access control mechanism. From a security implementation standpoint, this type of system is much better than a packet-filtering router or gateway. Because it represents an extension of packet filtering, implementation of a stateful inspection system is nearly identical to that of a packet filter (in theory).

Because stateful inspection implies the construction of a firewall, we will momentarily defer discussion of its implementation. Section 4.5 describes the configuration of a typical firewall product in greater detail.

Pros and Cons of Stateful Inspection: Following are some advantages of using stateful inspection as a network access control:

1. Stateful inspection offers much better security than a packet filter because *communication* between hosts is inspected and verified against the security policy. A stateful inspection system goes beyond the limitations of packet filtering to actually "track" conversations.

2. Because a stateful inspection system examines the entire packet contents, it is cognizant of the application using the packets for communication between hosts. As a result, the system can anticipate the application's responses and behavior. Applications such as FTP and DNS can be supported with greater security than packet filtering because the stateful

inspection system knows what to expect from the conversations of these applications. It can therefore identify abnormalities and hence weed out potential attacks.

3. Stateful inspection systems are generally faster at screening traffic than application gateways or circuit proxies. The greater speed is possible because the stateful inspection system does not act as a proxy and regenerate packets on behalf of the clients.

4. Today's firewall vendors place much emphasis on transparency. Like a packet filter, the stateful inspection system does not require modifying the client in any fashion.

There are also a few disadvantages to using stateful inspection:

1. Stateful inspection is generally found only in server-based firewall products. Some exceptions exist, as vendors rush to market with hybrid router-based firewall products. From a corporate viewpoint, a firewall is considered an "additional" purchase while the purchase of a router is considered mandatory. Stateful inspection firewalls are simply more expensive than standard packet-filtering routers.

2. Stateful inspection does not offer the full advantages of an application gateway. Although it reviews the entire packet contents, it does not screen these data as precisely as an application gateway.

4.4.5 Network Address Translation

Network address translation (NAT) is another technology that provides network access control. (Refer to the Appendix A for a fuller description of NAT operation.) Although NAT provides additional IP addresses for use in your networks, it also hides the IP addresses of your hosts from the Internet.

Typical Implementation: When used to provide additional security, NAT is typically deployed in firewall products. Recently, however, some router manufacturers have begun providing NAT in their software. You should use NAT if you want to hide the IP address "identity" of your network hosts, whether they are your internal users or servers. For instance, administrators may assign private, local IP addresses to

...ιι nternet servers (for example, a web server or FTP server). In these cases, the NAT server appears between the servers and the Internet.

Pros and Cons of Network Address Translation: The exterior device involved in the communication is the NAT server, not the host using the translated IP address. As a result, NAT provides a degree of security making it more difficult (but not impossible) for crackers to directly infiltrate and attack your network. This protection is the major advantage of using NAT as an additional security technique.

On the other hand, NAT does not provide any screening functionality. Thus it cannot be considered a full access control mechanism. It must therefore be deployed with another network access control technology if it is to provide security.

4.5 Firewall Products Explained

By definition, a **firewall** is a system or group of systems that enforces security policies. Firewall systems may consist of packet filters, circuit proxies, and application gateways. Some incorporate stateful inspection and NAT as additional network access control mechanisms. Although you may correctly refer to a system of packet-filtering routers as a firewall, the term also denotes a new generation of products that enable you to implement security. Today, a firewall appears to denote a singular system offering security services.

Your best bet for building Internet security *quickly* is to invest in a commercial firewall product, even if you have implemented packet filtering at your Internet router. This approach offers several benefits:

1. Firewall products incorporate added functionality to screen out common attacks, which cannot be accomplished using generic packet filtering.
2. Firewall products usually include predefined lists of Internet services. Although these lists may not be 100% complete, they are usually quite extensive and will save time during rules configuration.
3. Firewall products can add **authentication** services to enable only "verified" users to send and receive packets through your

Internet connection. They can also include **encryption** services to ensure that unauthorized parties cannot read the packet contents.

4. Unlike generic packet filters, firewalls can keep track of who is using the connection and log various events, including intrusions.

5. Firewall products now include support for items such as virtual private networks and NAT.

The remainder of this section discusses generic features commonly encountered in today's firewall products. The intention is to give you some idea of the possibilities with these products so you can assess if a product meets your needs.

4.5.1 Configuring

Most firewalls operate on a server platform or router using stateful inspection as the network access control. Because a firewall is essentially a software program, the most common platforms are UNIX or Windows NT workstations.[2] Additionally, firewalls are available for routers. Most router vendors now include a group of firewall services in their system software. On a router, the availability of these parameters is intended to facilitate construction of a firewall. The scope of these parameters, however, can be limited to common Internet services.

Although some variations exist between products, most seem to look and feel roughly the same. In essence, you configure your security policy from a graphical user interface (GUI) that enables you to create rules just as you would for a packet filter. Typically, you select predefined Internet services from drop-down lists to build individual filter rules. Although the GUI is intended to make the configuration process easier, it is still possible to misconfigure rules and leave holes for an attacker.

Unlike packet filters that require you to specify IP addresses, ports, and similar information, firewalls enable you to build rules using more logical names. For instance, Table 4-3 outlines a policy that supports

---

2. The Windows NT operating system has been regarded as a less secure platform than UNIX for performing firewall duties. This reputation resulted from some publicized cases in which the NT platform did not fare well when subjected to trivial denial-of-service attacks.

Table 4-3 Typical Firewall GUI

Number	Source	Destination	Services	Action	Log
1	Internal_nets	All	DNS	Permit	No
2	Internal_nets	All	HTTP	Permit	No
3	Internal_nets	All	Telnet	Permit	No
4	All	FTP server	FTP	Permit	Yes
5	All	All	All	Deny	Yes

DNS, HTTP, and Telnet from the internal networks to the Internet. In addition, it allows inbound FTP to an FTP server. The final rule enforces the default stance.

4.5.2 Attack Screening

One attractive feature of firewalls is their capability of screening for common attacks. Packet filtering alone cannot derive sufficient information from a packet to effectively prevent all of today's attacks, because these assaults exploit other vulnerabilities in servers and communication processes using valid TCP/IP packets.

Although many types of attacks exist, the more common ones usually attempt to bypass security on generic packet filters (that is, routers) and either launch a denial-of-service attack or retrieve information about your networks that can be used later for a different attack.

Common attacks screened by firewalls include the following tactics:

- Source address spoofing
- SYN flooding
- IP fragmentation
- IP options manipulation (source routing, record route)
- ICMP probes

No firewall can screen as-yet-undeveloped attacks with 100% certainty. As new attacks are discovered, however, firewall vendors are sure to include additional services to protect networks from them.

Source Address Spoofing: In source address spoofing, the attacker sends packets to hosts in your network with source IP addresses from your assigned IP address space.[3] The hope is your security policies will inspect the destination and source IP addresses and execute a rule as if the packets originated within your network. That is, your security policy may apply a rule assuming the sending station (the cracker) is actually a trusted host. Figure 4-4 shows source address spoofing.

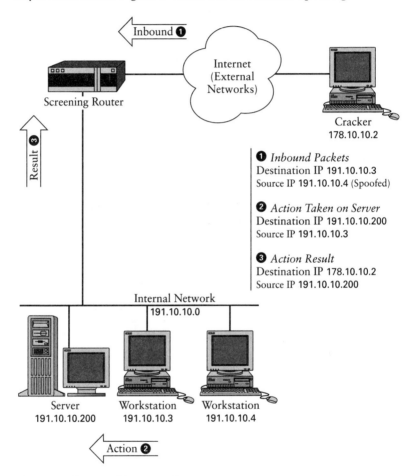

Figure 4-4 *Source address spoofing*

---

3. Authentication of users based on IP address is very weak. IP is not an authenticated protocol and thus the origin of a packet from within the Internet is not guaranteed to be the source address. Other authentication mechanisms must be employed to verify the identity of the sender.

The cracker will never receive any direct responses to the packets it sends into your network, because the source address claims to be another host within your network. Instead, response packets will be sent to the spoofed internal address. So why do crackers use source address spoofing to launch denial-of-service attacks? The answer lies in the fact that most operations involving TCP have predictable results. A skilled cracker can therefore send packets into your network that cause an internal device to take some action on another internal device. For instance, in Figure 4-4 the internal host 191.10.10.3 tells the server to mail its password file to 178.10.10.2. Presto! The cracker has succeeded.

Firewalls thwart this type of attack by applying interface information to the filtering process. For example, you can configure a firewall to deny incoming packets with a source IP address matching any of your interior network addresses. To apply this type of logic, a firewall must know through which interface a packet was received and then accordingly apply the source address spoofing logic.

SYN Flooding: Another attack that can be difficult to detect using generic packet filters is **SYN flooding**. The first packet in a TCP connection has its synchronize (SYN) flag set. When a server receives such a packet, it allocates a certain amount of memory for the ensuing data connection. The server replies to the client per the normal three-way handshake for TCP connections.

By flooding packets at a server with the SYN flag set from a spoofed external address, a cracker hopes to force a server to allocate memory for multiple incoming connections. Because the external address is spoofed, the server cannot complete the handshake, which results in a lot of half-open connections. Eventually the server will exhaust its memory pool and either deny any new connections or crash. In either case, the cracker has successfully launched a denial-of-service attack.

Some firewalls contain special services that look for SYN flooding. The filter looks for suspicious activity, such as multiple SYN packets originating from the same source address. In addition, it tracks the duration of a three-way handshake. If the last packet in the handshake from the client to the server takes too long to arrive, the handshake is assumed to be a hack attempt. The best protection from SYN flooding is to ensure that the operating systems of your hosts are immune to such problems, although screening for such attacks is always helpful.

IP Fragmentation: According to RFC 1858, "the Internet Protocol allows fragmentation of packets into pieces so small as to be impractical because of data and computational overhead. Attackers can sometimes exploit typical filter behavior and the ability to create peculiar fragment sequences in order sneak otherwise disallowed packets past the filter." The best option in this event is disallow fragmented packets through your firewall.

IP Options: Although ICMP is the most common method of discovering a network's architecture, exploiting the options fields in the IP header may also return information about your network that can be used later for an attack. Additionally, the cracker may manipulate IP options fields to allow dangerous packets into your network once authentication of the first packet occurs. Two IP options are often used for such attacks:

- **Source routing** is a method of routing packets between hosts using a path specified in the packet, as opposed to a path determined by routers. Source routing is rarely used today in the Internet in normal configurations. Crackers may use source routing because it enables them to see the results of forged packets. Your firewall should disallow source-routed packets.
- **Record Route** is an IP option that causes a packet to keep a log of the routers it crosses as it travels to its destination. Record route is extremely useful for normal network operators, because it works much more rapidly than the traceroute utility. On the other hand, a cracker can use this feature to discover the architecture of your networks. Typically, you have no reason to divulge this information to either an intruder or a legitimate user outside your network. We recommend that you deny packets with the record route option set.

ICMP Probes: Eliciting ICMP replies from your network, or any of its devices, is another method of launching a denial-of-service attack. In a manner similar to SYN flooding, a cracker can flood your network with ICMP echo request packets. By directing ICMP echo request packets at key servers or routers, it is possible to force these devices to respond only to the echo requests—thereby dropping legitimate data packets from other hosts. This process creates a denial-of-service situation.

Because ICMP is designed to provide information to the requestor about the status of network routing, crackers may find it a very useful tool when they are on reconnaissance operations. For this reason, it is prudent to limit or deny *incoming* ICMP request packets into your network. Life is never so easy, however. In some cases, you may wish to support ICMP echo requests to key web or FTP servers. In addition, wholesale disabling of ICMP may prove harmful to the performance of some operating systems that rely on ICMP for things like path **maximum transmission unit (MTU)** discovery.

The bottom line: If you need to support ICMP, a firewall can help screen for denial-of-service attacks that use ICMP. This screening is normally accomplished by throttling the number of ICMP packets into your network (for example, allowing no more than ten packets per second.) The type of ICMP protection varies according to firewall product.

4.5.3 Authentication

TCP/IP itself lacks any method of validating the identity of an IP address. Thus it is not possible to verify the identity of a user based on his or her IP address. To overcome this problem, many firewalls include additional authentication services that force users to identify themselves before they may transmit packets through the Internet gateway.

By authenticating the user through a trusted mechanism and *not* the IP address, firewalls can securely support users who reside outside of your networks but wish to access interior resources—for example, nomadic users and virtual private networks. Of course, the authentication process must itself be secure to ensure that the bad guys cannot masquerade as one of your trusted users.

Popular methods for providing user authentication include the following:

- User name and password
- One-time passwords
- Security tokens

Although various methods for authenticating user identities exist, the most common authentication approach involves submitting a user name and a *digital hash* of the password. Most often, the user name and password are tested against the values held on a **Remote Authentication Dial-In User Service (RADIUS)** system, operating system or internally in the firewall. The use of passwords without digital hashing is not recommended, as most are easily guessed and transmitted in a clear text format that can be captured by eavesdroppers.

Other methods include one-time passwords such as the S/Key system developed by Bellcore for use on UNIX systems. Also available are security tokens about the size of a PCMCIA card, such as the SecurID card manufactured by Security Dynamics. The user must attach the token to the workstation to authenticate himself or herself at the firewall.

4.5.4 Encryption and Virtual Private Networks

Many firewall products include support for one or more encryption technologies. Although a number of applications for encryption exist, the most popular these days is the virtual private network (VPN), which most firewall vendors now support. (Appendix B includes a description of VPNs. If you are unfamiliar with this technology and need a quick primer on the subject, take a few minutes to read it now.)

To enable you to set up a VPN, firewall manufacturers offer VPN-ready products. In addition to performing its duties as the endpoint of a tunnel, the firewall encrypts the contents of the tunneled packets. Bear in mind that the devices at the two ends of the tunnel must know how to decrypt one another's encrypted packets. Although VPNs are relatively new, their standardized encryption schemes enable product interoperability between vendors.

Various methods are available to encrypt data in VPNs. The most common practice is to implement **public-key encryption,** in which each node possesses two keys—a **public key** that it shares with other nodes and a **private key** that it does not share. The nodes exchange their public keys, and then use a third party called a **certificate authority (CA)** to verify the integrity of the sender's public key. Each node then generates a **secret key** by combining its private key with the sender's public key. Interestingly, the resultant secret keys are identical, and apparently it is mathematically unfeasible for a third party to forge this secret key. The secret keys are then used to provide the bulk of data encryption in the VPN.

This very basic description of public-key encryption barely skims the surface of the topic. For more information you may wish to read *Internet Cryptography* by Richard E. Smith, which provides a description of public-key encryption.

Most firewalls support encryption through one or both of the following technologies:

- Secure IP (IPsec)
- Simple Key-Management for Internet Protocols (SKIP)

IPsec is the standard protocol for encryption in VPNs. It includes a number of features that make it the first choice for deploying security within VPNs. For instance, IPsec provides standards for encryption and encapsulation of the entire packet into the tunneled packet. In addition, it authenticates that the sending station is indeed the proper sender.

Although IPsec is an Internet standard, a few aspects of this protocol have not yet been standardized. You should therefore make certain the vendor will update your firewall software later, when these last portions of IPsec are standardized.

SKIP is a variant of IPsec that addresses some shortcomings of the Secure IP standard. In particular, it resolves the issues that arise because of IPsec's use of fixed keys for the duration of the connection and its lack of a mechanism for exchanging keys.

In addition to IPsec and SKIP, some firewall vendors provide their own proprietary encryption schemes for VPNs and other applications. Typically they developed these proprietary encryption schemes when IPsec was not standardized. If you implement one of these schemes instead of IPsec or SKIP, remember that it may not be interoperable with another firewall product's encryption.

4.5.5 Event Logging and Intrusion Notification

In addition to filtering common attacks, other nice features of firewall products include event logging and intrusion notification. Event logging records the actions of the firewall on a per-packet basis. Periodically administrators should inspect the event logs to look for evidence of intrusions or attempted attacks. Today's firewalls typically provide secure event logging and methods of searching the volumes of recording to find suspicious activity.

In particular, you should pay attention to requests not supported at your Internet connection. Repeated attempts by external hosts to ping or traceroute into your network may constitute evidence that someone is trying to gain access to your interior networks. External hosts that request information via *finger* and *whois* should always be viewed with suspicion if you do not support these services.

Finally, some firewalls can detect an intrusion while it occurs. These security features that provide intrusion notification have predefined "suspicious activities." You can configure the firewalls to take various steps upon detection of an intrusion, such as ceasing to forward packets, paging you, sending e-mail to you, and so on.

4.5.6 Other Integrated Services

The fierce competition in the firewall marketplace has prompted vendors to include ever more features in their wares. In addition to acting as hybrid packet filters and circuit proxies, many firewalls now incorporate application gateway features. Beyond that, some even include server-related functions.

NAT: Network address translation (NAT) is now a common feature in firewall products. As discussed earlier, using NAT at your firewall may not only resolve IP address issues in your interior networks, but also screen your interior hosts from the Internet. In other words, your firewall becomes a circuit proxy by default when it performs NAT duties.

Virus Filtering: Firewalls can now screen the data payload within packets for virus definitions. Traditionally, viruses were spread by means of games and Trojan horse programs. Today, however, they may ride within mail messages as file attachments. Some viruses even hide in the macros of Microsoft Word documents. It is not possible to screen attachments for viruses with 100% accuracy. For instance, viruses can reside within an encrypted mail message that cannot be deciphered by the firewall.

Screening for viruses is a never-ending process. Implementing virus filtering at the Internet connection should be only one part of a virus eradication campaign. You should also consider virus scanning packages for both your file servers and workstations.

URL Filtering (Policing): In all likelihood, you will support HTTP traffic for your user community—without it, the web will remain out of reach. You may find it necessary to restrict your user community from accessing particular web sites—to prevent individuals from accessing pornographic sites, for example. Whatever your reason for policing web surfing, it will be very difficult to implement filter policies based on IP addresses.

The solution provided by a few firewalls involves URL filtering. In this security feature, the firewall looks into the payload portion of the HTTP packet and determines the destination URL. If the URL is part of a restricted list, it drops the packet. Although some management of the URL lists may be necessary, this option is far easier than managing IP addresses. In addition, filtering against URLs is a pliable mechanism that accommodates IP address changes of servers and Internet hosts.

The efficacy of such a filtering mechanism is questionable, however. Administrators of "undesirable" sites occasionally go to great lengths to use names that will bypass URL filters looking for keywords. Also, a trend toward using IP addresses in URLs has recently emerged.

Split DNS: One problem many administrators face when connecting their sites to the Internet relates to DNS. If you wish to hide the names of the interior workstations and system from the Internet, you need to maintain two DNS servers. One resolves names for your interior users; the other performs the same function for Internet users. Typically, the naming information on the exterior server is a subset of the interior server. Maintenance of two DNS servers is known as a **split DNS** configuration.

Operating a split DNS becomes an issue when exterior hosts perform reverse and double-reverse lookups on your interior hosts' IP address. It is common for server sites to attempt a verification of the client by executing either of these challenges. In the reverse lookup, the server asks your DNS to resolve the IP address into a name. If the server receives an answer (any answer), it grants the connection. In a double-reverse lookup, the server first conducts a reverse lookup. Then it queries your DNS again using the name it received from the reverse lookup. If the server does not receive the same IP address used for the first lookup, it blocks the connection.

Reverse and double-reverse lookups are relatively weak security mechanisms. First, reverse lookups do not authenticate who is actually using the service. Second, administrators with split DNS configurations must fill their host tables with fictitious names for the external DNS. When these mechanisms are employed, you must ensure that your external DNS responds consistently to both the reverse and double-reverse lookup. Many firewall vendors provide a DNS server that runs on the firewall server, working in conjunction with your interior DNS server to provide split DNS functions.

4.5.7 Vendors

Every day more vendors jump into the game of selling firewall products. As a result, you should probably do some independent research to narrow the field of contestants. Before you begin shopping for a firewall product, however, ask yourself whether a firewall is absolutely necessary. More specifically, does the router connecting your sites to the ISP have reasonable filtering capabilities? It is quite possible it may already include some "firewall" features.

If you decide to enhance your site's security by adding a firewall to the network, then you will need to do some homework and research available products. It is recommended that you look at the following sources of information to get a handle on available firewall products:

- Conduct some searches using the web. Many review articles can be found online through the web. The author started with a quick web search using the keywords *firewall Internet vendors* and managed to find some very useful links.

- Visit the library and find some industry magazines and journals with articles reviewing firewalls.
- Ask your ISP to recommend a firewall product for your site. Even though the ISP may provide limited choices for products, getting its recommendation is a quick way to begin assessing firewall products.

A quick web search revealed the following sites that listed firewall products:

- A good hit was CSI's Free Firewall Resource at http://www.gocsi.com:8080/firewall.htm. This site listed about 40 reviewed firewall products.
- The site http://www.greatcircle.com/firewalls/vendors.html contained a large list of firewall products categorized by commercial products, freeware, resellers, and so on. Great Circle Associates was founded by D. Brent Chapman, the coauthor of *Building Internet Firewalls,* referenced at the beginning of this chapter.
- Another good site is Internet Firewalls Frequently Asked Questions maintained by Marcus J. Ranum at http://www.clark.net/pub/mjr/pubs/fwfaq. This FAQ site offers many good links to other security sites.

Commercial Products: As you might guess, most firewalls are commercial products that you must purchase. Generally these firewalls come with documentation, distribution CDs, and technical support as you would expect with any software package. Many are sold indirectly through resellers, reflecting the notion that a local group or organization will be better able to serve your needs than a large software company.

Freeware: The amount of freeware firewall software is far more limited than available commercial products. If you are savvy in UNIX and willing to spend time configuring the firewall software, a freeware package may be in your future. If you are not versatile in TCP/IP networking, we do not recommend that you attempt to build your own firewall using freeware.

Freeware firewall packages include the following:

- The Internet Firewall Toolkit from TIS, available at ftp://ftp. tis.com/
- Freestone from SOS Corporation, available at http://www. soscorp.com/
- Mediator One Firewall from Comnet Solutions, available at http://www.comnet.com.au/htmls/mediator1.html

U.S. Export Policies: Some forms of encryption sold by companies in the United States cannot be exported to other countries. If you need an encryption technology for deploying VPNs or perhaps user authentication, check with the vendors to make certain the technology can be sold in your country.

4.5 Typical Policies

The following section gives security recommendations on the common Internet services you will likely support. You should view these guidelines as a starting point for your security policy, realizing that you may need to modify them to meet your specific needs.

4.6.1 Outbound Traffic

You should limit the services you permit in the outbound direction to only those necessary. Although it is generally safe to allow outbound packets for TCP-based services such as Telnet and HTTP, even supporting these options might incur some risk. In particular, client-side bugs in web browsers cause some exposure to hacks.

Apart from DNS, try to stay away from supporting UDP-based services when possible. Using a firewall that employs a variant of stateful inspection can lessen the risk with UDP-based services, as it filters UDP packets as if they were part of a connection.

A few services absolutely should not be permitted from your networks—**X-Windows, Network Files System (NFS)**, and the r-services such as rlogin, rexec, and rsh.

Keeping a tight policy on outbound services is a good idea because it enables you keep track of the traffic on the Internet connection. Moreover, you can protect the Internet from overzealous users in your networks who might, for instance, try to use SNMP tools to discover and manage the Internet! Not only do you want to protect your networks from the bad guys in the Internet, but you also want to protect the Internet from the bad guys in your networks![4]

4.6.2 Inbound Traffic

When allowing traffic into your network, you need to differentiate between response packets destined for your interior hosts and other packets bound for other hosts. Here are some general rules:

1. Inbound TCP packets are acceptable if they are part of an *established* connection. Other incoming TCP traffic should be limited to your servers, which would optimally be located on your perimeter network.

2. Inbound UDP packets should be denied unless they are absolutely necessary. Make certain that you limit inbound UDP packets to particular source ports. Because UDP packets (and ports) can be easily forged, you should use a firewall product to track UDP conversations as if they were TCP connections.

3. Inbound ICMP should be blocked. Allowing responses to your interior hosts is acceptable, and you may choose to allow ICMP echo requests to your perimeter network servers to help users in the Internet determine their status.

4. Other IP protocols such as IP-Tunnel and IGMP should be blocked unless you really need them.

4.6.3 Service-Specific Recommendations

The discussions that follow provide recommendations for the standard Internet services supported at today's Internet connections, noting the server port numbers.

DNS (TCP and UDP Port 53): How you support DNS depends on the location of the DNS server used by the clients in your networks. There are essentially three cases you may need to consider:

---

4. Most security breeches are perpetrated by employees (or ex-employees) who have deeper knowledge of a network's systems, and hence its weaknesses.

1. *No internal DNS server.* In this case, the clients on your LANs will need to access an external DNS server (most likely that of your ISP).

2. *Internal DNS server with no secondary external server.* In this scenario, clients don't need to access external servers, but your internal DNS server does. External servers will need to query your internal DNS server.

3. *Internal DNS server with secondary external server.* This situation requires zone transfers between the primary and secondary DNS servers. The zone transfer will be requested by the secondary server. You will need to support incoming TCP connection requests from the secondary server to the primary server. External servers will need to query your internal DNS server.

For case 1, we recommend that you limit outbound queries from internal clients to the external server. You should permit replies from the server to the internal clients.

In case 2, you should limit outbound queries to only those between the internal server to external servers. You can permit replies from external servers to the internal server and allow external servers to query the internal server.

The recommendation for case 3 is the same as that for case 2, but with the following addition: You should restrict incoming requests to the primary for zone transfers to the secondary servers.

File Transfer: Several services are available for copying files from one host to another using TCP/IP. The most common are *File Transfer Protocol (FTP), Trivial Transfer File Protocol (TFTP),* and *Network File System (NFS).*

For FTP (FTP 20, 21, random port greater than 1023), we recommend that you use a firewall to support the protocol. In standard FTP, the server opens the data channel with the client, which is an undesirable security situation, as an external device needs to open a TCP connection into your network. In PASV-mode FTP, the client opens the data channel with the server, which is better because the TCP connection originates within your network. In either case, the client uses a random port greater than 1023. Writing generic packet filters to screen FTP is not a trivial exercise. Your best bet is to let a firewall screen your FTP traffic using stateful inspection.

TFTP (UDP 69, random port greater than 1023) is a simpler version of FTP that includes no user authentication or login protection. As a result, you should not support it through your Internet connection.

NFS (UDP 2049) is the staple method of transferring files between UNIX systems. Because NFS has some severe shortcomings with authentication, you should not support NFS through your firewall.

ICMP: As mentioned previously, ICMP can allow crackers to gather information about your networks. This protocol also helps you get the status of IP routing in the Internet.

We make the following recommendations for ICMP support:

1. Allow outbound ICMP echo requests (type 8), which enables you to ping external hosts.
2. Allow outbound ICMP echo response (type 0) and time exceeded (type 11) for external users pinging or tracerouting to your servers.
3. Allow inbound ICMP echo response (type 0), destination unreachable (type 3), and time exceeded (type 11). External hosts will be able to answer your ping requests.
4. Allow inbound ICMP echo request only to your servers that must support external hosts. Use a firewall to ensure that this protocol can't be used for a denial-of-service attack.
5. Do not support other ICMP services.

Mail: Several services permit a client to read Internet mail from a server—IMAP4, POP3, and POP2. Only one service allows servers to exchange mail with one another—SMTP.

IMAP4 (TCP 143): If your ISP provides mail hosting for your site and the server supports *IMAP4*, you should enable your interior hosts to connect using TCP destination port 143 to the mail server. Limit incoming packets to source port 143 with the ACK bit set.

POP3 and POP2 (TCP 110, 109 respectively): If your ISP provides mail hosting for your site and the server supports *POP3*, you should enable your interior hosts to connect using TCP destination port 110 to the mail server. If you enable *POP2*, then you should support outbound TCP packets to port 109. Limit incoming packet to source port 110 with the ACK bit set for POP3, and to source port 109 with the ACK bit set for POP2.

SMTP (TCP 25): Because so many security holes have arisen with *SMTP* server daemons on UNIX systems, maintaining a SMTP mail server in your network is a major task. If you must maintain this type of server, allow the server to create only outbound connections to other servers. If your mail server resides outside of your network, then your clients must create outbound SMTP connections to it. Similarly, allow incoming connections using destination port 25 to your mail server.

NNTP (TCP 119): Because the server software for NNTP has been prone to weakness, crackers have been able to send embedded characters and commands, causing the servers to divulge information. If you maintain a news server, make certain it runs the latest server software. Allow the server to create only outbound connections to other servers—there's no need for clients to perform this function. Similarly, allow incoming connections using destination port 119 to your news server.

Routing Protocols: A basic Internet connection should not require the exchange of routing information with the ISP's router. The ISP knows how to route to your networks, and you simply need a static route to the ISP. Do not run a routing protocol on your Internet connection unless explicitly instructed to do so by the ISP.

SNMP (UDP 161, 162): The **Simple Network Management Protocol** (**SNMP**) is a protocol used to manage network devices. (If you wish to learn more about SNMP, read Darryl Black's book, *Managing Switched Local Area Networks: A Practical Guide.*) When used within your own networks, SNMP is a wonderful tool, but it is pointless to deploy SNMP to learn about the network devices in the Internet for two reasons. First, you probably won't be able to manage those devices without the proper passwords (called **community strings**). Second, SNMP applications poll devices periodically to learn about networks. If you allow your user community to poll the Internet, you will waste your connection's bandwidth. Consequently, you should not allow SNMP through your Internet connection in either direction.

Telnet (TCP 23): Generally, your interior hosts can freely use Telnet outbound to the Internet. Nevertheless, you should make your user community aware of the fact that Telnet (like other protocols) transmits information in cleartext format. Thus the passwords and login names used to access devices in the Internet are readable to eavesdroppers. Screen incoming Telnet packets to ensure that their source port is 23 and the ACK bit is set. Try not to support inbound Telnet to your networks unless you have an explicit reason to do so. (Telnet is a fabulous tool for crackers.) Use a firewall with user authentication to verify the user's identity.

RealPlayer (TCP 7070, UDP 6970–7170): The RealPlayer client by Real-Networks is a software package that enables a user to receive video and audio feeds from the Internet. The RealAudio client service works as follows:

1. The client initiates a TCP connection with the RealPlayer server using destination port TCP 7070.
2. After some negotiation, the server begins streaming UDP packets to the clients in the port range of 6970 to 7170 (inclusive).

Although you can restrict the incoming packets to TCP port 7070, it will likely degrade the performance, as the TCP packets require handshaking whereas the UDP packets do not. If you wish to support RealAudio, we recommend that is you invest in a firewall that can screen specifically for these types of connections. In particular, the firewall must be capable of tracking the outbound request from the client and then anticipating the incoming UDP packet stream.

HTTP (TCP 80, 8080): HTTP is the workhorse of the web. The majority of HTTP connections use TCP port 80, though port 8080 has been designated as an alternate. In recent years, we have seen more use of TCP ports 81, 8000, and 8002 for HTTP requests.

There's no problem in allowing your interior hosts to send HTTP requests outbound to the Internet. You should, however, screen incoming HTTP packets to ensure that their source port is 80 TCP and the ACK bit is set. You can also support the other ports on a case-by-case basis. If you have a web server, you should limit incoming HTTP connections to the server's IP address.

SSL (TCP 443): Recommendations for this service are the same as those for HTTP.

4.6.4 Problematical Services

By far the easiest Internet services to filter at your Internet connection are those based on TCP. The TCP header includes the ACK bit, which indicates whether the packet is part of an established connection. From this information, you can derive direction without resorting to a firewall product. Other common services may prove more difficult to screen with generic filters, including the following:

- UDP
- FTP
- ICMP
- IP-Tunnel

Your best bet for supporting these services safely is to use a firewall product that can employ complex filtering and stateful inspection.

4.7 Security Auditing

4.7.1 Need

Once you have finished implementing your security policy, you need to test it. Then, when you have finished testing it, you should test it again. In addition to testing your policies as a host connected to your interior network, try hacking your Internet connection from the Internet. Having a dial-up account with another ISP is very useful for this purpose.

When you think you have your security set, consider asking an outside party to verify it as well. The market for security auditing has become a big business, with many large organizations hiring auditors to ensure that their security policies are correctly implemented and enforced.

4.7.2 Software Tools

A new breed of commercial software tools is capable of either auditing your security or detecting intrusions. Some products perform both functions.

Security auditing packages usually contain a suite of common attacks that you launch against your network and its hosts. Some of these tools also provide some programming capabilities so that you can build your own tools.

Other intrusion detection packages look for ping sweeps, SATAN scans,[5] and other tell-tale signs of probing or actual attacks. These packages notify you via paging or e-mail that an attack is in progress. Some of these tools can take corrective actions and stop the attack.

A key factor in determining the value of any of these tools is the strength of the company building it. The company should be extremely knowledgeable about how attacks work and able to duplicate or detect them. In short, the effectiveness of each tool depends on the strength of the database of known attacks and how up-to-date it is kept.

If you opt not to purchase a software tool for auditing, the Telnet application can be used in a limited manner to verify some of your security policies. This option will be truly helpful only if you can launch Telnet from an IP address outside your network. By specifying a TCP port other than 23, you can verify whether your filters weed out incoming TCP connections on nonsupported ports. Do not consider this procedure a substitute for real auditing, however.

4.7.3 Auditing Services

If you do not want the hassle of installing software for intrusion detection or auditing, you can turn to companies that perform auditing services. For a fee (and it can be a large one), the auditor will probe your

---

5. Security Administrator's Tool for Analyzing Networks (SATAN) was a freeware tool that probed firewalls and hosts for the most common security flaws. In fact, some firewalls now protect your network from SATAN scans in case a cracker is using the same tool to probe your network. The tool is no longer supported.

network for weaknesses and launch attacks against it where applicable. At the end of the audit, the company will provide a report indicating where it found problems and making suggestions for correcting them. An increasing number of companies are delving into this business, which borders on security consulting. If you are interested in this option, first consider the auditing services offered by your ISP. After that, a web search or recent magazine reviews are good ways of locating an auditor.

4.8 Keeping Current

At the beginning of this chapter, we noted that security is an ongoing concern. Once your site is operational, you will need to update your security knowledge periodically. A few information sources for security that you may find helpful in this respect are described here:

- Bugtraq is a very useful resource for security on the Internet. This mailing list has been in operation for many years and has become the de facto clearinghouse for security information on the Internet. You can send your subscription request to bugtraq-request@netspace.org.
- Firewall-1 Mailing List is CheckPoint's associated mailing list for its Firewall-1 product. It is helpful not only if you use Firewall-1, but also if you would like to access the conversations between users about general security questions. CheckPoint's web site has instructions for subscribing at http://www.checkpoint.com/.
- SANS is an organization with a mailing list (and associated web site http://www.sans.org) that performs a similar function to Bugtraq. Typically, the SANS newsletters summarize security risks with URLs, pointing to more in-depth coverage of particular topics.
- The Computer Emergency Response Team (CERT) Coordination Center provides a newsletter and web page with security advisories on recent attacks and steps to prevent recurrent attacks.[6] Its web site is http://www.cert.org.

---

6. CERT typically does not provide any detailed information about attacks. Usually you must look at another source to obtain any substantive information.

4.9 Checklist—Security

Network Access Control Methods

❏ Which access control method will you use to enforce your security?
  ❏ Packet filtering either as a router or firewall (most common)
  ❏ Circuit proxy by means of a firewall
  ❏ Application gateway
  ❏ Stateful inspection
  ❏ Network address translation
❏ Have you determined the services you need to support?
❏ Have you researched how the supported services function (for example, passive FTP, Telnet)?

Firewall Products Explained

❏ Can the firewall screen for UDP communications?
❏ Does the firewall screen for common attacks?
  ❏ Source address spoofing
  ❏ SYN flooding
  ❏ Tiny fragments
  ❏ Source routing
  ❏ Record route
  ❏ Other IP options
❏ Does the firewall screen for and throttle ICMP?
❏ Does the firewall provide event logging and intrusion notification?
❏ Does the firewall have user authentication capabilities? Which ones are supported?
  ❏ User name and password
  ❏ One-time passwords
  ❏ Security tokens
❏ Does the firewall support VPNs? Which tunneling protocol is used?
  ❏ Using PPTP
  ❏ Using L2TP

❑ If VPNs are supported, how is the data encrypted in the tunnel?
   ❑ Proprietary Symetric key encryption
   ❑ IPsec
   ❑ SKIP
❑ Does the vendor sell encryption that can be exported to your country?
❑ Does the firewall support network address translation?
❑ Does the firewall include other integrated services?
   ❑ Virus filtering
   ❑ URL filtering
   ❑ Split DNS

Firewall Network Architectures

❑ Will you deploy a screened host subnet architecture using two screening routers or one?
❑ If you have servers that need access to external hosts, can you place them on the perimeter network?

Typical Policies

❑ Will you support DNS through your Internet connection?
   ❑ DNS server is located in your network
   ❑ DNS server is located with ISP
❑ Will you support FTP through your Internet connection?
   ❑ Standard FTP
   ❑ Passive FTP
❑ Will you support ICMP through your Internet connection?
❑ Will you support IMAP4, POP3, or POP2 to an external mail server?
❑ Will you support SMTP between an internal mail server and the Internet?
❑ Will you support NNTP?
❑ Will you support RealAudio?
❑ Will you support Telnet?
❑ Will you support web access (HTTP and SSL)?

Designing Your Network Architecture

5.1 Chapter Overview

At this point you are ready to start designing the network architecture that will connect your LAN to the Internet. The preceding chapters covered the background information you will need as you design the network. Now it's time to apply this information.

In many cases, designing a network is an iterative process. Of course, you will seek to minimize the number of iterations, but do not be too concerned if you find yourself working on your third or fourth version of a design. To help keep your design efforts focused, you should follow the steps outlined in Table 5-1. The remainder of this chapter discusses these steps in further detail.

Table 5-1 Overview of the Design Process

Step	Description
1	Delineate your service objectives
2	Assess your design factors
3	Select a prototype design
4	Determine your IP architecture
5	Select your equipment
6	Reiterate from step 2 as needed

After reading this chapter you should be able to answer the following questions about designing your network:

1. What services do you plan to support and will you need to locate any servers on-site that will be shared with the Internet?
2. How do security and cost concerns influence the network design?
3. What are the key features, benefits, and drawbacks of the prototype designs provided in this chapter?
4. How do IP addressing, subnetting, and routing influence your architecture?
5. What should you select for your router, firewall, and WAN premises equipment?

5.2 Delineate Your Service Objectives

In designing a network, you need to know what its intended purpose will be. Otherwise, you may end up over- or under-designing the network. Determining your site requirements is the first step in the design process. In particular, you must decide which Internet services your site will support, if you have not done so already.

5.2.1 Services Accessed from the Internet

First you should figure out which services you wish to access *from* the Internet, and then compile a list of those services, as shown in Table 5-2. This step creates a shopping list of services you intend to purchase from the Internet "supermarket." To put this issue in the proper framework, ask the following question: "What services will my internal hosts need to access from external hosts in the Internet?" Note that Table 5-2 is merely a basic list of services; you may wish to add other services to the list as your situation warrants.

We have already discussed the typical lineup of Internet services. In particular, Chapter 1 gave descriptions of the basic services that constitute the bulk traffic within the Internet. Chapter 4 discussed some of these services from the security perspective.

Table 5-2 Basic Internet Services

Category	Service	IP Protocol	Port
Domain Name System	DNS	UDP, TCP	53
File transfer	FTP	TCP	20, 21
Mail	SMTP	TCP	25
	IMAP4	TCP	143
	POP3, POP2	TCP	110,109
News	NNTP	TCP	119
Security/encryption	SSL	TCP	443
Terminal emulation	Telnet	TCP	23
Web	HTTP	TCP	80, 8080

To a large extent, your "shopping list" will dictate your security policy with respect to outbound traffic and the associated inbound replies. For instance, if you allow your internal hosts to access external web servers, you will need to support HTTP packets in the outbound direction for connection requests and queries, and HTTP packets in the inbound direction for replies. You would *not* need to support inbound connection requests.

5.2.2 Services Provided to the Internet

Next, you need to delineate the services you will provide to the Internet. You will share these services with external hosts and servers. As with the services you take from the Internet, the services you provide to the Internet dictate your inbound security policies. For instance, if you maintain an FTP server, then you must account for inbound connection requests and associated outbound replies in your security policies.

Although your choice of services to provide to the Internet is largely optional, several mandatory services exist that you *must* provide to have your site function properly on the Internet. These services include DNS and mail:

- Providing DNS information to the Internet is necessary to allow external hosts (at minimum) to resolve how to send mail to your mail server. Also, if you maintain other servers, external hosts must be able to resolve the names of these servers into IP addresses. For security reasons, the DNS information you provide to the Internet is usually a smaller subset of the database you reference internally (for example, split DNS).
- If you wish to receive e-mail from other Internet hosts, you must provide a mail server where external servers can deposit incoming mail for your site. Although this server does not need to be the same one that sends mail to the Internet for your site, it often is.

For small sites, the ISP typically provides these two services to the Internet on your behalf. The DNS and mail servers are located at the ISP and used by customers other than you. The primary advantages of using the ISP's servers are that you do not need to provide server setup and maintenance, and you do not configure security policies to the servers. As mentioned in Chapter 2, the ISP is normally responsible for assisting in configuring DNS and mail for your site. This service should be included in the installation and setup of your connection.

In some circumstances, however, you may want these servers to be located on-site. In almost all cases the underlying reason is to gain greater control, information security, and bandwidth conservation. Although the ISP's servers are most certainly safe havens for DNS and mail, you may have a large and dynamic environment with many users accessing these services. Simply locating the servers on-site helps minimize Internet traffic and enhances your control over the servers. On the other hand, it places many more responsibilities on your shoulders, including maintenance, configuration, and security.

Other services you may wish to provide to the Internet are called "optional" to distinguish them from DNS and mail, both of which are mandatory. These days, optional services you provide to the Internet usually include the following (though you could support many more):

- World Wide Web (HTTP)
- FTP
- News (NNTP)

Technically, you are not required to provide a web server. Your management, however, may not view the web server as an optional item—it may be the major reason you are building an Internet connection. If this construction is your first Internet connection, you may wish to consider having your ISP host these services for you. Having your ISP do the hosting, at least initially, will alleviate some of the complexity in your design. Chapter 2 discussed web-hosting options with ISPs.

5.2.3 Other Services

Besides the core services you take from the Internet and the few you provide to the Internet, you may have a few other requirements at your site. Some common ones include the following services:

- Virtual private networks (VPNs)
- Remote access via the ISP
- Multicast and MBone
- Faxing

At this point, you should have developed a list of services you will support to the Internet, including the mandatory items of DNS and mail as well as any additional services, such as HTTP and FTP. Perhaps you may be planning to support VPNs as well.

5.3 Assess Your Design Factors

Although many items will influence the details of your design, only a few will actually drive the design. These items, which are known as the design factors or conditions, govern your choice of architecture, equipment, and network access policies. The Internet services you delineated in Section 5.2 are your objectives. Now you must think about designing a network that delivers these objectives while meeting the constraints of your particular situation, which are usually related to security and cost.

5.3.1 Security

Our discussion keeps returning to security, largely because this requirement governs your design. Certainly, providing decent security is a design objective, just like supporting Internet services. Changing your security requirements, however, can change your network design more so than, for example, adding another TCP-based protocol to your lineup of supported Internet services. In effect, your security policy influences your design.

When assessing security requirements for a site, the following items should shape the ultimate security policies:

1. **Service Objectives**—Your security must match your Internet service objectives. If you plan to deploy a very basic list of Internet services, then your security policies will likely be (refreshingly) simplified. In these cases a hybrid packet-filtering router may suffice for security. On the other hand, if you elect to support some security unfriendly services (for example, FTP, UDP-based services), then you may need to deploy a full-featured firewall. Take some time to research the services you plan to support and really understand how they operate. Determine how their functioning will affect your security policies.

2. **Location of Servers**—Where you choose to locate your servers that share information with the Internet is a significant factor in your security, and hence in the system design. The location determines whether you must support inbound connection requests or queries from the Internet into your network. At minimum, you will need to decide where your DNS and mail servers will be placed. Will you locate these at the ISP, on-site, or split between locations?[1] Also, will you maintain other servers on-site, such as a web or news server?

3. **Budget**—Because most of today's security solutions are commercial products, your available budget usually governs your design and equipment selection. Although purists might say

---

1. Many smaller sites choose to locate their DNS servers at the ISP. In this way, they can offload the DNS configuration and maintenance to the ISP, which are not trivial tasks.

money should never be a factor in security designs, for most of us it is *the* factor that drives our designs.[2] In layman's terms, your available cash will determine if you can deploy security using router-based packet filtering, circuit proxy, application gateway, or a firewall using stateful inspection. What budget do you have available to invest in security?

Answering these questions will help shape your security policy and selection of a network access control mechanism. At least you will know the conditions with which you are working when deploying your security.

5.3.2 Cost

Lucky readers will not be constrained by cost when designing their networks. For most of us, however, cost is the primary constraint of the design. Cost also influences security, as previously mentioned. The items in Table 5-3, in particular, can account for major line items in a design budget.

Table 5-3 Major Budgeting Items

Equipment	Use	Min. Cost
Workstation (UNIX or PC)	Firewall	$2,500
Server equipment (UNIX or PC)	Servers, gateways	$2,500
Software	Firewall, application gateway, and so on	$2,500
Router	Packet filtering, WAN connectivity	$1,500
Switch (bridge)	Building network segments	$1,500
Hub (repeaters)	Building network segments	$1,000
WAN premises equipment (CSU/DSU, NT1, and so on)	WAN connectivity	$1,000
Uninterruptable power supply (UPS)	Network equipment, servers	$500

---

2. Many administrators underestimate the cost of insufficient security. Convey to your manager the importance of security and explain the risks of insufficient security. It should help you negotiate a larger budget for the security component of your design.

The last column in Table 5-3 indicates the approximate minimum cost for the equipment item in U.S. dollars. As you can see, if you are not careful your budget for equipment can get quickly out of control. The important point is to assess what financial resources you have at your disposal before you design your network.

As you select your prototype design, do a rough cost analysis of its components to ensure that you are not building something you cannot afford. Although the detailed cost analysis should wait until after you have selected a prototype design, there's no point in creating your dream network when your budget dictates otherwise.

5.4 Select a Prototype Design

Once you have your design objectives listed, and your constraints and design criteria in hand, you may begin tinkering with your prototype designs. This section provides several prototype designs that you can use as starting points for your own designs. Your job will be to add the necessary details to these designs, thereby generating a unique solution that matches your particular requirements in terms of services, costs, and security.

Several standard designs have proved to be extremely robust in providing security. These strategies are commonly referred to as **screened subnets.** To keep matters simple, we will provide two examples of screened subnets that represent good foundations for security. In these examples, the term "router" denotes both a real router and a firewall device.

The type of design you deploy really depends on how much security you want, and whether you need to provide services to the Internet. The overriding philosophy in most Internet architectures is to keep traffic between external hosts and your servers separate from your interior networks. In these designs, we assume that everything outside of your interior networks has had its security compromised.

The discussions of the following designs concentrate on the placement of internal hosts, filters, and servers. In particular, they focus on the DNS and mail servers, because they are mandatory items for any Internet connection. You can place additional servers next to the DNS or mail servers in these designs and apply similar security policies to those servers. In addition, our discussion provides a very basic policy list that you may use as a starting point in defining your own security policy.

Keep in mind that your ISP is potentially a very good resource for validating your design and resolving questions. ISPs are in the business of Internet connectivity and can likely offer you some design suggestions that match their architecture and yours. Do not hesitate to ask your ISP for a prototype design.

5.4.1 Design 1—Single Filter for Screening Internal Hosts

Figure 5-1 shows one of the more common network designs using a single filter. This basic design includes internal users and external mail and DNS services. This architecture has the following features:

1. All hosts are located within the interior networks behind the filter. The filter usually comprises a packet-filtering router or workstation-based firewall.[3]

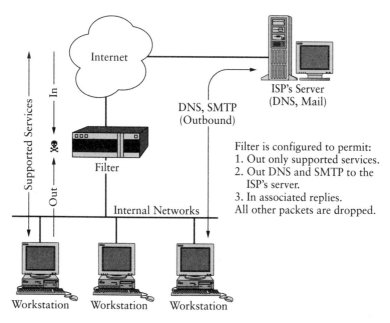

Figure 5-1 *Single-filter design*

---

3. Some ISPs provide packet-filtering services deployed on their end of the WAN Connection. In effect, this approach allows the ISP to protect your site without modifying the configuration of your on-site equipment. You may wish to consider this method of augmenting your own security.

2. All servers are located at the ISP. The ISP is therefore responsible for configuring and maintaining these servers, as well as providing security for them.

3. This economical design minimizes your amount of on-site equipment and configuration tasks. Keep in mind, however, that it does increase your fees to the ISP, as the ISP is hosting and maintaining servers on your behalf.

4. The design provides only a single element of network access control. If a cracker manages to infiltrate the filter, your network security is likely compromised.

The nice thing about this design is that most external hosts do not need to initiate TCP connections to hosts within your networks. The glaring exception to this is standard FTP (see Chapter 1). Overall, your security policy in this design governs the outbound traffic from internal hosts to the Internet, and the associated replies. Table 5-4 gives a quick rundown of a security policy for this design.

Table 5-4 A Security Policy

Service	Comment
SMTP	1. Permit outbound communication for all clients to mail server 2. Permit inbound replies to clients from mail server (ACK bit set)
DNS	1. Permit outbound communication for all clients (UDP only) to DNS server 2. Permit inbound replies to clients (UDP only) from DNS server
Other services (HTTP, Telnet, FTP, POP3, IMAP4, SSL, and so on)	1. Permit outbound packets for other supported services 2. Permit inbound replies to clients (ACK bit set)
ICMP	1. Permit outbound echo request 2. Permit inbound echo reply, destination unreachable, time exceeded
Default stance	1. Drop all packets either inbound or outbound

A few considerations that you must take into account with this architecture follow:

1. In this configuration, your internal clients will likely access their messages from the mail server using either the POP3 or IMAP4 protocols. To send messages, however, they will need to connect to the mail server using SMTP.

2. With this single-filter design, you must pay attention to your policies for FTP support. Remember, supporting standard FTP will require the server to initiate an inbound data connection to the client using an source port of 20, while supporting passive FTP will require the client to initiate a connection to the server using a destination port greater than 1023.

3. The ISP may ask for you to support several inbound services from hosts in its network to your router (that is, ICMP). If the ISP manages your on-site router, then it will take care of this task for you. In fact, you probably will not need to worry about router security configurations until you assume control of the router.

5.4.2 Design 2—Single Filter for Screening Servers

Figure 5-2 shows another common network design using a single filter but with one or more servers located within the interior networks. This basic design includes internal users as well as internal mail and DNS servers. Its primary advantage is that it puts you in control of your server(s). Keep in mind that placing a server within your internal network increases your risk of being attacked.

This architecture has the following features:

1. All hosts are located within the interior networks behind the filter.

2. With respect to DNS and mail, the internal servers communicate with external servers throughout the Internet (not just the ISP's servers). External servers must query and connect to your server to deliver mail and resolve names. Your internal hosts communicate with only the internal server for mail and DNS; they do not communicate with external hosts to obtain those services.

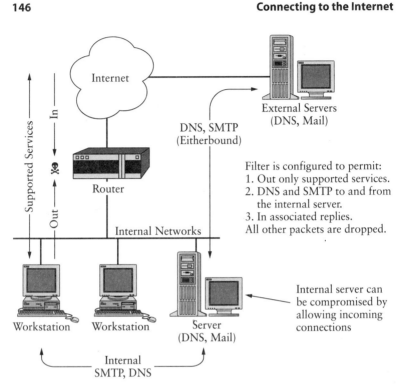

Figure 5-2 *Screened server*

3. This economical design minimizes your amount of on-site equipment and configuration tasks. Unlike the previous design, however, it decreases your ISP-related fees because the ISP no longer maintains servers on your behalf. On the other hand, you now incur the cost of maintaining servers.

4. It provides only a single element of network access control. If a cracker manages to infiltrate the filter, then your network security will likely be compromised. Furthermore, the cracker then has a convenient platform from which to attack other internal hosts.

Unlike the previous design, this single-filter architecture requires external hosts to initiate connections to the servers within your networks. Thus your security policy governs not only the outbound traffic from internal hosts to the Internet and the associated replies, but also the traffic to and from the servers. Table 5-5 gives a basic security policy for this design.

Note the following points about this security policy:

1. Because your server is located behind the filter within you internal network, it is a convenient location from which a cracker can launch attacks against internal hosts. You should "lock down" the server and remove unnecessary services such as Telnet,

Table 5-5 Basic Security Policy

Service	Comment
SMTP	1. Permit outbound communication from mail server to Internet 2. Permit inbound replies to mail server from Internet (ACK bit set) 3. Permit inbound connections to mail server from Internet 4. Permit outbound replies from mail server to Internet
DNS	1. Permit outbound queries (UDP) from DNS server 2. Permit inbound replies (UDP) to DNS server 3. Permit inbound queries (UDP) to DNS server 4. Permit outbound replies (UDP) from DNS server 5. Permit inbound connections (TCP) to DNS server from secondary servers (for zone transfer) 6 Permit outbound replies (TCP) from DNS server to secondary servers (ACK bit set)
Other services (HTTP, Telnet, FTP, POP3, IMAP4, SSL, and so on)	1. Permit outbound packets for other supported services 2. Permit inbound replies to clients (ACK bit set)
ICMP	1. Permit outbound echo request 2. Permit inbound echo reply, destination unreachable, time exceeded
Default stance	1. Drop all packets either inbound or outbound

X11 (X-Windows), FTP, NFS, and NIS from it. For maximum
security, you should only allow root login from the console.[4]

2. With an on-site DNS server, it may be necessary to support secondary zone transfers with external DNS servers. The primary reason for employing zone transfers is to ensure that another copy of your name database remains available to the Internet should your primary DNS server become unavailable. A zone transfer occurs when the external secondary server connects to your server (using TCP) and retrieves a portion of the name database. You should enable only inbound TCP connections from the secondary servers. You can ask your ISP for help with zone transfers, as it will likely maintain a secondary server.

3. In this configuration, your internal clients will not access their messages from an external mail server. You may not need to support POP3 or IMAP4 protocols through the filter. Furthermore, you should not need to support SMTP from the clients to external hosts.

4. You must pay attention to your policies for FTP support to account for the differences in standard and passive FTP.

5. The ISP may ask you to support several inbound services from hosts in its network to your router and the server (that is, ICMP).

5.4.3 Design 3—Single Filter with Screened Subnet

Figure 5-3 shows a single-filter design with an additional network for the servers. This network is known as a **perimeter network,** or **demilitarized zone (DMZ).** Its primary advantage is that it places your server on a separate network from your interior hosts. As a result, you can enhance the security policy governing the traffic between the server and the Internet, and between your internal hosts and the server. In effect, this strategy better separates external traffic from internal traffic.

---

4. Many books discuss practical UNIX and Windows NT security administration. Instead of diverting our discussion from the task of building the Internet connection, we defer to these texts as better sources of information.

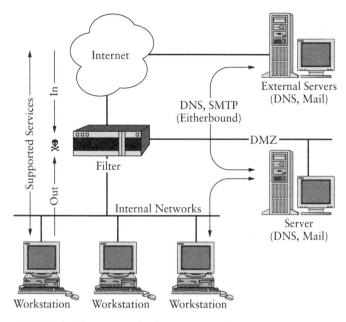

Figure 5-3 *Single-filter screened subnet*

This architecture has the following features:

1. Hosts are located within the interior networks behind the filter. The server also resides behind the filter but on its own network (DMZ), which is assumed to be compromised.

2. With respect to DNS and mail, the server communicates with external servers throughout the Internet. External servers query and connect to your server to deliver mail and resolve names. Your internal hosts communicate with the servers on the DMZ for mail and DNS; they do not communicate with external hosts for those services.

3. The server cannot initiate communication with the interior hosts. The DMZ is assumed to be part of the Internet, and the policy governing exterior traffic to interior hosts is therefore applied from the DMZ to the interior network as well. (This effect is the major advantage of this design.)

4. This moderately economical design minimizes your amount of on-site equipment and configuration tasks. Compared with the previously described designs, however, it increases your costs because of its requirement for additional network equipment. This equipment includes an additional LAN interface in your filter plus networking equipment such as a repeater or switch for the DMZ network.

5. It provides only a single element of network access control. If a cracker manages to infiltrate the filter, then your network security will likely be compromised. If your server is compromised, however, then the cracker cannot necessarily attack your internal hosts. The filter should block any attempt to infiltrate the internal networks.

This design really does not have value unless you maintain an on-site server. As in the previous design, inbound queries and connections will be restricted to the server. The internal hosts must be able to do the same to the server on the DMZ. Table 5-6 gives a basic security policy for this design.

Table 5-6 Basic Security Policy

Service	Comment
SMTP	1. Permit outbound communication from mail server to Internet
	2. Permit inbound replies to mail server from Internet (ACK bit set)
	3. Permit inbound connections to mail server from Internet
	4. Permit outbound replies from mail server to Internet
	5. Permit outbound communication from internal hosts to mail server
	6. Permit inbound replies from mail server to internal hosts
DNS	1. Permit outbound queries (UDP) from DNS server
	2. Permit inbound replies (UDP) to DNS server
	3. Permit inbound queries (UDP) to DNS server
	4. Permit outbound replies (UDP) from DNS server
	5. Permit outbound queries (UDP) from internal hosts to DNS server

(*cont.*)

Table 5-6 Basic Security Policy (*cont.*)

Service	Comment
	6. Permit inbound replies (UDP) from DNS server to internal hosts 7. Permit inbound connections (TCP) to DNS server from secondary servers (for zone transfer) 8. Permit outbound replies (TCP) from server to secondary servers (ACK bit set)
Other services (HTTP, Telnet, FTP, POP3, IMAP4, SSL, and so on)	1. Permit outbound packets for other supported services from internal hosts 2. Permit inbound replies to internal hosts (ACK bit set)
ICMP	1. Permit outbound echo request 2. Permit inbound echo reply, destination unreachable, time exceeded
Default stance	1. Drop all packets either inbound or outbound

The following concerns apply to this policy:

1. You should "lock down" the server and remove unnecessary services such as Telnet, X11 (X-Windows), FTP, NFS, and NIS from it. Consider allowing root login only from the console.

2. With an on-site DNS server, it may be necessary to support secondary zone transfers with external DNS servers.

3. In this configuration, your internal clients will not access their messages from an external mail server. But you may need to support POP3 or IMAP4 protocols through the filter to the server on the DMZ. Furthermore, you should not need to support SMTP from the clients to external hosts, but only to the mail server on the DMZ.

4. You should pay attention to your policies for FTP support to account for the differences in standard and passive FTP.

5. The ISP may ask you to support several inbound services from hosts in its network to your router and the server (that is, ICMP).

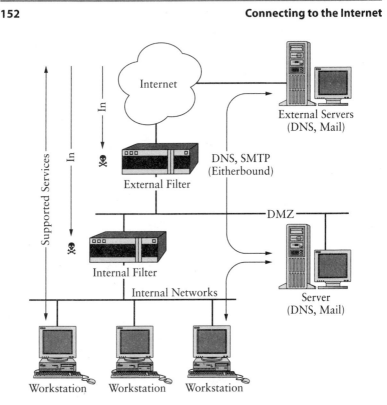

Figure 5-4 *Single-filter screened subnet*

5.4.4 Design 4—Dual Filter with Screened Subnet

The design depicted in Figure 5-4 is a classic screening architecture discussed in detail in Chapman and Zwicky's *Building Internet Firewalls*. In this setup, two **screening routers** filter traffic between your interior networks and the Internet. The router facing the Internet is your exterior router, while the one attached to your interior network is the interior router. The servers you share with the outside world reside on the network in between—that is, the DMZ. The servers are dubbed **bastion hosts** as they are assumed to be expendable if compromised.

The major features of this architecture are as follows:

1. The two screening routers make intrusion into your interior networks twice as difficult. A cracker would need to compro-

mise the security policies on both systems to gain access to your interior networks.

2. If your exterior router becomes compromised, the interior router continues to screen traffic (and holds the fort).

3. You can configure the interior router to accept only response packets destined to interior hosts. This approach prevents exterior hosts and hosts on the perimeter network from launching attacks at your internal networks.

4. With respect to DNS and mail, the server communicates with external servers throughout the Internet. External servers query and connect to your server to deliver mail and resolve names. Your internal hosts communicate with only the internal servers for mail and DNS; they do not communicate with external hosts for those services.

5. This design is potentially expensive because it increases your amount of on-site equipment and configuration tasks. You must provide an additional filter device (router or firewall) plus networking equipment such as a repeater or switch for the DMZ network.

We highly recommend this architecture if it fits within your budget. It gives you the flexibility of adding servers to your site. Keep in mind that the screening routers in this design can be replaced by other firewall products. For instance, instead of using a real router as your interior screening device, you could deploy some sort of firewall product.

Because of the presence of the two filtering devices, you will maintain two security policies. Although they are basically the same, some subtle differences do exist between the two. In short, the external filter does not need to support any policies governing how internal hosts access the DNS and mail servers on the DMZ. Similarly, the internal filter does not need a policy regarding traffic between the server and the Internet. Tables 5-7 and 5-8 outline the basic security policies for this design.

Table 5-7   External Filter

Service	Comment
SMTP	1. Permit outbound communication from mail server to Internet 2. Permit inbound replies to mail server from Internet (ACK bit set) 3. Permit inbound connections to mail server from Internet 4. Permit outbound replies from mail server to Internet
DNS	1. Permit outbound queries (UDP) from DNS server 2. Permit inbound replies (UDP) to DNS server 3. Permit inbound queries (UDP) to DNS server 4. Permit outbound replies (UDP) from DNS server 5. Permit inbound connections (TCP) to DNS server from secondary servers (for zone transfer) 6. Permit outbound replies (TCP) from DNS server to secondary servers (ACK bit set)
Other services (HTTP, Telnet, FTP, POP3, IMAP4, SSL, and so on)	1. Permit outbound packets for other supported services from internal hosts 2. Permit inbound replies to internal hosts (ACK bit set)
ICMP	1. Permit outbound echo request 2. Permit inbound echo reply, destination unreachable, time exceeded
Default stance	1. Drop all packets either inbound or outbound

Table 5-8   Internal Filter

Service	Comment
SMTP	1. Permit outbound communication from internal hosts to mail server 2. Permit inbound replies from mail server to internal hosts
DNS	1. Permit outbound queries (UDP) from internal hosts to DNS server 2. Permit inbound replies (UDP) from DNS server to internal hosts
Other services (HTTP, Telnet, FTP, POP3, IMAP4, SSL, and so on)	1. Permit outbound packets for other supported services from internal hosts 2. Permit inbound replies to internal hosts (ACK bit set)
ICMP	1. Permit outbound echo request 2. Permit inbound echo reply, destination unreachable, time exceeded
Default stance	1. Drop all packets either inbound or outbound

The same notes from the previous design apply here as well.

1. Be careful about which services you support through the external filter to your internal networks. We suggest that you do not enable any significant services inbound through the external filter, such as Telnet, FTP, and so on. Enable only internal hosts to connect to the external filter.

2. You should "lock down" the server and remove unnecessary daemons and services.

3. With an on-site DNS server, it may be necessary to support secondary zone transfers with external DNS servers.

4. In this configuration, your internal clients will not access their messages from an external mail server. Therefore, you may not need to support POP3 or IMAP4 protocols through the external filter. Furthermore, you should not need to support SMTP from the clients to external hosts.

5. You should pay attention to your policies for FTP support to account for the differences in standard and passive FTP.

6. The ISP may ask you to support several inbound services from hosts in its network to your router and the server (that is, ICMP).

5.5 Determine Your IP Architecture

After selecting a prototype design, your next step is to determine your IP architecture. This process entails assigning IP addresses to your design and figuring out how to configure routing from your LAN to the Internet.

5.5.1 IP Addressing

The first step in building your IP architecture is to obtain addresses for the hosts in your network. Of course, this task requires that you have a reasonably accurate idea about the number of hosts in your LAN that will require access to the Internet. Start by counting the number of hosts or users. Then, determine how many IP subnets your design will include. For instance, in the four prototype designs given in Section

5.4, the first two required only a single IP subnet and the last two included DMZ networks and thus required two IP subnets.

Once you know your required number of hosts and subnets, you can obtain IP addresses from your ISP or the local regional registry of the Internet Assigned Numbers Authority (IANA). (Appendix C offers an extensive discussion of how the Internet is managed, including information about these regional registries.)

Today, most organizations get their IP address space through their ISP. Although you could obtain your addresses directly from a regional registry, these organizations currently allocate subnet ranges with a network prefixes no longer than /19, which gives a mask of 255.255.224.0. This range is equivalent to 32 class C networks or 8,128 hosts. Such a policy effectively bars smaller organizations, which require far fewer addresses or subnets, from obtaining addresses directly from the regional registries. For their part, ISPs allocate addresses in far smaller chunks, such as class C networks that have 254 usable addresses.

When you obtain your address space from an ISP, you potentially face two problems either immediately or in the future:

- The ISP many be unable or unwilling to allocate a sufficient quantity of addresses for your hosts or subnets. Although this situation arises only rarely, you nevertheless need to plan for the expected growth (or contraction) of your organization. Telephoning the ISP every few weeks because you need another class C network will be problematic.
- Because the ISP merely *loans* you address space while you remain its customer (a policy known as **address lending**), you must return the addresses to the ISP if you change providers. If you have a large organization and correspondingly large deployment of IP addresses, this transition could be very painful.

To overcome some of the headaches associated with IP address depletion (scarcity of addresses), address revocation, and the general management of address space, you should consider using one or more of the following technologies.

Network Address Translation (NAT): Effectively, NAT allows you to assign an arbitrary range of IP addresses within your networks and

Table 5-9   Private IANA Addresses

Start	End	Comment
10.0.0.0	10.255.255.255	1 class A
172.16.0.0	172.31.255.255	32 class B
192.168.0.0	192.168.255.255	256 class C

translate these addresses into globally unique IP addresses for use with the Internet. The recommended practice is to use the IANA private addresses within your own networks, shown in Table 5-9. The addresses you deploy internally are called local addresses. (Appendix A gives a fuller description of NAT.)

Several compelling reasons exist for using NAT:

1. NAT provides flexible and possibly inexhaustible IP address space for your use. It allows you to alleviate problems associated with address space scarcity and depletion. For instance, instead of requiring several class C addresses from the ISP for your networks, you can use NAT and require far fewer globally unique addresses.

2. NAT allows you to keep your internal addressing intact if you switch ISPs or change the global addresses used to communicate with the Internet. Also, if you have borrowed addresses from an ISP and must now return them, NAT can help ease the transition. By translating the previously loaned addresses into new global addresses, it allows you to extend the transition indefinitely—or at least until you are able to reallocate new addresses within your networks.

3. NAT adds a degree of security to your networks because it hides the true IP address of your internal hosts from the Internet. This approach doesn't render these hosts immune from attack, but it makes them harder to find. The DMZ is a logical place to use NAT because it adds security and does not require obtaining another network address from the ISP for a typically small subnet.

In short, you can use NAT anywhere inside your external router with the following caveats. First, the servers on the DMZ should probably have one-to-one mapping with a global IP address. Because your servers will likely be accessed by hosts in the Internet, you must provide a DNS entry for each server at a global IP address. Second, some implementations of NAT have limitations. You should read the document first before deploying a particular NAT product.[5]

IPv6: Around 1993, the Internet's designers began to respond to the fear of address depletion by developing a new version of IP with larger addresses. The result, introduced in 1996, was **Internet Protocol version 6 (IPv6)**.

One of the largest shortcomings of IPv4—the current version of IP—relates to its limited address space. IPv6 overcomes this limitation by greatly expanding the size of the IP address, thereby providing "infinitely" more addressing. In truth, it is not infinite, but 128-bit IP numbers will nevertheless permit the assignment of IP addresses for every person currently living on earth with plenty left over for future expansion in the next several millennia.

Today network equipment manufacturers are building routers that support IPv6, making it possible to deploy such a network in your own LAN. Those who implement IPv6 internally must convert the IPv6 packet to an IPv4 packet before it is transmitted to the Internet, and vice versa for packets coming into the internal network. (In some ways, this approach resembles NAT.)

IPv6 is a huge and complex subject worthy of its own book. Most experts agree that the migration to IPv6 will be slow, as other solutions dealing with the address depletion problem have already hit the market—namely NAT and DHCP. We'll probably start seeing more IPv6 implementations in the next several years.

DHCP: Dynamic Host Configuration Protocol (DHCP) dynamically assigns an IP address when requested by a host. It represents an extension of the **Bootstrap Protocol (BOOTP)**, which has been around for

---

5. This approach seems backward for most of us, who read the documentation only after things don't work!

some time. In loose terms, DHCP is a process in which the client broadcasts a request into its subnet asking for an IP address. (Appendix D covers the details of DHCP.)

In addition to providing an IP address, DHCP provides mask, gateway address, DNS server address, domain name, and WINS server address. The benefit of this protocol is that it automatically assigns an address when necessary. This tactic removes the need for administering IP addresses at the workstation. Furthermore, it enables users to move their workstations between DHCP-enabled subnets without reconfiguring their IP addresses.

Another benefit is that DHCP allows you to support a user group with a smaller address pool than if you had to support the same group with static addressing. For instance, you could possibly support a group of 100 network users with 70 dynamic addresses. In practice, you assume that only a portion of the 100 users will need simultaneous access to the Internet. Consequently, you can "get away with" assigning a smaller number of addresses. Of course, you should assess whether this approach will work for your particular situation. To further extend your addressing space, you can couple DHCP with NAT.

Protocol Gateways: Another piece of equipment that can help alleviate an IP address crunch is a protocol gateway. This device converts the data of non-TCP/IP-based protocol packets into TCP/IP packets for transmission to the Internet, and vice versa. In short, this protocol translator removes the necessity of assigning unique IP addresses to the hosts that access the Internet. Of course, a protocol gateway adds some delay to the connection process, but it can be a very useful method of adding Internet access to a user community that has an existing protocol other than TCP/IP.

The most common application of a protocol gateway is the IPX-to-IP gateway. With such a large deployment of IPX networks throughout the world, it makes sense to enable IPX hosts to access the Internet through this method. Novell's intraNetWare is one well-known IPX/IP gateway.

With protocol gateways, you must keep in mind that the applications used on the workstations expect an underlying TCP/IP protocol stack. Consequently, a shim driver needs to exist between the application and the network protocol (in this case, IPX) that "fools" the application into believing that the underlying protocol is TCP/IP. (This shim is an extra software driver inserted between the application and network layers.)

Protocol gateways have tremendous potential in enabling non-native TCP/IP clients to access the Internet. Furthermore, because the native protocol within the LAN is not TCP/IP, it is much more difficult for crackers to infiltrate and damage such LANs. The only major disadvantage with this approach is the overhead associated with translating between protocols at the gateway, which usually means slower performance.

5.5.2 IP Subnetting

Another component to designing your IP architecture is determining where you will deploy these subnets. When you deploy IP subnets, you must use a router to forward packets between subnets. Because this book assumes you have some knowledge about IP addresses, and thus about the process of defining IP networks, we will dispense with a tutorial and focus on only the most important points.

Most simple LANs consist of a single IP subnet without any internal routing. The WAN router between the LAN and the Internet constitutes the only router. Figure 5-5 shows such a case where the single internal subnet is routed to the Internet.[6] The internal network is assigned the address 192.168.10.0 with a mask of 255.255.255.0. This subnet architecture matches the first two prototype designs provided earlier in this chapter.

The other example designs included two subnets: the internal network with the users and the DMZ. In these designs, one or more routers forward packets between the internal networks, the DMZ, and the Internet. Figure 5-6 shows an example of this type of subnetting. The internal network is assigned an address of 38.10.1.0 with a mask of 255.255.255.0. Similarly, the DMZ has an address of 192.168.1.0 with a mask of 255.255.255.0.

---

6. Perhaps you recognized that the addresses used in Figure 5-5 belonged to the block of private IANA addresses. This setup would indicate NAT was used internally.

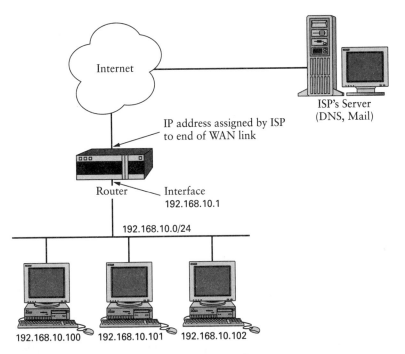

Figure 5-5 *Single internal subnet routed to the Internet*

You should be familiar with several important terms in IP subnetting:

- *Gateway* is the address in the subnet that leads to other subnets. In Figure 5-6, the router interfaces 38.10.1.1 and 192.168.1.1 are the gateway addresses for their respective subnets. These interfaces lead to other subnets and (most importantly) the Internet. Sometimes more than one gateway from a subnet can exist if you have more than one router attached to the subnet.
- *The subnet mask* is the mask that distinguishes the network component of an IP address from the host portion of the address. The examples in this chapter use a natural class C mask of 255.255.255.0. This mask indicates that the first three octets of the address are the network portion and the last octet is the

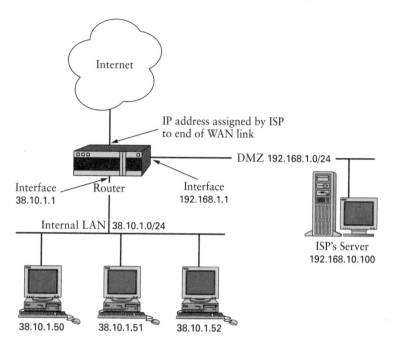

Figure 5-6 *Multiple internal networks routed to the Internet*

host portion. A device with an IP address of 38.10.1.51 therefore has a network address of 38.10.1 with a host address of 51.

When configuring your router, pay attention to masks. If the masking is flawed, your routing may not work. Be especially cautious of masks when you define your security policies. A misconfigured mask in a policy could unduly allow packets into a network that you had intended to block. For instance, if you wanted to restrict incoming packets to your internal LAN of 38.10.1.0 with a mask of 255.255.255.0, but accidentally wrote the policy with a mask of 255.255.0.0, you would inadvertently allow in all packets with a network address of 38.10.0.0.

Smaller organizations will require only a single internal IP subnet, though larger outfits might need more. Usually the ISP will loan you one or more class C addresses that you will deploy with a corresponding mask of 255.255.255.0. This approach gives you roughly 254 host addresses per subnet.[7]

It is becoming more common to deviate from the standard class C mask of 255.255.255.0 and use variable subnet masking, especially now that switched packet networks and high-speed uplinks to routers are considered mainstream. Network engineers have found that they can create large IP subnets in switched networks without impacting performance, a process known as **flattening** a network. For example, a building with 1,000 users could be supported by using a single IP subnet with a mask of 255.255.252.0 applied to an address of 192.168.120.0. This strategy would consolidate four class C networks (120.0, 121.0, 122.0, and 123.0) into one subnet with 1,024 nodes. An address of 192.168.122.78 would have a network prefix of 192.168.120.0 and a broadcast address of 192.168.123.255.

5.5.3 Configuring IP Routing (Tips and Traps)

After you have defined your IP addressing schemes and assigned subnet numbers to the segments in your design, you need to address the issue of routing. We had a brief encounter with routing in Chapter 1, when we explained its concepts. Now we will move on to deal with how you configure routing in your design.

Traveling Outbound to the Internet—Default Route: To reach the information superhighway, outbound packets must first find the path from their hometown (that is, your LAN) to the nearest highway onramp (that is, your ISP). In routing terms, the outbound packets follow the **default route** toward the Internet. The default route is the path that a packet takes if the router has no other entries that can better route the packet.

---

7. Avoid using the network and broadcast addresses in a subnet. For a class C subnet with a mask of 255, these host addresses are 0 and 255. In the past the .0 address was unsupported by many routers. Although you can use it as a network address, its use as a host address is still bad planning. The 255 address is considered the broadcast address. When a station needs to broadcast a message to all IP stations on a subnet, it does so by addressing the packet to host 255, which is all hosts.

As an administrator, you must ensure that each of your routers has a proper default route that forwards packets toward your ISP. At minimum, this responsibility means manually configuring the default route on your Internet router(s). A manually configured entry in the routing table is called a **static route.**

Figure 5-7 shows our prototype network design with assigned IP addresses. In this design, we configure your router's default route to point to the ISP's router at IP address 38.10.99.26. The routing table for your router would appear as shown in Table 5-10. The first route in the table is the default route; the other routes are the directly attached networks.

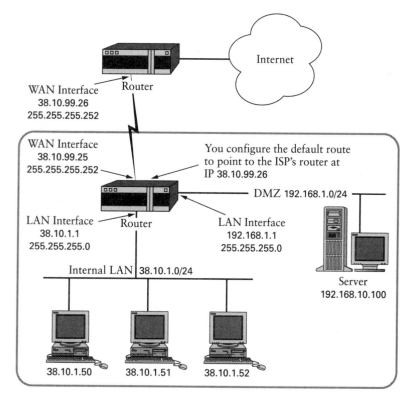

Figure 5-7 *Example routing configuration*

Table 5-10   Routing Table

Destination	Mask	Gateway	Metric	Status	TTL	Source
0.0.0.0	0.0.0.0	38.10.99.26	1	—	—	Static
38.10.1.0	255.255.255.0	38.10.1.1	0	Up	—	Connected
38.10.99.24	255.255.255.252	38.10.99.25	0	Up	—	Connected
192.168.1.0	255.255.255.0	192.168.1.1	0	Up	—	Connected

For smaller organizations, Figure 5-7 and Table 5-10 will basically account for the routing architecture. Without any other internal routers, configuring the default route and outbound routing to the ISP is simply a matter of entering the default route on your router.

If your network employs more than one internal router, then you must ensure that these routers also have proper default routes. You can accomplish this goal by either propagating the default route into your networks using a routing protocol such as RIP or manually adding the default to each router. Figure 5-8 shows a more complex version of our example with several internal routers, each of which has a default route pointing to the next router that can forward the packet to the Internet.

If you elect to use a routing protocol to advertise the default route into your internal network, you should be aware of the following potential problems:

1. A rogue routing device or misconfigured router might propagate an incorrect default that your routers will learn. Although this type of event is uncommon in smaller environments, it is more common in larger networks, where someone might easily make a mistake in configuring a router or workstation. The solution is to restrict your routers to accepting the default route only from trusted hosts—namely, your routers.

2. In large companies that have multiple Internet connections, the network may include multiple default routes within the routing tables pointing to separate gateways. This setup will cause major problems for the following reasons. First, your ISP will route only your packets and not those of your colleagues' in

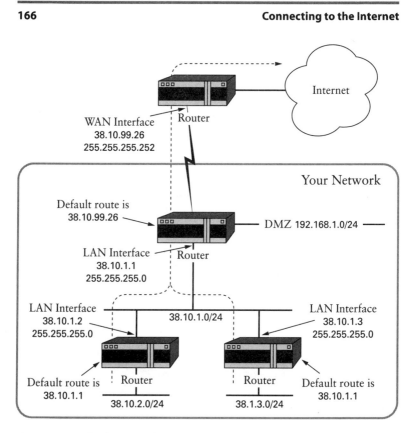

Figure 5-8 *Multiple Internal Routers*

other locations.[8] Second, your firewall should drop outbound packets that do not match the addresses of your LANs. Similarly, if your packets start following a default route to another Internet gateway, they will most likely be dropped before they reach the Internet.

Of course, using static default routes on all your internal routes will avoid the aforementioned issues. Unfortunately it, will also result in your routers being unable to handle route changes if you have multiple

---

8. In advanced configurations it's possible to have multiple Internet gateways acting as backups to one another.

paths to the Internet gateway within your LANs. You may nevertheless prefer to use static default routes versus learned ones within the networks you manage. Although it takes some time initially to configure the routers, rogue devices and renegade engineers cannot affect the default routing to any large degree.

Here are some pointers about outbound routing to the Internet:

1. Configure your exterior Internet router with a default route pointing to the WAN interface of the ISP's router. (See dual filter design.)

2. If you have an internal Internet router, configure its default route to point to the LAN interface of the external Internet router.

3. If your LANs include other routers, these routers must also have a default route pointing to your Internet connection. Take care to avoid the previously mentioned potential problems if you choose to have these routers learn the default route.

Traveling Inbound to Your LAN: Inbound routing from the Internet to your LANs raises the following issues:

1. Your Internet router will be able to route inbound packets to its directly attached networks.

2. If you have other networks within your LANs not directly connected to your Internet router, you will need to ensure that the Internet router has proper entries in its routing table for these networks. Making static entries in the routing table or using a routing protocol to learn the routes from the other routers can accomplish this goal.

3. You do not need to advertise routes internally if no other routers need to learn the routes.

Your ISP is responsible for advertising your IP networks to the Internet. When packets travel to your network, your ISP will eventually route them to the WAN interface on your router. For the most part, you simply need to ensure that your Internet router knows how to route packets to hosts within your networks. No equivalent of the default route for inbound packets exists, because the ISP handles this issue for you.

Life becomes a bit more interesting when you have multiple routers on-site. In that case, you must ensure that the router connecting to the ISP has complete knowledge of your IP networks. The router can then forward inbound packets to other routers deeper in your LANs.

You have two options for configuring the Internet router so it has entries for your internal hosts and networks. One method is to learn the routes from the internal routers using a routing protocol. Common routing protocols used in the LAN environment include RIP, IGRP, and OSPF.

Another method is to configure static routes for the internal networks. If your networks are not too large, this option might offer a simple solution. Most administrators, however, use a routing protocol, enabling each router within the network to learn how to get to the other networks.

Routing on the WAN: A few more points about some specific topics of routing to the Internet are provided below:

1. With a basic Internet connection, no routing protocol is generally used on the WAN between your on-site router and the ISP's router.

2. You configure a static default route pointing toward the ISP's router, and it, in turn, configures static routes pointing traffic to your IP networks.

3. If you advertise your networks to the ISP via a routing protocol, it's quite likely that the ISP will not listen to these advertisements and you will merely waste bandwidth on your WAN circuit.

Nevertheless, in some cases you will use a routing protocol with your ISP. This situation usually occurs when you make multiple connections to the ISP for redundancy reasons. When you run a routing protocol on your WAN with the ISP, it is likely to be BGP or OSPF. These advanced routing protocols will require you to do more homework.

Route Advertising Pitfalls: Two very peculiar problems are worth mentioning in connection with route advertising. For the most part, they apply only to large organizations with either multiple Internet gateways or reckless users who create havoc with the routing tables. These two problems are as follows:

- Advertising the ISP's WAN network
- Advertising foreign addresses within your LANs

The first problem involves advertising the ISP's WAN segment via RIP into a network with multiple Internet gateways. In this case, your internal routers will include an address for the ISP's network in their tables. If propagated internally using RIP, this address class may become larger than the actual WAN subnet, causing large amounts of Internet traffic from the other internal sites to become diverted to your site.

Obviously, this diversion is not a good idea. When configuring your WAN router in a multiple Internet gateway organization, we suggest that you do not advertise the WAN segment into your internal networks, regardless of which routing protocol you use. First, you do not need to advertise this segment because it does not contain any hosts. Second, it could confuse routing in other parts of your network.

A similar problem arises with advertising foreign routes within your networks. In particular, if a user or device begins advertising routes that have not been assigned to you by the ISP (or through a regional registry), packets destined to those addresses within your internal networks that should really go to the Internet may be diverted.

We recommend that you periodically review the contents of your routing tables to identify all the subnets contained therein. You might find some unexpected surprises, especially in a large organization. One tool that is particularly helpful in resolving the owner's identity of a network is the whois portion of ARIN's web site.

Firewalls and WANs: Chapter 4 covered typical firewall products, describing how their use significantly improves your Internet security. Although some firewalls are router-based, most run on a UNIX- or Windows NT-based workstation. Because these workstations are LAN devices, determining how to support a direct WAN connection to a workstation-based firewall can represent a challenge. For instance, how should a UNIX workstation support a V.35 serial connection from a CSU/DSU? And which software drivers and functions are necessary to support such a connection?

When using a workstation-based firewall, you may need to place the firewall behind the WAN router and connect the two via a LAN connection, especially if your WAN is based on an E1- or T1-speed connection. If your WAN is based on an ISDN BRI, however, you might be able to install a native ISDN NIC in the firewall workstation. Figure 5-9 shows the placement of the firewall behind the WAN router.

In this configuration, the WAN router and firewall connect to one another using a LAN connection such as an Ethernet segment. In effect, because the firewall also acts as a router, two routers lie in the path between your internal networks and the Internet. Thus the seg-

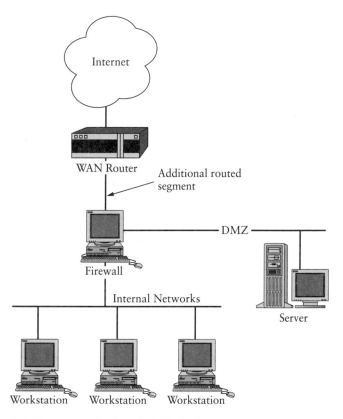

Figure 5-9 *Placement of a firewall behind a WAN router*

ment between the WAN router and the firewall constitutes an IP network, requiring you to assign yet more addresses to the LAN interfaces of these devices.

Several methods are available for configuring these devices together. For example, you can play a little trick and assign a private IANA network to the segment between the firewall and the router. Because this network does not include any hosts, it is not necessary to assign global addresses here. As long as the default route on the firewall sends packets to the WAN router, and the WAN router knows how to route packets back to the internal networks and the DMZ, all should be set.

For instance, the LAN interface of the WAN router would receive an address of 192.168.100.1 and the corresponding interface on the firewall would have an address of 192.168.100.2. The firewall's default route would then be configured to point to 192.168.100.1. The WAN router would either learn the local routes via a routing protocol or be configured with static routes to forward packets to the internal networks by sending them to 192.168.100.2.

If you think critically about this configuration, you might realize that a limitation exists here. Specifically, a problem arises if you use NAT for any of the subnets attached to the firewall. In short, you cannot use NAT effectively unless the NAT devices have global IP addresses facing the Internet. For instance, if your DMZ is the subnet 192.168.1.0, then translating this address with 192.168.100.0 will not work.

Consequently, you may prefer another method of assigning addresses to this new subnet—asking the ISP for a global fractional class C address to use between the router and firewall. In essence, the segment would be addressed like a WAN circuit with the only two addresses assigned to the segment. For instance, the router might get an address of 38.10.1.1 and the firewall receive an address of 38.10.1.2, with both using a mask of 255.255.255.252. In this situation, your NAT configurations would work correctly.

5.6 Equipment Selection

After you have assigned IP addresses to your design and decided on the routing of packets within it, you must then select the equipment to perform the tasks in the network. If you have an existing LAN, some of this equipment may already be in operation. Most likely, this equipment will include Ethernet repeaters or switches for your proposed internal networks. Depending on your design, you will need to select one or more routers, and a firewall if you are serious about security.

When the time comes to make equipment selections, you may find that your prototype design is too expensive. You will therefore need to start with another prototype and work through the design sequence. If this situation arises, do not feel like you have failed. This revision is a normal step in network design.

5.6.1 Routers

In your network design you will need at least one WAN router connecting your networks to the ISP's router. You can select a router from any vendor you like, although most ISPs maintain a list of preferred products to ensure that their equipment is compatible with your equipment. This compatibility issue seems to surface only when the WAN routers need to communicate a routing protocol. Otherwise, with static routes on both ends of the link, the routers simply send each other properly formatted packets according to the WAN protocol (such as Frame Relay or PPP).

Of course, your ISP will be more than happy to sell you a router. As mentioned in Chapter 2, ISPs offer several options with respect to routers:

- Purchasing the router outright from the ISP and configuring and managing it yourself
- Purchasing the router from the ISP and engaging the ISP to manage and configure it
- Leasing the router from the ISP and engaging the ISP to manage and configure it

In truth, selecting a WAN router is not particularly difficult. Although some of the following suggestions may appear to be common sense, not everyone has equal experience in purchasing network equipment. Tips on router selection for the WAN follow:

1. The router should support one or more WAN interfaces and several LAN interfaces. In the prototype designs given in this

chapter, the WAN router required only one WAN interface and at most two LAN interfaces. Many affordable small office routers on the market have fixed configurations (for example, one V.35 serial WAN interface, one ISDN BRI WAN interface, and two Ethernet LAN interfaces). Make certain that the router you select supports your immediate needs as well as those anticipated in the future.[9] For example, it's helpful to purchase equipment that can be used for multiple WAN technologies such as Frame Relay and point-to-point circuits.

2. Look for routers that are reasonably easy to manage and upgrade. If you have never purchased a router before, you may find it impossible to assess these features with any certainty. The good news is that more networking companies are shipping products with embedded web servers that allow you to configure and manage the devices from a browser. This capability augments the standard command-line management of network equipment via Telnet. In regard to upgrades, find out before you purchase a router exactly how its software is upgraded. Also, removing a system from operation to drop in new chips on its motherboard is too much work. Stick to software upgrades, changes to PCMCIA cards, or similar upgrade strategies.

3. Look for routers with advanced software features. Your WAN router to the Internet should, at minimum, support packet filtering. You might also prefer a router that includes "firewall" features such as stateful inspection and predefined security services. You may wish to find a router that supports NAT, VPNs, and DHCP. Other attractive advanced features include the routing protocols BGP and OSPF.

When it comes to selecting a product for your interior router (if applicable) or another LAN router, nearly all of the same tips apply. The only exception arises in that these routers do not require WAN

---

9. We prefer purchasing routers with modular interfaces, but only because we continually cycle through equipment and change WAN and LAN configurations from time to time. Routers with configurable interfaces are more expensive, however—sometimes a lot more expensive.

interfaces. Consequently, the LAN routers should have a fuller complement of LAN interfaces.

5.6.2 WAN Interfaces for Routers

Chapter 3, which focused on provisioning the WAN, discussed equipment selection for each particular WAN technology. The router that you select must have an interface capable of connecting to the WAN premises equipment. Usually, this requirement means the router supports one or more of the following:

- Serial connection to a CSU/DSU for WAN technologies using a T1. Typical serial connections are V.35, RS-232, RS-449, and X.21.[10]
- An RJ48 connector supporting a G.703 interface, in the case of the WAN technologies using an E1.
- An RJ45 interface to support an ISDN BRI connection. In the United States and Canada, this equipment should be a U-interface; elsewhere, it should be an S/T-interface.

Make certain that you have the proper cables to connect the interface on your WAN router to the premise equipment.

5.7 Reiterating the Design Process

Sometimes during the design process, you may find that the pieces do not fit together very well. Colleagues will occasionally hear us say, "This one is fighting me all the way!" When this situation occurs, it is a warning sign that you should stop and reassess your efforts.

---

10. Many small office routers now come with onboard CSU/DSU functions that permit you to connect the incoming circuit from the telecom directly to your router using a Category 5 straight-through cable.

Your ability to recognize major design problems will improve with experience. It also improves dramatically when you make mistakes and learn from them. Here are some general items that usually indicate a design problem:

- The boundaries between the internal networks, the DMZ (if applicable), and the Internet are unclear or poorly defined.
- IP addressing problems arise, including insufficient IP address space to serve your user community.
- You are experiencing tremendous difficulty selecting equipment because of uncertainty about which functions the equipment must perform. (You will likely experience some trepidation when making equipment purchases for the first time.)

If your network design fails to meet your expectations in some respects, then you should consider making another pass through the design process. Sometimes you can make corrections that do not require a redesign. For example, adding services to your policies does not necessarily warrant a redesign. In fact, it should not—as you will need to handle service changes later when your connection becomes operational. You may find, however, that the architecture you selected does not fit your objectives. Then it is time to start again and select another architecture.

To stay organized, we recommend that you start the process again at step 1, where you assess your service objectives. As you proceed through the process this time, you can use your previous work to speed your efforts. For example, if you need to reassess your service objectives, then you can make your changes to your existing list. This task is far easier than starting with a clean page and building an entirely new list. See Table 5-1 (page 135) at the beginning of this chapter to review the steps in the design process.

Most design problems stem from incomplete work during the initial steps. That explains why the steps where you delineate your service objectives and assess your design factors are so crucial. You must have a clear and detailed vision of what you want to achieve. In network design, the cliché "the devil is in the details" is very true.

5.8 Checklist—Network Architecture and Equipment Selection

The following checklist is a guideline to use when designing your network architecture—that is, a list of things to consider as you proceed through the design process.

Delineate Your Service Objectives

Services Accessed from the Internet

❑ What protocols will you need to support to access various services in the Internet?
  ❑ DNS
  ❑ FTP
  ❑ HTTP
  ❑ IMAP4
  ❑ NNTP
  ❑ POP2
  ❑ POP3
  ❑ SMTP
  ❑ SSL
  ❑ Telnet

Services Provided to the Internet

❑ How will you configure the mandatory services? On-site servers or servers at the ISP?
  ❑ DNS
  ❑ Mail (SMTP)
❑ Which additional services will you provide to the Internet?
  ❑ Web (HTTP)
  ❑ FTP
  ❑ Telnet
  ❑ News (NNTP)

Other Services

❑ Which other special services will you require or support?
  ❑ Virtual private networks (VPNs)
  ❑ Faxing

❑ Remote access via the ISP
❑ Multicast and MBone

Assess Your Design Factors

Security

❑ How do your service objectives affect your security?
❑ Will any of the services you plan to support require specialized security?
❑ Where will your servers be located?
❑ How will the budget affect your selection of security products?

Cost

❑ Have you considered the cost of the following items?
  ❑ Router
  ❑ Workstation (UNIX or PC)
  ❑ Server equipment (UNIX or PC)
  ❑ Software
  ❑ Hub (repeaters)
  ❑ Switch (bridge)
  ❑ WAN premises equipment (CSU/DSU, ISDN NT1, and so on)
  ❑ Uninterruptable power supply (UPS)

Select a Prototype Design

❑ Will your network design be based on a single-filter/router configuration without any servers on-site?
❑ Will your network design be based on a single filter/router with servers located within your internal networks?
❑ Will your network design be based on a single filter/router with a DMZ?
❑ Will your network design be based on dual filter/routers with a DMZ?
❑ Have you detailed how you will configure your security policies based on your design? In particular, have you addressed how DNS and mail are handled?

IP Addressing

❑ How many hosts in your networks must you support?

❑ How many subnets must you configure?

❑ Can you obtain the required IP address space from your ISP or regional registry?

❑ If you are borrowing addresses from an ISP, have you considered the consequences of the addresses being revoked?

❑ Have you considered implementing NAT?

   ❑ On the interior networks?

   ❑ On the DMZ?

❑ Have you considered using IPv6 internally?

❑ Have you considered using DHCP to help manage your internal addressing?

❑ Can a protocol gateway offer any help in providing additional access to the Internet?

IP Subnetting

❑ Have you assigned IP addresses to the networks in your design?

   ❑ DMZ?

   ❑ Internal networks?

❑ Have you taken care to assign proper masking consistently in your design?

Configuring IP Routing (Tips and Traps)

❑ Have you assigned the default route to your design?

❑ If you have more than one internal router, how will these devices have the default route configured?

   ❑ Static

   ❑ Learned via a routing protocol

❑ How will your WAN router (and any other Internet router) determine how to route packets to your interior networks?

   ❑ Static

   ❑ Learned via a routing protocol

❑ Will you need to support a routing protocol on the WAN segment with your ISP?

❑ Have you taken care not to advertise the ISP's network into yours?

Firewalls and WANs

❑ How will the placement of a firewall affect your IP addressing?
    ❑ Will you need to obtain another subnet from the ISP?
    ❑ Can you use a private IANA address?

Equipment Selection

Routers

❑ What interfaces does the router support?
    ❑ How many LAN interfaces and type?
    ❑ How many WAN interfaces and type?
❑ Will the router handle your current needs and possibly your future ones?
❑ Is the router easily managed and upgraded?
    ❑ Can a web browser as well as Telnet manage it?
    ❑ Are system upgrades hardware- or software-based?
❑ Will the router support advanced services?
    ❑ IP packet filtering
    ❑ Firewall features
    ❑ NAT
    ❑ VPNs
    ❑ DHCP
    ❑ Advanced IP routing protocols, OSPF and BGP

Wan Interfaces for Routers

❑ Do the WAN interfaces match your premises equipment?
❑ Do you need to purchase additional cabling to connect your WAN equipment to the premises equipment?

Staging and Testing Your Design

6.1 Chapter Overview

The purpose of this chapter is to help you stage and test your design prior to going "live" with the ISP. Before conducting the tests given in this chapter, we recommend that you have all of your network equipment and diagnostic tools available so as to spend your time troubleshooting and verifying much more efficiently. This chapter also discusses which diagnostic tools are particularly helpful in this process.

Prior to turning on your connection to the ISP, you should test the following features within your internal networks, the DMZ (if applicable), and the WAN segment leading to the ISP:

- Routing
- Filtering and security
- Mandatory services (that is, DNS, mail)

Ultimately, if your network is in good order before you activate your Internet connection, the final process of going live with the ISP will flow smoothly without too many obstacles.

After reading this chapter you should be able to answer the following questions (there will be a test later!):

1. Which tools do you need to conduct basic testing of your routing, security, and additional services?
2. How can you stage your equipment so as to simulate an Internet connection?
3. What are good ways to test your routing?

4. What are good ways to test your security?

5. How can you test DNS, mail, and other services for proper operation?

Although this chapter is short, it provides some operational tips that you will not find elsewhere—except by word of mouth. Not everything in networking is common sense, and sometimes it helps to get a few tips from your friends.

6.2 Assemble Your Tools

Before you can test your assembled design, you need tools that can test and measure various components of your network. Administrators typically use software tools on a daily basis to test, prod, and poke their networks, as well as some hardware-based tools such as network analyzers and **remote monitoring** (**RMON**) probes.

6.2.1 Software Utilities

A handful of software utilities serve as standard tools, including the ping, traceroute, nslookup, arp, ipconfig, netstat, and Telnet utilities. Now that TCP/IP is becoming the de facto communication protocol, most of these utilities come as standard applications within today's operating systems. Table 6-1 lists these common applications and tools.[1]

Table 6-1   Useful TCP/IP Tools and Applications

Windows 95	Windows NT	UNIX	Macintosh
ping	ping	ping	MacPing
tracert	tracert	traceroute	
winipcfg	ipconfig	ifconfig	
route	netstat, route	netstat, route	
arp	arp	arp	
	nslookup	nslookup	TCP Watcher
Telnet	Telnet	Telnet	NSCA Telnet

1. If the utility is not a command delivered in the operating system, there's a very good chance that someone has created a freeware program to perform the task.

A brief description of these utilities follows.

- ping is a tool used to test reachability and round-trip response time between devices within IP networks.
- traceroute reports the routing path that a packet takes through an IP network as it travels toward its destination.
- winipcfg, ipconfig, and ifconfig are utilities that show the currently assigned IP addresses assigned to a workstation's interfaces.
- route and netstat are command lines that display the contents of a routing table on a host. These two commands are invaluable if you must configure a workstation as a router and need to view the routing table. They also allow you remove and add routes.
- arp is a utility that displays and manages the ARP cache on a host. The ARP cache was discussed in Chapter 1.
- nslookup is a UNIX utility that allows you to perform DNS queries. It's a useful tool for debugging name-to-IP address resolution problems. Unfortunately, no equivalent exists for the Windows world, unless you find a freeware version.
- The Telnet program allows you to connect to another network device and enter commands at its console as if you were sitting in front of the system. You may prefer Telnet packages that enable you to use a TCP destination port other than port 23, which is the default for Telnet. In later chapters, we'll see how Telnet can be used to simulate various TCP-based connections.

A nice product for Windows 95 and Windows NT that wraps many of these utilities into a single software package is Sam Spade by Blighty Design. This freeware can be obtained at http://www. blighty.com/products/spade/. If you are still looking for additional software tools, try some of the following web sites for freeware. Also, you may wish to evaluate copies of commercial software.

- Stroud's freeware web site (http://cws.internet.com) is a good source for many useful downloads. In particular, it contains server freeware for HTTP, SMTP, FTP, and Telnet, as well as a small section on network utilities.
- Another good site is http://www.shareware.com.

- Public domain security tools can be found at the following sites:[2]
  ftp://ciac.llnl.gov/pub/ciac/sectools/unix, ftp://ftp.cert.org/pub/
  tools, and ftp://ftp.win.tue.nl/pub/security.

6.2.2 Network Analyzer

A **network analyzer** is a device that listens to traffic on your network, interprets this traffic, and then presents its analysis to you in a readable format in a process sometimes called decoding. Most analyzers can interpret traffic for particular protocol stacks, such as TCP/IP and IPX/SPX. In short, these tools allow you to view the network traffic coming and going through your Internet connection. Because "a network analyzer does not lie," it is a great troubleshooting and verification tool.

Many types of analyzers are available, ranging from moderate models ($1,000) to very expensive models (more than $10,000). Try searching the World Wide Web (WWW) using the keywords "network troubleshooting," "protocol analyzers," and "network analyzers" to find such tools. The simplest packages are software-based, using the network interface card (NIC) in a PC or workstation to capture data from the network. At the top end of the range are advanced hardware systems that with specialized PCs placed into a box with various types of network interfaces, such as Gigabit Ethernet, FastEthernet, FDDI, and Token Ring.

The author uses the Sniffer Network Analyzer products from Network Associates and the Transcend LANsentry Manager from 3Com Corporation, and has been tinkering with Surveyor from Shomiti Systems. The network traces shown in this book were made with the Sniffer Analyzer. Shop around and make an investment that suits your needs. Here are some popular network analyzers:

- tcpdump is a freeware program available for UNIX systems that can analyze most TCP/IP packets. The program understands TCP, UDP, most routing protocols, and ARP packets. It also is

---

2. These sites for public domain security tools are reproduced from the SANS 1998 Network Security Roadmap.

helpful for analyzing DNS queries. One particularly nice benefit of using tcpdump relates to its brevity, which can be helpful in diagnosing busy LANs.

- etherfind and snoop are software programs delivered with Sun OS 4.x and Solaris 2.x, respectively. They decode TCP/IP packets in real-time.
- LANwatch by Precision Guesswork is a commercial software package that enables a DOS PC to become a network analyzer.
- EtherPeek by the AG Group is another software package that provides network analysis functions to both Windows and Macintosh systems.
- Surveyor by Shomiti Systems is a powerful, integrated analyzer plus monitoring application for Gigabit 10/100 Ethernet and 4/16 Token Ring networks.
- Sniffer Nework Analyzer by Network Associates is a suite of network analyzer products, ranging from software packages for PCs to specialized systems operating on portable platforms or distributed network units.
- Transcend LANsentry Manager from 3Com Corporation is a software package that runs on UNIX and Windows platforms and analyzes data captured by distributed RMON probes.

For Ethernet- and FastEthernet-based networks, the NIC used by a network analyzer must operate in promiscuous mode. In network terms, this operation means that the NIC listens to all packets on a network segment, including those that are not addressed to it. Check with your NIC manufacturers to ascertain the operation mode of the NIC.

6.3 Routing Diagnostics

One of your first steps after assembling your network design is testing the IP routing between the various LAN segments. To test routing, you should have some of the following tools:

- ping—You will use this application to ensure that devices in your network are reachable from other devices.
- traceroute—This application will record the route that a packet takes as it travels toward its destination. It is useful for validating

that packets follow the intended default route and for testing inbound routing.[3]

- ARP—Some operating systems provide an ARP command that shows the contents of a workstation's ARP cache. On routers, you can often display the contents of the ARP cache through a menu. Inspecting the ARP cache can help determine whether a network host has successfully resolved an IP address into a MAC address.

- Network analyzers—As noted earlier, these software or hardware products listen to the traffic on the network and report various information in real-time about the network traffic. These tools are extremely helpful in determining whether a packet is being transmitted in a subnet.

6.3.1 Server Applications

One simple way to test whether a client can access a server through your network is by configuring an actual server and placing it on the network. Instead of spending lots of money on commercial server software, we recommend that you pay less and use freeware server applications. Keep in mind that your goal is simply to test whether your internal hosts can access servers on the DMZ or Internet. Thus feature-rich server software is not a necessity when testing.

Server applications that you can use for this type of testing include FTP, web, mail (SMTP, POP3, and IMAP4), and Telnet.

6.3.2 Client Applications

When testing connectivity from clients to servers, you can use several tools on the client:

- ping for testing connectivity using ICMP.
- traceroute for determining the route from the client to the server. (See Table 6-1 for the various names and incarnations of traceroute.)

---

3. If you have only one router in your design, the traceroute utility will not provide any additional information beyond that provided by ping. Once you go live with your connection, however, both will be useful tools.

- A web browser for testing access to a web server.
- Mail clients for testing access to a mail server. Try to find a client that supports POP3 and IMAP4, if necessary. (A mail client may be included with the browser software.)
- Telnet for testing access to a Telnet server, as well as for testing TCP connectivity to the server. With Telnet, you can specify another destination port besides 23. For instance, you can use this application to connect to a mail server by specifying that port 25 be used. The server will see this link as a normal connection using SMTP on port 25.

6.3.3 Network Hardware

When you stage and test your design having a small Ethernet repeater can be very helpful (if your network is Ethernet-based). By connecting the repeater to your exterior router or firewall, you can simulate a network in the Internet.

6.4 Staging Equipment

Before activating your connection with the ISP, you will want to assemble and configure all of your equipment. The point of this exercise is to find and resolve problems before they become crises. (Plus, you need an excuse to play with your new equipment!)

Concentrate your efforts on configuring the Internet routers, DMZ network (if applicable), and the connection to your internal networks. You should first assign IP addresses to the hosts and networks, then focus on configuring your security policies and filtering. After assembling and configuring your equipment, you will then go through the paces of testing it to ensure that it works properly.[4]

---

4. To interconnect your equipment, you must obtain the necessary cabling beforehand. For the most part, the network equipment manufacturers do not supply this equipment for you. You will need to purchase most of these odds and ends from another supplier. Some household names in the network industry for cabling in the United States are Anixter, Dicar, and Black Box. You can also ask your wiring vendor for the names of local cable suppliers.

In preparation for testing, you may want to create a mock Internet network off your external router or filter. This setup allows you to test how your design both routes and filters traffic to and from the Internet. This mock Internet connection will act as an exterior network to yours.

Figure 6-1 shows a mock Internet connection with a LAN segment consisting of an Ethernet repeater. When assigning a network address to the "external" network, use one that is not already found within your internal networks. Although it doesn't matter which addresses you deploy, the private IANA addresses will not interfere with globally unique addresses that need to be routed to the Internet. Furthermore, they are easy to find when searching a large routing table.

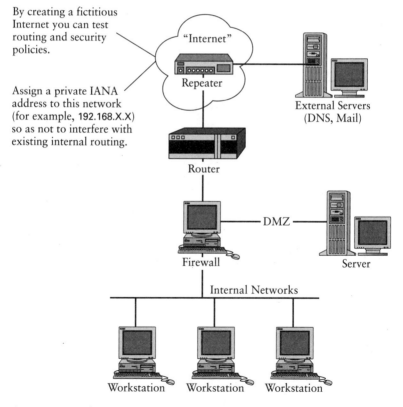

By creating a fictitious Internet you can test routing and security policies.

Assign a private IANA address to this network (for example, 192.168.X.X) so as not to interfere with existing internal routing.

Figure 6-1 *Mock Internet connection*

	Source	Destination	Comment
Table 6-2	**Routing Test Matrix**		
1	Interior	DMZ	Test outbound routing to DMZ
2	Interior	Exterior	Test outbound routing to Internet (default route)
3	DMZ	Interior	Test inbound routing from DMZ
4	DMZ	Exterior	Test outbound routing from DMZ
5	Exterior	Interior	Test inbound routing from Internet
6	Exterior	DMZ	Test inbound routing to DMZ from Internet

Finally, before testing routing, security, and the mandatory services, you should configure those "special" IP addressing services that are unique to your situation, such as NAT and DHCP, if applicable.

6.5 Test Your Routing

When you have finally assembled and configured your equipment, you should test its routing capability. *Remember that many elements of your Internet connection depend on proper routing, especially your security policies, which are enforced by the network access control devices. If the routing is faulty, then other operations will be flawed as well.*

Start your testing by creating a test matrix as shown in Table 6-2. This table, which lists the various combinations in which traffic flows between networks in your design, is a test matrix for the design in Figure 6-1. Tailor your matrix to your design. For instance, if you do not have a DMZ, then you need not test traffic from your interior networks to the DMZ. Test routing in each direction as listed in your matrix.

Prior to actually testing your routing, make certain you do several things:

1. Turn off filtering and security enforcement to eliminate these features as a source of problems.

2. Place hosts on your destination subnets that are properly configured for IP. This strategy will eliminate the host as a source of problems.

3. If you will be using NAT, turn it off temporarily until you have verified that basic routing works between subnets. You can then activate NAT and test routing to translated IP addresses from a mimicked exterior network. Make certain NAT is enabled when you test your security policies.

To test the routing in your design, you should use the ping and traceroute utilities. (Be certain to use IP addresses—and not DNS names—with ping and traceroute until DNS has been configured.) From a host such as a workstation in the source network, use ping to test the reachability of a host on the destination network. Follow these steps:

1. Telnet to your router (or routers) and display the routing table to ensure that you have configured a default route.

2. Ping the TCP/IP stack itself on the testing device to ensure that you have configured TCP/IP properly. You can ping either the host's IP address or the loopback address of 127.0.0.1.[5]

3. Ping the IP address of another device on the same subnet. This action will confirm that your workstation's IP configuration is correct and that it is properly connected to the network.

4. Ping the gateway address on the subnet. This action is normally equivalent to pinging the router's LAN interface. It will ensure that the workstation and the router can communicate.

5. Ping the IP address of a target host on another subnet. If this attempt fails, try pinging another host on the target subnet. If a second host is not available, ping the gateway address of the destination subnet, which is really the router on the subnet. If the second ping succeeds, something is likely amiss with the target host's IP configuration, such as masking. If the second ping fails, a routing problem may exist between the subnets.

If you suspect a routing problem, try using other tools or looking for additional information. Solving network problems is much faster if you take a divide-and-conquer approach to testing. Try the following:

---

5. The loopback address is a nonrouted address within the Internet. It is deployed within the TCP/IP software on a host and used for diagnostic purposes.

1. The traceroute utility is a very handy tool for determining the path that a packet takes as it travels toward its destination, especially when you have multiple routers. To use traceroute, simply enter the address of the destination node. The utility will then report the routers that the packet went through on its way to the host. (Use traceroute with the option that forces it to *not* resolve addresses to host names in the output until DNS is configured and operational. For example, in UNIX specify "traceroute –n <IP>"; in Windows 95, use "tracert –d <IP address>".)

2. If traceroute does not return any enlightening information, examine the routing tables of each router between the source node and the destination node. In particular, verify that each router has an entry for the destination network. Normally the traceroute and ping commands will return the "Destination Unreachable" message if a router along the way does not know how to route the packet.

3. Other potential tests performed from the router include pinging the node directly from the router and inspecting the ARP cache. If you can ping the destination node from its nearest router but not from the source network, a masking problem may exist with the destination host. If you can't ping the host from the router, then something is probably wrong with the host. Examine the ARP caches of the router to see if an entry exists for the destination host. If it is not listed after attempting a ping, then you need to determine why the router and host cannot communicate.

4. If you wish to be completely certain that packets are being routed correctly, place a network analyzer in the destination network and capture the ping packet you send from the source host. Recall that ping uses ICMP and traceroute can use ICMP or UDP packets with high port values. This information should be helpful in limiting the packets you capture.

Table 6-3 provides a list of common symptoms and causes of routing problems. In most cases your Internet connection and associated routing will work properly if you configure your devices with consistent masks and IP addresses. If you do run into problems, use the ping methodology to isolate the source of your problem.

Table 6-3 Routing Symptoms and Causes

Symptom	Causes
Unable to ping a host on the same subnet	1. Host is not properly connected to the network 2. Host does not have proper IP address for the subnet
Unable to ping gateway address on the same subnet	1. Gateway address used in ping is incorrect 2. Gateway is not attached to subnet 3. Either gateway or host does not have proper IP address for the subnet
Unable to ping address on destination subnet	1. Destination host is not reachable from its local gateway 2. Packet is routed incorrectly between the source and destination networks 3. A router between the source and destination networks does not have "knowledge" about the destination network

6.6 Test Your Security (Filtering)

After concluding your routing tests you should test the operation of your security policies. As with the routing test, you should devise a test matrix like that shown in Table 6-4 that tests your security policies in each direction packets may travel. Using a matrix will help you keep

Table 6-4 Security Test Matrix

	Source	Destination	Comment
1	Interior	DMZ	Test outbound security to DMZ
2	Interior	Exterior	Test outbound security to Internet (default route)
3	DMZ	Interior	Test inbound security from DMZ
4	DMZ	Exterior	Test outbound security from DMZ
5	Exterior	Interior	Test inbound security from Internet
6	Exterior	DMZ	Test inbound security to DMZ from Internet

track of your progress so you may be certain that each component of your network security has been tested.

In addition to the test matrix given in Table 6-4, you will need to create a detailed matrix addressing the particular elements of your security policy. For each line of your security test matrix, you should develop a sublist of all particular services and security policies you need to test. Table 6-5 provides a list of typical services.

The list in Table 6-5 contains permitted policies. Unless you explicitly deny a service in your policies, it does not make too much sense to list denied services. Instead, conduct a few tests verifying that your policy denies unsupported services. The list should be tailored to the specifics of your security policies. For example, it may not make sense to test inbound POP3 from the exterior to your DMZ if you support only HTTP inbound. Simply proving that HTTP works and, for example, Telnet fails will probably be sufficient.

When testing your security policies, the following tips may prove helpful:

1. Place servers on your mock external network for testing outbound traffic from your internal networks and the DMZ. Run

Table 6-5 Services Test Matrix

Service	Policy	Test Result
DNS	Permit	
FTP	Permit	
HTTP	Permit	
ICMP	Permit	
IMAP4	Permit	
POP3	Permit	
SMTP	Permit	
SSL	Permit	
Telnet	Permit	

freeware server packages for services such as HTTP, SMTP, FTP, and Telnet. Do not get sidetracked with server content—you simply want to test connectivity between the host and the server.

2. UDP is very difficult to test. Thankfully, the majority of your supported services, will be TCP-based. To test UDP services, you will need to use a network analyzer to confirm that the packets are being blocked or transmitted. Place the analyzer in the destination network.

3. Try specifying destination addresses for networks that are not part of your "internal" networks. Logic errors often occur when policies deny various services to the internal network, but inadvertently allow the same services through to other networks that are not part of the "internal" network's definition. This problem is especially evident in large organizations with multiple Internet gateways. Logic errors in one gateway can expose the internal networks of another site to attacks. For instance, suppose you define your internal networks as 192.168.10.0 in your security policies. You might then try sending packets inbound to the network 191.10.10.0 to see whether they squeak through your policies. Figure 6.2 shows this scenario.

The following points describe how to conduct basic tests of your security policy during start-up. After your connection is built and operational, you may wish to engage the services of a security auditing company or purchase auditing software, as discussed in Chapter 4. During start-up, however, a few basic tests will do:

1. *Use the ping and traceroute utilities.* The utility ping will test your ICMP policies. You can also test these policies with traceroute, although you should remember that some UNIX versions of traceroute send UDP packets with high ports values and low TTL values.

2. *Use actual servers and clients.* Where feasible, use the actual application to test connectivity to a server in the destination network. For instance, use your web browser to test HTTP access to a web server.

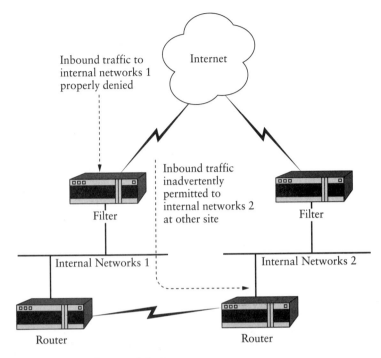

Figure 6-2 *Internal network logic error*

3. *Test using variable ports.* When you can no longer test connectivity with an actual server, use the freeware servers and configure their listener ports to another value. Then, use the Telnet or web client and specify the port you wish to test when communicating with the server. For instance, to test POP3 on port 110, configure a web server to listen to 110 instead of 80. Using a web browser, enter the server's IP address with ":110" appended to specify port 110. The client must then communicate with the server using the specified port. The same process can be undertaken with a Telnet server and client combination. (This method is useful for testing only TCP, unless you find a server and client that support UDP as well.)

4. *Test unsupported services.* After testing the services you wish to support, devise a few tests to verify that unsupported services are

properly denied. For instance, use the client/server test and specify TCP ports for an unsupported service. Also, try specifying ports greater than 1023 to expose any logic errors with accepting these values, because they may belong to a client.

5. *Set up a network analyzer to test difficult services.* Ultimately, by placing a network analyzer in the destination network (or, even better, on the destination side of the filter), you can verify that packets are properly denied or permitted. If you capture a packet that should have been denied, then a problem exists with the policy.

Testing your security policy is a task that requires prior planning and methodical execution. Of all the tips and tools mentioned, the network analyzer is perhaps the most valuable. The time you invest upfront in learning how to use this tool will pay off handsomely down the road.

6.7 Test Mandatory Services

There are two services you may wish to test prior to activating your connection with the ISP—DNS and mail. Of the two, DNS poses a greater challenge, because it is UDP-based and difficult to mimic with standard tools such as a Telnet client. You might consider configuring a DNS server and placing it on the DMZ (if applicable), which would enable you to test inbound and outbound policies to and from the server. Keep in mind that the server will be able to resolve only names within its tables until it can query other DNS servers in the Internet. If you manage to configure a local DNS server, then testing access to it is simply a matter of configuring a client to point to this device for name resolution.

If you do not plan to provide a local DNS server and will use the ISP's DNS, then you should apply a network analyzer to your testing. Place the analyzer on the destination side of your filter, then configure the client with DNS information for a fictitious server on the destination network. Try pinging a device by name, and watch for either denied or permitted DNS queries in the destination network from your client as it tries to resolve the name to IP address.

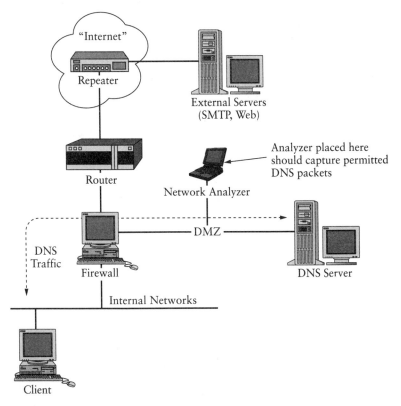

Figure 6-3 *Testing DNS*

Figure 6-3 shows the location of the network analyzer in relation to the DNS server. This location applies whether the server exists or not. Obviously, it is advantageous to have a real server to respond to the client's requests, as you can then test DNS policies from the server to the client.

The other service, mail, is somewhat easier to test. In a basic mail test, you can set a server in the destination network that mimics port 25. A good candidate is a Telnet server listening to port 25 instead of 23. By using a Telnet client and specifying port 25, you can mimic a mail session (or at least the TCP connection).

If you are really ambitious, you can configure a real mail server on the destination network and test connectivity with a genuine mail client. Several freeware mail server packages that you can use for this purpose are available on the Internet.

If you do capture a mail exchange between the client and the server, it will resemble the following code. The >>> symbol indicates a command entered by the client on the server. The numbered lines are responses from the mail server (that is, **220, 250, 354**). When you Telnet to a mail server, you can enter these commands for your test. If the responses match those shown here, then you configured the mail server successfully.

```
tequila{drew}% andrew_wardward@example.org . . . Connecting to
gilligan.example.org. (ether) . . .
220 Example.org ESMTP Sendmail 8.8.5/8.8.5; Tue, 16 Jun 1998
06:38:09 -
0400 (EDT)
>>> HELO tequila.
250 Example.org Hello [192.168.10.1], pleased to meet you
>>> MAIL From:<drew@tequila>
250 <drew@tequila> . . . Sender ok
>>> RCPT To:<andrew_ward@example.org>
250 <andrew_ward@example.org> . . . Recipient ok
>>> DATA
354 Enter mail, end with "." on a line by itself
>>> .
250 GAA16148 Message accepted for delivery
>>> QUIT
221 Example.org closing connection
andrew_ward@example.org . . . Sent (GAA16148 Message
accepted for delivery)
```

6.8 Checklist—Staging and Testing

Assemble Your Tools

❑ Have you obtained the basic software tools for your operating system and learned how to use them?
  ❑ ping
  ❑ traceroute, tracert

- ❑ winipcfg, ifconfig
- ❑ route, netstat
- ❑ arp
- ❑ nslookup (UNIX)
- ❑ Telnet
- ❑ Have you obtained evaluation copies of some of the commercial network analyzer products (if available)?
  - ❑ LANwatch
  - ❑ EtherPeek
  - ❑ Sniffer Nework Analyzer
  - ❑ Transcend LANsentry Manager
  - ❑ Surveyor
- ❑ Will any freeware tools be useful?
  - ❑ Tcpdump (UNIX)
  - ❑ Etherfind (UNIX – Sun OS and Solaris)
  - ❑ Snoop (UNIX—Sun OS and Solaris)

Routing Diagnostics

- ❑ Have you assembled your routing diagnostic tools?
  - ❑ Network analyzer
  - ❑ ping
  - ❑ traceroute
  - ❑ arp

Server Applications

- ❑ Have you obtained the following server applications for testing client/server communications?
  - ❑ FTP
  - ❑ Web
  - ❑ Mail (SMTP, POP3, and IMAP4)
  - ❑ Telnet
  - ❑ Other (Gopher server, and so on)

Client Applications

- ❑ Have you obtained the following client software for testing client/server communications?
  - ❑ FTP
  - ❑ Web

❑ Mail (SMTP, POP3, and IMAP4)
❑ Telnet
❑ Other (Gopher server, and so on)

Network Hardware

❑ Have you obtained some inexpensive additional network hardware for mimicking exterior networks and other such testing?
❑ Small Ethernet repeater

Staging Equipment

❑ Have you interconnected and configured your network equipment?
❑ Have you created a mock external network that you can use for duplicating routing to the Internet?

Testing Your Routing

❑ Have you created a routing test matrix that will help you keep track of your progress when testing?
❑ Have you temporarily shut down your filtering or network access control to eliminate unnecessary variables when evaluating your routing?
❑ Have you have temporarily shut down NAT (if applicable) during testing to eliminate it as a variable? Were you certain to reenable it and test routing with NAT?
❑ Are the hosts you placed on your network properly configured for IP?

Test Your Security (Filtering)

❑ Have you created your test matrices for verifying that the security policies work as desired in the directions that network traffic will travel?
❑ Did you test routing in your security policies?
❑ Did you test client/server communication in your policies?
❑ Did you test your policies using variable ports to ensure that they permit desired packets and deny those you wish to block?

❑ Did you verify that your security policies work by using a network analyzer?

Test Mandatory Services

❑ Have you devised a way of testing DNS? For instance, if you will support a local DNS server, did you configure it and place it on the perimeter network? Did you actually test communication with this server?

❑ Have you have tested communication with a mail server? For example, did you configure a mock mail server on the DMZ or external network and connect to it from internal clients?

Implementing and Validating
Your New Connection

7.1 Chapter Overview

This chapter is about putting all the pieces together and making your Internet connection usable. Implementing your connection is the event in which you simultaneously apply your knowledge of TCP/IP, WANs, security, and network design. After reading this chapter you should be able to explain the following:

1. What to expect from the ISP and the telecom in the final stages of WAN provisioning.
2. The steps you will take to make your Internet connection operational, and how you and your ISP will verify that everything is functioning properly.
3. Troubleshooting of your WAN connection if it fails to work properly.
4. The procedures to validate that your connection is fully operational and your security is working properly.

7.2 Complete the WAN Circuit

Once your network design is deployed and tested, you should undertake the final steps to make your connection live. Usually the last major hurdle in the connection process is completing the WAN circuit and verifying its operation.

One key piece of information is the date that your circuit will be complete. The telecom provides an order completion date to the customer during the initial stages of WAN provisioning, indicating when the WAN circuit should be completely operational and released for use. This target is not always reliable. If the circuit construction process is smooth, then the completion date may move up (earlier). Occasionally snags in provisioning may cause delays and the date will slip (later). You should be prepared for all eventualities.

If your circuit is being ordered through the ISP, ask the ISP to relay the completion date to you. You should expect the telecom's completion date and the ISP's activation date to be identical, because the activation with the ISP usually occurs immediately upon completion of the circuit.

Prior to the completion date, the telecom will likely visit your facility and build the local loop portion on the circuit infrastructure. Once you order a WAN circuit (either directly or indirectly through the ISP), you should expect the telecom to show up at any time during normal business hours to build the circuit.[1] On a "clean" installation, this step may require only a single visit from the telecom. Do not be too concerned if it takes several visits, however. Sometimes new equipment must be installed and configured.

Once the physical infrastructure has been built and tested, the telecom conducts the switch programming necessary for the particular circuit technology (for example, point-to-point, Frame Relay). Also, before the circuit is released to the customer, the telecom verifies its operational status. In the case of a T1 or E1 circuit, the telecom tests the connection with a combination of special equipment and **loop tests**. In the case of an ISDN circuit, the circuit technicians actually place calls from your facility to the local CO in addition to validating the circuit with their test gear.

---

1. A word of advice: Your organization should not admit telecommunications personnel into your wiring closets without your prior permission or notification. This policy will prevent a rogue user from installing a circuit "behind your back" and possibly circumventing your security. Furthermore, although most telecommunications personnel are skilled professionals, not all meet such standards. You should always ask the technician to explain the nature and extent of the work when he or she arrives at your facility.

Typically, troubleshooting the WAN does not occur unless *you* suspect a problem. Most commonly this situation arises because you and the ISP failed to successfully connect your networks together during activation. (Because this failure usually follows an attempt to activate your connection with the ISP, WAN troubleshooting tips will be discussed later in this chapter.)

As a preparatory step, you should assemble your WAN premises equipment before the telecom's completion date. Also, until you are ready to go live with the ISP, you should either disconnect your exterior router from your LAN or disable this router. This strategy will prevent any routing "mishaps" while the ISP or telecom completes the configuration work.

If you haven't removed your test equipment or configurations from your network, you may wish to do so prior to the ISP's activation date. This step may require changing IP addresses on some interfaces of your exterior router or firewall.

Following the installation of the WAN, you should obtain the circuit ID. The circuit ID is an alpha-numeric designator that identifies your particular circuit. If you ordered the circuit directly from the telecom, then it should provide this information to you. Otherwise, get the circuit ID from the ISP.[2] Whenever you contact the telecom about your WAN circuit, its first question will be, "What is the circuit ID?" Keep this information handy for future reference.

If you ordered the circuit through the ISP, ask to be made an official site contact on the circuit with the telecom. The telecom will then treat you as the customer, rather than just the ISP. Keep in mind that if you purchased bundled provisioning from the ISP then the ISP is responsible for the WAN circuit. If anything goes wrong call the ISP first.

---

2. Circuits built using multiple telecom providers will have more than one ID. For instance, the local loop will have an ID from the local exchange carrier (LEC), while an interoffice channel (IOC) may use another carrier and have another ID.

7.3 Going Live with the ISP

Before activation, you should interconnect all your equipment with its final IP and routing configuration. This step also applies to the connections between your LAN and the WAN premises equipment. Everything should be in place, just as it will be during normal operation.

The ISP will most likely have an established test procedure that it uses to activate your connection. You may want to ask for a copy of this activation plan so you can keep track of its progress. In any event, you can probably expect it to follow the general process given in Table 7-1.

7.3.1 Deactivate Your Security

Your first step in the activation process should be to deactivate your security. Although a slightly unorthodox maneuver, initially deactivating your security will eliminate its policies as a source of problems until you verify that the network and its routing are operational.[3] Troubleshooting an Internet connection can be a complex task when security is active. Once your connection is tested, you will reactivate security.

7.3.2 Test WAN Connectivity

Next, you should test the WAN connectivity. Use ping to assess the connectivity between your exterior router and the ISP's router[4] and

Table 7-1 General Activation Steps

Number	Step
1	Temporarily deactivate security
2	Test WAN connectivity
3	Test routing to the Internet
4	Test DNS and mail
5	Reactivate security

---

3. Security gurus will likely object to this tactic, as it may expose your network (albeit briefly) to unnecessary risk. Keep your shields down only as long as necessary to verify that your routing and architecture are correct.

4. When using ping and other utilities like traceroute, be certain to use IP addresses and not names. You have not yet tested DNS.

confirm that the WAN circuit is operational. Your ISP will also conduct a ping test to ensure that its router can communicate with yours. (See Section 7.4 on WAN troubleshooting if this step fails.)

7.3.3 Test Routing to the Internet

From the exterior router, try pinging a device in the Internet such as ns.nic.ddn.mil (192.112.36.4).[5] Another good test is to traceroute to a host in the Internet. Also use traceroute to test routing from your DMZ and interior networks.

7.3.4 Test Connectivity to DNS and Mail Servers

If the ISP provides DNS and mail services for your organization, you will first validate DNS resolution, which is fairly straightforward to test. Try resolving names using the nslookup utility, if available, for your operating system. You can also use ping with names such as those of your favorite web sites. Confirm that names are resolved into IP addresses. The following code shows a ping that resulted in a name being resolved into an IP address:

```
C:\WINDOWS>ping www.awl.com
Pinging pop.awl.com [192.207.117.2] with 32 bytes of data:
Reply from 192.207.117.2: bytes=32 time=77ms TTL=247
Reply from 192.207.117.2: bytes=32 time=43ms TTL=247
Reply from 192.207.117.2: bytes=32 time=44ms TTL=247
Reply from 192.207.117.2: bytes=32 time=44ms TTL=247
```

In the case of testing mail, the ISP will have configured your organization's mail accounts ahead of time. Testing mail is also fairly logical. For example, you can try sending mail to a friend or the technician who is working with you at the ISP. Have these people send mail back to you. If you have a separate ISP account set up for testing, try sending mail to yourself at that address. Similarly, you can use your account to send mail back to yourself. If the ISP hosts your mail server, getting mail to work merely consists of ensuring that your internal users can make SMTP connections to the mail server. Similarly, your

---

5. Be careful about your conclusions following failed pings to the Internet. The administrator of the host may have configured the security policy to block inbound echo requests.

users will need to make IMAP4 or POP3 connections to the same server to receive mail.

On the other hand, troubleshooting becomes a bit more involved when your mail server is located on-site. If either the sending or receiving process fails, use a network analyzer to verify that packets are routed to and from your network as required. Although entire books have been written on mail systems and how to troubleshoot them, you can start with the assumption that something is wrong at the network layer. Use your network analyzer to answer the following basic questions:

- Are internal clients able to make SMTP connections to the server and send mail?
- Does the mail server make SMTP connections to other servers for sending mail?
- Does the mail server receive incoming SMTP connections from other servers?
- Can internal clients connect to the server using POP3 or IMAP4?

If no network layer (routing) or transport layer (TCP connection) problem exists, try testing whether the mail server is properly configured. Keep in mind that sometimes servers will exhibit strange behavior that you might interpret as a transport layer problem, but in actuality reflects a configuration problem. For instance, a server that constantly resets new TCP connections may have a problem allocating memory.

7.3.5 Reactivate Security

When you have verified that your network communicates properly with the Internet, or if you need to stop testing for a period, then you should activate security. Perhaps you found a few problems that require more work. Depending on the problem you may need additional help from the ISP—do not be afraid to ask for assistance.

If all your tests to this point have worked properly, the ISP may pronounce your Internet connection operational. This achievement is a major milestone. Before you run off to take up your favorite activity, do not forget that you still need to ensure that the connection operates properly with security active.

7.4 Troubleshooting the WAN

As mentioned earlier in this chapter, your installation may become side-tracked if the WAN is built incorrectly or the premises equipment on either end is configured incorrectly. Usually a WAN problem is obvious—your router cannot communicate with the ISP's router. Typically, you do not discover the problem until you and the ISP attempt to activate the connection. Until that time, both you and the ISP will likely be busy building equipment and networks. Thus the activation date is sometimes your first opportunity to test connectivity between routers.

When troubleshooting the WAN, you need to be as knowledgeable as possible about your specific WAN equipment. Some words of advice: Try to read the documentation on your equipment before you activate your connection, because this knowledge will help you later. Of course, the ISP and the telecom will assist in troubleshooting the WAN.

Normally the ISP will have a technician ask you to perform tests, and you will whiz through menus without really understanding the process. If you find yourself in this situation, try to slow down and take notes about each test you conduct. Not only will you be smarter later on, but you also will understand how your current problem was solved.

The following is a general list of WAN troubleshooting tips:

1. On most routers, the interface with the WAN connection will report "UP" if the router can communicate with the router on the opposite end of the circuit. This characteristic applies to most circuit technologies such as point-to-point, Frame Relay, and ISDN.

2. If working with a T1 or E1 span, check your premises equipment for proper configuration. If you have a question about a specific parameter, ask your ISP for clarification. For instance, check that your framing and line coding selections are correct on the CSU/DSU. Also, check that your channel selections are correct if you are using a fractional circuit.

3. If the router reports the WAN port to be "DOWN," and both you and the ISP believe your equipment is configured properly,

then you must call the telecom. Remember that the ISP will make the call if it owns the circuit.

4. If working with a T1 or E1 span, be prepared for the telecom to conduct loopback tests.[6] These tests will confirm that each physical component of the circuit has been built properly. Take time to learn how to operate the loopback tests on the CSU/DSU, if you have one in your setup.

5. If working with Frame Relay, check for correct DLCI values in your equipment configuration. Also, check whether LMI is being used.

6. If working with ISDN, try using the equipment to dial another number besides that of the ISP. Make certain your equipment is configured properly to dial the ISP's ISDN telephone number.

If something is really wrong with the construction of the circuit, the telecom will be required to rectify the problem. This repair can take some time, as isolating WAN problems can prove difficult. Usually things get resolved quickly once a technician is on-site with the proper diagnostic tools.

7.5 Validating Operation and Security after Start-Up

After your Internet connection becomes active, you change gears slightly and focus on verifying that the services you wish to support remain available when your security is active. When you initially tested your connection upon activation, security was disabled to eliminate your security policies as a source of problems. Now that you have activated your security, you need to test the policies to ensure they work in a real environment.

---

6. A loopback is a diagnostic test in which selective equipment in the WAN returns transmitted signals to the sending device. By comparing the transmitted signal with the return signal, problems can be isolated on the WAN. Your premises CSU/DSU will have a loopback function that enables this feature. Normally the telecom will send a signal to your CSU/DSU that activates the loopback function.

Table 7-2 Security Test Matrix

	Source	Destination	Comment
1	Interior	DMZ	Test outbound security to DMZ
2	Interior	Exterior	Test outbound security to Internet (default route)
3	DMZ	Interior	Test inbound security from DMZ
4	DMZ	Exterior	Test outbound security from DMZ
5	Exterior	Interior	Test inbound security from Internet
6	Exterior	DMZ	Test inbound security to DMZ from Internet

To validate the operation and security of your connection, you should revisit the test matrices you created earlier when testing your design and its security. Table 7-2 gives the security test matrix used to verify your security policies in the directions that packets travel through your Internet connection.

Similarly, Table 7-3 provides a representative test matrix of the service policy that you support in each direction. The only difference between the testing you did earlier and the testing conducted now is that your Internet connection is live and you can test connectivity to real sites in the Internet.

When testing your inbound policies, it may prove very helpful (if not necessary) to use a separate ISP account from which you can launch services requests at your network. If your ISP provides a guest

Table 7-3 Services Test Matrix

Service	Policy	Test Result
DNS	Permit	
FTP	Permit	
HTTP	Permit	
ICMP	Permit	
IMAP4	Permit	
POP3	Permit	
SMTP	Permit	
SSL	Permit	
Telnet	Permit	

server account, you can use it for testing. The point of this exercise is to validate your security and, in the process, verify that your connection supports services as you intended.

If you encounter problems, use the divide-and-conquer approach to problem solving. Take advantage of the tools you have at your disposal. In particular, your network analyzer will become your best friend in debugging problems. When troubleshooting problems with particular services, ask the following questions:

1. Is DNS name resolution working properly? For instance, if you are trying to traceroute to www.example.org, is this name being resolved into an IP address? To check this feature, you might use ping with an option to resolve names.

2. Is the outbound packet being routed properly to the Internet? You might try a traceroute to see the path taken by a packet.[7] You can also use a network analyzer to verify that outbound packets reach your exterior router.

3. Is the inbound packet being routed properly to your network? In this case, a network analyzer is the best method of verifying the identity of the packets that reach your network.

4. Is the site actually available at the moment? Try accessing another site.

5. Is your security policy blocking a service that you intended to support? Try configuring your network access control devices (such as a firewall) to log all packets that it denies, then sift through the logs looking for these entries.

6. Did you misconfigure your security policy? Check whether your policy uses the correct port values for the services. Also, check the policies for errors with specified source and destination IP addresses. Improper subnet masks and addresses can sometimes be the culprits.

Once you have tested all of your services, it's time to release your masterpiece to the user community. In some respects, true validation of

---

7. This tactic assumes that you have configured your security to permit internal users and hosts to traceroute and ping devices with the Internet.

your work comes only when you announce to your user community that the Internet connection is open for business.

After you finish polishing off a few beverages in your local watering hole, you should seriously consider having an external resource validate your security, as discussed in Chapter 4. At the very least, ask your ISP to review your policies and test connectivity to your network.

7.6 Checklist—Implementation and Validation

Complete the WAN Circuit

❑ Has the order completion date been obtained?

❑ Has the activation date of Internet connection been obtained?

❑ Is the WAN premises equipment assembled and operational prior to circuit completion?

❑ Is the WAN router disconnected from LAN during completion phase?

❑ Are test equipment and configurations removed from your network?

❑ Have you obtained the circuit ID from the telecom or ISP?

❑ Have you asked to be a contact on the circuit with the telecom?

Going Live with the ISP

❑ Is the equipment set up with its final IP and routing configuration before activation?

❑ Did you temporarily deactivate security?

❑ Did you test WAN connectivity?

❑ Did you test routing to the Internet?

❑ Did you test DNS and mail?

❑ Did you reactivate security?

Troubleshooting the WAN

❑ Did you check the WAN router for status of circuit (UP or DOWN)?

❑ If working with a T1 or E1 span, did you check your premises equipment for proper configuration?

❏ If working with a T1 or E1 span, are you prepared for the telecom to conduct loopback tests?

❏ If working with Frame Relay, did you check for correct DLCI values in your equipment configuration?

❏ If working with Frame Relay, did you check whether LMI is being used?

❏ If working with ISDN, did you try using the equipment to dial another number besides that of the ISP?

❏ If working with ISDN, did you make certain your equipment is configured properly to dial the ISP's ISDN telephone number?

Validating Operation and Security after Start-Up

❏ Have security test matrices been created for testing?

❏ Is a separate ISP account used for testing? Is a guest server from ISP available?

❏ Do you need troubleshooting services?

   ❏ DNS resolution works properly

   ❏ Outbound routing works properly

   ❏ Inbound routing works properly

   ❏ Internet site is available

   ❏ Security policy is blocking services

   ❏ Security policy is misconfigured

   ❏ Connection released for general use

Managing Your Connection

8.1 Chapter Overview

Once the installation of your Internet connection is complete, your focus switches from construction to management. This chapter discusses some of the common tasks and issues you are likely to address as you manage your Internet connection. After reading this chapter you should have some idea about the following:

1. Techniques for evaluating new services before implementing them.
2. The common methods used to check for security breaches or lapses.
3. Tactics for monitoring the usage of the Internet link.
4. Major things you should consider if you change ISPs.

8.2 Evaluating New Services

A very common task in managing an Internet connection is responding to requests to support new services. In all likelihood, you will already support the "core" services, such as HTTP, SMTP, FTP, Telnet, and so on. As members of your user community become increasingly savvy, however, they will explore the Internet and find new applications that require the connection to support additional services.

Your job will be to evaluate new services and assess the risk that they pose to your security. Indeed, much of your support of an Internet connection involves security management. For this reason (and some others), you should *not* immediately support a new service until you fully understand its purpose and its functioning.

First, you need to recognize when a user is asking for a new service versus having difficulty with an already-supported service. Usually questions come in the form of "Do we have some kind of firewall that stops Application x from working?" Get as much information as possible from the user about the application he or she was using when difficulties arose. Typically, you should ask for the name and manufacturer of the software application before beginning to evaluate a new service.

The task of evaluating a new service puts you in the role of detective. Your job is to find out as much as possible to answer the following basic questions:

- Which IP protocol does the service use? If it uses TCP or UDP, which ports does it use?
- What risks does the service pose to your site security?

You do not need to smoke a pipe and sleuth around town with a magnifying glass to obtain the answers to these questions. Simply check some or all of the following resources to get your information:

1. Check IANA's web site for port and IP protocol numbers. You may be able to find the service in one of these lists (assuming the service has a name and you know what it is).

2. Check your firewall software for a predefined service. Many firewall packages come with lists of services, which you can update frequently from their web sites. Again, this step assumes that you know the name of the service.

3. Check the web site of the organization using or providing the service. It may have a description of the firewall configuration necessary to support the desired services. The better software companies generally provide good descriptions of how their services work and what you must do as an administrator to support them. In some cases it may be very difficult to find any information, especially if the application consists of freeware.

4. Use a network analyzer to dissect the service as it is used. To carry out this analysis, you will need to download and install the application. Sometimes the installation directions provide information about the services required for the application to work. With the network analyzer you can intercept outbound packets from the client and determine which ports and IP protocol it uses.

5. Ask the ISP for recommended configurations for a particular service. Chances are good that someone at the ISP has dealt with the application, unless it was just released.[1]

Once you have some background information about how the service functions, assess the security risks associated with this new service. In the end, if the security risk outweighs the benefits of the service, then you should not support the service. Ask yourself the following questions to gauge the impact of a service on security:

1. Can this service enable an external host to set up a connection into the interior network or DMZ? Avoid such services. Permit only controlled incoming connections to your servers.

2. Is the service based on TCP, UDP, or another IP protocol? If based on TCP, will allowing outbound connections suffice? If UDP-based, will your network access control handle unsolicited inbound packets? If another IP protocol, how will the network access control handle the situation?

3. Does the service carry any known security risks? Check security web pages such as http://www.cert.org and http://www.sans.org. Other security information sources, such as mailing lists, can also provide useful information.

Other things to consider as you assess a new service include the following:

1. Will the service require or consume significant bandwidth? Sometimes you do not know until you actually implement the service.

---

1. Literally thousands of Internet applications exist. Do not be ashamed to admit you have never heard of an application. Your job is to administer your connection, not surf the web for hot applications.

2. For your organization's structure, does the service need to be business-related? Some organizations require that supported Internet services have strictly business purposes.[2]

3. Normally the ISP will support all standard Internet services, but it is possible that the requested service may be a nonstandard or additional fee-based service. For instance, if a user asks for an MBone feed, you will need to assess not only how to support the service through the firewall, but also how to pay for it.

You should support a new service only after researching and building an additional policy to control it. Typically the task of supporting the new service requires nothing more than adding a policy to your security. When implementing a new service, take the following steps:

1. Verify that the security policies control the service. Use a network analyzer to confirm that security features work properly. Try launching a hack at your network to ensure that your policy works.

2. Actually use the application that requires the service. You can learn a lot about things by simply tinkering with new applications.

8.3 Checking for Security Breaches

Another common task that you should undertake after your Internet connection becomes operational is a review of your site's security. Periodically check for evidence that someone is trying to infiltrate or has gained access to your network. Your efforts should focus on containing and documenting any incursions, and preventing new ones.

You might want to read some of the many books on practical Internet security, which provide detailed descriptions of how to review your site's security. In addition, the SANS web site, found at http://

---

2. In some cases, employees have been asked to resign because their day consisted of web surfing in the morning, eating lunch, surfing in the afternoon, and then going home!

www.sans.org/roadmap.htm, offers an excellent summary of security issues, common breaches, and links to other sources of information. The CERT web site, at http://www.cert.org, also has a section on intrusion improvement, detection, and response.

In summary, here are a few actions you can take to review your security periodically:

1. Inspect the log of your firewall and look for *repeated* attempts to access your network through unsupported ports or services. This suggestion assumes that you are logging the packets dropped by your firewall. You should also look at who is gaining access to the firewall. Realistically, only you and perhaps a few other administrators should be able to access information on the firewall.

2. Check the logs or your servers for any suspicious activity from external hosts. The list of what constitutes "suspicious" is huge. Keep in mind that any activity outside of the server's purpose should be considered suspicious. For instance, evidence that the /etc/passwd file on your UNIX web server was mailed to a host in the Internet should be regarded with distrust.

3. Look for evidence of security breaches on the servers, such as modified system binaries and directories.

4. Search your servers for network analyzer software. Sometimes hackers place the packages on servers to collect more information for their next attack.

5. Keep learning about security issues. Although the majority of tips on server security apply to UNIX, much more information is now available about Windows NT security. Subscribe to security mailing lists, such as Bugtraq and CheckPoint's Firewall-1 (described in Chapter 4).

If you believe that one or more of your systems has been compromised or is the focus of an attack, take the following steps:

1. Immediately assess the risk to your organization's operation and conduct triage. Depending on the type of incursion, you

may opt to temporarily remove the compromised system from the network or take your site off the Internet. Although this last action seems very drastic, it may be necessary, especially if you are in the throes of a denial-of-service attack.

2. Call your ISP to report the situation. Your ISP should have staff trained in security responses. At a minimum, you can obtain additional information on how to proceed. Often the ISP will help you contain the incursion or attack. More importantly, it should be able to suggest ways to prevent the incident from occurring again.

3. Document the intrusion. Keep "evidence," such as logs. If you plan to bring legal action against the perpetrators, you will need solid proof on hand.[3]

4. Consider reporting the incident to CERT. In addition to your ISP, CERT can offer some technical assistance and guidance in dealing with your problem. Also, it will help track such incidents and possibly help you contact other administrators who have experienced the same problem.[4]

5. Communicate the situation to your management.

6. Once you have a handle on the situation, take immediate steps to rebuild, further protect, or sanitize the affected systems. Then go about the process of restoring service.

With luck, you will never have to respond to a security incident, but the prudent course is to have a defined plan before you have a security incident. You may wish to roll this plan into your disaster recovery plan, which is also now called business resumption planning.

---

3. The decision to prosecute hackers and crackers should not be taken lightly. Depending on the legal system in your country, this situation could become an expensive and involved experience.

4. Because of CERT's limited staffing and the increasing number of security incidents, you may not receive any assistance at all. At this point, it appears that CERT responds to only major incidents.

8.4 Usage Monitoring and Baselining

Yet another task in managing an Internet connection is usage monitoring and baselining. In simple terms, this duty involves monitoring the utilization levels on your Internet WAN circuit over the course of several weeks or months. This information helps you and the ISP determine whether the WAN circuit is sized properly to accommodate your Internet traffic. Also, it defines the "normal" utilization levels on the WAN and can be used to define an operational baseline.

The ISP will monitor your WAN utilization. In most cases, it uses this information to ensure that your site is not underpaying for the service it uses, especially if you have a usage-based billing plan. The ISP, however, will also monitor your usage to ensure that your connection is not running consistently at or near its maximum utilization. If it is, the ISP may suggest that you increase your WAN capacity.

Tools for monitoring WAN utilization are SNMP-based. Technically, these tools are classified as network management reporting packages. Some router manufacturers provide such tools, usually in a reselling arrangement with a software manufacturer. Other commercial companies like Concord Communications (http://www.concord.com/) and DeskTalk Systems (http://www.desktalk.com/) have developed software that reports utilization and many other interesting things about your network segments, but remains vendor-neutral. Common to all of these tools is their ability to generate trend reports and graphs that show utilization over time. Figure 8-1 depicts a utilization graph for the day in the life of a fictitious Internet connection.

Traditionally, you received a printed graph of your circuit's monthly utilization. Today, however, many ISPs are investing in web-based front ends to their reporting tools that allow the customer to generate such reports on demand. Ask your ISP if it offers this service.

In any event, you may decide to invest in a package, especially if you manage a large connection and LAN. Some good reasons exist to buy such a reporting tool:

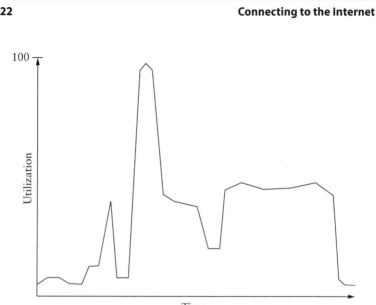

Figure 8-1 *Utilization graph*

1. You can obtain a baseline showing the normal utilization of the WAN. Thus, if you experience any problems with the circuit, you at least know the "normal" usage levels.
2. If you have usage-based billing, you can compare the ISP's reports with your own. The two should match, but if not then you have some information to present in your favor.
3. Baselining helps you plan for future growth. If your connection is currently operating near its maximum capacity and your organization plans to add 50 more employees, then you may need to increase the WAN capacity.
4. A reporting tool can help you manage the utilization on all your networks, not only on the Internet WAN link.

When you examine your WAN usage, do not be alarmed if you see usage near 100% from time to time throughout a day. In most cases, "bumping the ceiling" will occur in the inbound direction when many users simultaneously pull information from the Internet.

Although the threshold for increasing WAN capacity is somewhat subjective, you should generally begin planning to increase capacity when the average utilization consistently hovers near 50% with frequent and sustained hits at 100%. Ask your ISP for its recommendation about when to increase capacity. Most can use their monitoring software packages to report your average or 95 percentile usage for a month. When viewed over time, you should be able to see trends that indicate whether your usage is remaining flat, falling, or rising.

8.5 Addressing Performance and Connectivity Issues

In addition to monitoring usage, you may find yourself dealing with performance and connectivity problems. It is not uncommon to experience glitches every once in a while. Do not worry if you are occasionally asked, "Is there something wrong with our Internet connection? I cannot get to the web site . . . ," or "Boy, the Internet really seems slow today! Is there something wrong with our connection?" Do not panic.

Most users presume that the network is the culprit with *all* Internet access problems. In particular, the local Internet connection is assumed to be guilty. Accept this presumption of guilt as human nature. Very few people actually understand how the pieces of the Internet fit together and function. Some of the problems reported will be "pilot error." Others will reflect problems in some component of your Internet connection or in a system within the Internet itself. In either case, you need to respond.

Internet problems can be classified into several categories:

1. *Performance degradation* occurs when one or more components within your Internet connection or the Internet itself fail to forward packets at normal speeds. Frequently this problem is attributed to bandwidth contention within WAN circuits. For instance, during some peak periods many hosts may simultaneously attempt to access or use an Internet resource. Although no outright failure occurs in the communication between hosts, the communication that does occur is so slow as to be unusable. Another source of performance problems is the

overburdened server. Too many connections to a server equate to bad performance.[5]

2. *Connectivity failure* involves an outright failure of some component in the network connecting your site to the Internet at large. Frequent sources of connectivity failures are down WAN circuits, including your WAN or those of your ISP. Keep in mind that your connectivity is only as good as that of your ISP. If it experiences problems, then you will, too. A connectivity failure may also reflect a routing problem. If any router between the hosts fails to work properly, a connectivity failure will occur.

3. *Server failure* is a failure of one or more servers or its processes. In a very simplified view, your network clients communicate with Internet servers. If one or more of these servers fail to function properly, then the client cannot use the service normally provided by the server. For the most part, server failures remain isolated events that most users can understand. Depending on the location and function of the server, however, the impact can be far-reaching. For instance, if your DNS server fails, you cannot resolve names into IP addresses, which will have a major impact on operations.

The divide-and-conquer approach to troubleshooting works best for solving these types of problems.[6] Keep your focus when troubleshooting. You need to answer the big question, "Does the problem lie within your systems or within the Internet?" How you fix or respond to the problem depends on the answer.

---

5. Some products perform bandwidth management to enforce time-of-day rules that restrict or open access to systems based on IP address. For instance, during the day you may wish to allocate 75% of your circuit's bandwidth to traffic for your internal users. If you have a web page at your site, at night you could restrict your internal users' access to 30% while improving external access to 70%.

6. To be blunt, the author does not recall ever learning of another diagnostic technique for troubleshooting technical problems other than this one. At least with networks, troubleshooting implies using this approach.

Here we will provide a general approach that should be familiar to you. You encountered a variation of this methodology when testing your design prior to activation. It may not solve all your problems, but it should point you in the correct direction. Table 8-1 gives an overview of the problem-solving process.

1. Understand the problem first. Spend some time getting the facts before you dive into matters. Ask the basic "who," "what," "when," and "where" questions. Answering the "why" question is your job.

   - Who is experiencing the problem?
   - What site or systems are unreachable?
   - What specifically does not work?
   - Are there problems with other sites in the Internet?
   - Are there problems with access to internal systems?
   - How long has this problem existed?
   - Where is the client's host located in the internal networks?

2. Conduct a quick systems check of your Internet equipment—a "sanity check." The specifics of a user's problem may have little

Table 8-1 Problem-Solving Methodology

Number	Step
1	Understand the problem
2	Do a systems check
3	Isolate internal problems
4	Check DNS
5	Check routing
6	Check performance
7	Conduct a reference check
8	Document
9	Find a resolution

relevance when your WAN link to the ISP is down. This check should involve a cursory glance at port status of your WAN router, perhaps a traceroute to an external site, and similar reviews.

3. Try to eliminate internal problems before testing for Internet problems. With some common sense and deductive reasoning, you may be able to isolate local problems that are confined within your internal networks or located in the host system itself.

4. Verify that DNS resolution of Internet hosts names works properly. Many problems in accessing the Internet reflect failed DNS queries or misconfigurations of the TCP/IP client. Use ping to verify that the host name is resolved into an IP address.

5. Verify that routing to a destination works properly. Use the traceroute utility to check the routing of the outbound packet to the Internet host. Pay attention to the path that the packet takes and not necessarily to the response of the destination node. Sometimes administrators configure their security policy to block incoming ICMP and traceroute, as mentioned in Chapter 4.

6. Look at the performance and response time between the client and the server (or between the hosts, as the case may be). Unlike with LANs, response times in the Internet can be quite long. Remember, the Internet is groups of WANs, which have higher latency than LANs do. Two types of tools are used to measure response time:

   - Commercial or freeware application response time tools
   - Network analyzers

You can also employ ping and traceroute to retrieve some basic information, but view any data gained this way with some skepticism. ICMP usually has a low priority within routers, so responses can be delayed. These utilities are more useful for verifying reachability and routing than for checking response time.

7. Conduct a reference check to discern whether the problem is isolated to one host or affects many hosts. If the user has

problems with only a single Internet host, the implication is that the destination host is sick or unreachable (a server failure). If the user has problems with many sites, then connectivity failure is probably at fault.

8. Document the problem when you isolate it. As good administrative practice, you should keep track of problems and the eventual resolutions. Such documentation is also helpful when you must share information with others outside of your organization, especially when you enlist the assistance of your ISP or another administrator. Try not to go overboard—simply identify the pertinent information. Expect to record traceroute results, DNS query results, portions of log files, and so on.[7]

9. Find a resolution to the problem. You can do little to fix performance problems that lie outside of your network or that of your ISP. Consider contacting the administrator of the destination network to report the problem. The Internet community is a fairly decent group, and most administrators will be glad to know about problems with their sites. The Whois database at ARIN's web site can help you find a contact for registered IP networks.

In general, performance problems are hard to diagnose and repair unless they are systemic. Take your daily operation with a grain of salt. Accept the possibility that you will experience some bad days along the way. Instead, focus on ensuring an efficient connection to the ISP's network and its servers.

Keep in mind that the Internet is a huge WAN. At the moment most ISPs have service level agreement (SLA) policies for their customers that guarantee certain standards for uptime and availability.

---

7. If you use a Windows-based PC, you may be stumped about how to record the results of ping and tracert as these utilities are launched from a DOS prompt. Thankfully, the creators of DOS were once UNIX nerds and added some UNIX-like functions to their operating system. To capture results to a file, append "> filename" to the command. For instance, the command "tracert www.awl. com > result txt" will write the results of the command to the file instead of the screen.

The elusive element to guarantee has been performance—namely, available bandwidth and response time between hosts. No mechanism currently exists that enables an ISP to reserve bandwidth within another ISP's network. The majority of your Internet traffic leaves your provider's network and, once it does, your ISP cannot provide any guarantees on it. (Note that some NSPs are partnering together to develop SLAs with one another.)

Consult with your ISP if problems persist for long periods. Also, look at performance problems if your user community reports widespread problems. For instance, if you consistently hear that a particular web site responds poorly, first you assume that the problem lies at the particular site. If your user community reports that many external web sites respond poorly, however, then you may face a general performance problem. Get help.

8.6 Moving to a New ISP

Another task you may experience over time is moving your connection to a new ISP. Common reasons for changing ISPs include better pricing and service. Before making the decision to switch ISPs, you should document in writing to the current ISP why you are not satisfied with its service and any other pertinent issues. Most will try to fix the situation and make you a content customer.

If things do not work out for your site, then you need to be proactive and make a change. Planning a move of your Internet connection to a new ISP can be a complex and stressful event. Here are the key points to consider when you switch ISPs:

1. *IP Addressing.* Will you need to readdress your interior networks? If you took an address range on loan from the ISP, then you must give it back upon termination of service. Unless you own your addresses, this step is inevitable. The careful use of NAT can help ease this transition or make it completely transparent to your user community.

2. *DNS Modifications.* The new ISP will need to modify the DNS information for your organization. This process involves changing the root level entries and MX records. Although this

operation should be transparent to you, it requires the ISPs to work together. The new ISP will need to inform the old ISP of the changes.

3. *Early Termination Charges*. What charges must you pay if you terminate a contract with an ISP before its completion? Do not expect to break a contract without monetary compensation to the ISP. This charge may include more than one component, as the ISP may have early termination charges. In addition, the telecom may bill the ISP for early termination charges on a WAN circuit.

4. *WAN Connectivity*. Can you use your existing premises equipment to connect to the new ISP? One preemptive move you can take when you purchase your first router is to ensure that it has two WAN ports. Although few devices on the market currently offer dual ISDN BRI ports, many have dual WAN serial ports. Alternatively, you may want to consider purchasing an additional router for connecting to the new ISP. You can then bring up this connection in parallel with the existing connection, and at the last moment cut over to the new WAN circuit and disable the old one.

8.7 Your Internet Connection on Autopilot

Once you finish building your Internet connection, you will find it acts much like any other system in your network. It will require some attention periodically. On balance, however, its management should not necessarily consume your time. The purpose of the connection is to provide service—to be a useful tool for your organization. Take the time to understand how it works so that you can control its systems, instead of them controlling you! Have fun and good luck.

Appendix A
Network Address Translation

Network address translation (NAT) is a technology in which globally unique IP addresses act as proxies for nonunique local IP addresses assigned to hosts in your LANs. It is typically deployed at the gateway between your interior networks and the Internet (for example, at a router or firewall). The primary advantage of NAT is that it enables you to deploy arbitrary IP addresses to the hosts and networks in your LANs, thus freeing you from the need to obtain unique addresses from your ISP or a regional registry. In addition, because the NAT server prevents the Internet from knowing the true identity of the sending station, it acts as a nice security tool. In many respects, a NAT server is an IP proxy server.

Table A-1 Private IANA Addresses

Start	End	Comment
10.0.0.0	10.255.255.255	1 class A
172.16.0.0	172.31.255.255	32 class B
192.168.0.0	192.168.255.255	256 class C

RFC 1631 provides the recommended configurations for NAT. In effect, common practice calls for using the IANA private addresses within your networks as shown in Table A-1. Note that these addresses are not routed within the Internet and are meant to be deployed arbitrarily by LAN administrators. In NAT terms, they are local addresses.

When internal hosts send packets to the Internet, the NAT server intercepts the outbound packets and replaces the local source address IP with its own global address. All outbound packets therefore have a globally unique source address as they leave your network. Response packets from the Internet return to the NAT server's global IP address. The NAT server then replaces the destination address with that of the local device's address and forwards the packet into the LANs. To the Internet hosts, the NAT server appears to be the device making the requests.

NAT can be implemented in several configurations. The most commonly encountered are one-to-one and one-to-many address mappings. One-to-one address mapping is characterized by a global address for every local address. One-to-many address mapping features a single global address that communicates on behalf of many local addresses.

Figure A-1 shows an example of NAT. In this configuration, the ISP has provided two global addresses, 138.8.0.1 and 138.8.0.2, which are assigned to the exterior side of the NAT server and routed within the Internet. To hosts in the Internet, all packets coming from this site appear to originate from one of these two addresses. (Normally your ISP will provide many more global addresses, such as a class C network.) The internal network is assigned a private address of 192.168.2.0/24 and the DMZ is assigned to the 192.168.1.0/24 network. In theory your selection of translated addresses is arbitrary, though we recommend that you use private IANA addresses shown in Table A-1.

The NAT device is configured for two types of translation: one-

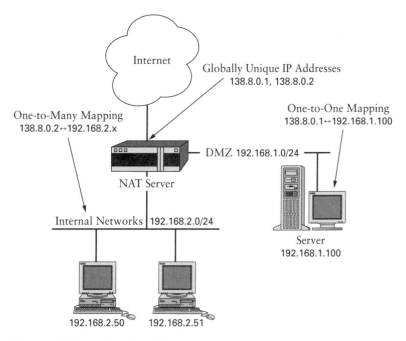

Figure A-1 *Network Address Translation*

to-one mapping for the server and one-to-many mapping from the internal hosts. The translation takes place on the interface to the Intenet. Thus, when external hosts communicate with the server at 192.168.1.100, they appear to be communicating with 138.8.0.1—a one-to-one mapping. When the internal hosts (192.168.2.x) communicate with the Internet, they appear as a single host, 138.8.0.2, because of the one-to-many mapping. When they communicate with the server, they address one another using the assigned private address—no translation is necessary. If the host, 192.168.2.50, needs to communicate with the server, it does so via the server's IP address of 192.168.1.100.

Although NAT is primarily intended to alleviate address space constraints in today's Internet, it is also being used as a load-balancing tool for web servers. With one-to-many mapping, a single global IP address can map to several servers with identical contents. When an external host initiates a connection to the server, the NAT device determines which server is least busy and then maps the connection to that server.

Until IPv6 is fully implemented, you should expect that more products will provide NAT support. If you are interested in learning more about NAT, read the pertinent RFC and check with network equipment vendors for white papers and tutorials on the subject.

Appendix B
Virtual Private Networks

A virtual private network (VPN) is an IP tunnel set up between your site and another site on the Internet. It carries network traffic as if it were a dedicated leased-line connection, such as a point-to-point circuit. VPNs take advantage of the Internet as a WAN backbone.

To date VPNs have been marketed primarily to replace leased lines between sites and thus minimize WAN costs. VPNs are also being used to support nomadic users as another form of remote access. Many other inventive uses of VPNs are also possible. VPNs appear highly attractive because of their relatively low cost. If you are already paying for an Internet connection and need to connect to another site through a dedicate link, a VPN may be a viable solution.

The Internet standard for VPN tunneling, the **Generic Routing Encapsulation (GRE)** protocol, is used by the Point-To-Point Tunneling Protocol (PPTP). A next-generation variant to PPTP, called Layer 2 Tunneling Protocol (L2TP), is also expected to become part of the tunneling standard in VPNs. PPTP uses IP protocol 47 for the data tunnel and TCP port 1723 for tunnel control (similar to how FTP uses data and control channels).

GRE encapsulates data within the payload. Specifically, it encapsulates the protocol data units (PDUs) of other protocols such as IP, IPX, and AppleTalk. As a result, PPTP permits you to set up a VPN across the Internet capable of carrying protocols beyond TCP/IP, such as IPX/SPX and Banyan VINES. Keep in mind, however, that PPTP does not itself provide encryption services.

Figure B-1 shows a basic VPN between the central office and a remote sales office. Both sites have an Internet connection. A VPN is configured between the sites using a tunneling protocol.

In another configuration, the VPN connects a user in the Internet to your network through the ISP's remote access infrastructure. In this setup, you configure a permanent VPN with a selected ISP and have your users connect via modem to that ISP's infrastructure. With this

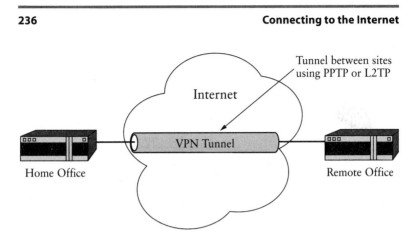

Figure B-1 *VPN between sites*

approach, you assume that the dial-up facilities of an ISP are less expensive, offer greater reliability, and have greater geographic availability than if you provide dial-up facilities yourself. In fact, some ISPs offer global remote access products.

In another take on this technology, you enable your nomadic users to create a VPN with your network on an as-needed basis. In such a case, you assume your mobile users maintain private accounts with an ISP and thus have access to the Internet.

Figure B-2 shows these two scenarios. Again, the VPN forms a tunnel between the Internet host and the home office.

VPNs will need to overcome two major hurdles to gain further acceptance as replacements for dedicated WAN circuits. The first is security, and the second relates to quality of service (QoS). In the first case, significant progress has been made in establishing Internet security standards. Chapter 5 discusses how VPN products use public-key encryption technologies to cipher the data payload. In particular, IPsec, SKIP, and proprietary encryption provide this type of security.

On the other hand, QoS remains an elusive goal. In short, this case requires a guaranteed bandwidth between stations and a prioritization of traffic based on protocol. Unfortunately, no standard mechanism exists by which ISPs can provide a subscribed data rate through the Internet between end stations. One near-term solution calls for ISPs to provide service-level agreements for traffic within their networks. Such

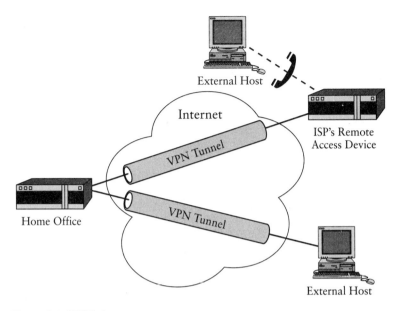

Figure B-2 *VPNs for remote access*

an agreement would cover a VPN constructed between endpoints in the provider's network. This form of QoS really derives from the ISP's construction of huge backbones, rather than through a traffic prioritization mechanism.

VPNs are a hot topic, and many books are devoted to the subject of configuring and maintaining such tunnels. In addition, an increasing number of vendors are developing VPN-ready products, so you can expect to see new and inventive uses of the technology over time.

Appendix C
How the Internet Functions

Have you ever wondered how the Internet enables people to communicate and exchange digital information from all corners of the globe? This appendix discusses how the Internet is constructed, how it provides services to its users, and what types of technical problems we face today as this global WAN continues to grow. Although some of this information may be "nice-to-know" stuff, the problems are real and may directly affect you when you build your connection.

C.1 Backbone Construction

Most Internet users remain blissfully unaware of the construction of the Internet backbone. They surf the web, never really pondering how the pieces of the puzzle come together to make the Internet work. In some ways, asking "What does my ISP do with my packets?" is like a six-year-old asking a parent "What happens to the dead goldfish when we flush it down the toilet?" Most people simply don't care what happens to the goldfish. Similarly, most don't care how their packets are routed through the Internet.

The Internet is actually a collection of many networks that are linked together as peers. When banded together, these networks form the Internet. The operation and maintenance of these networks falls upon groups called network service providers (NSPs). The most common NSPs include the following organizations:

- Tier one Internet service providers
- U.S. government organizations
- Telecommunications providers (such as British Telecom, MCI, and AT&T)
- Universities

Each NSP maintains its own WAN infrastructure and equipment. At the edges of this network, it connects to other providers. Although NSPs have a large list of responsibilities, fundamentally they perform the following functions:

- They exchange routing information with neighboring providers.
- They route traffic through their own network for neighboring providers.
- They route traffic for networks directly attached to their infrastructure.

Consequently, you will often hear ISPs discussing how they plan to upgrade their backbones. This type of upgrade not only helps them serve their customers better, but also expedites the routing of traffic between providers. In short, NSPs act as peers that help one another relay network traffic between hosts.

In actuality, NSPs enable connectivity between **autonomous systems (ASs)**. An autonomous system is a self-contained routing domain defined by the **Border Gateway Protocol (BGP)**. BGP is the routing building protocol used in the Internet, much like RIP is used in most LAN environments. Unfortunately, the details of BGP lie beyond the scope of this book. For more information on BGP, we suggest you read *BGP4*, by John Stewart, published by Addison-Wesley.

When you purchase Internet connectivity from an ISP, the ISP arranges for your TCP/IP networks to be advertised to the Internet from a particular AS. Generally, you don't need to know the details of this advertising unless you plan to build advanced Internet connections involving multiple ISPs. The end result is that the AS constructs routing tables with information about how to get to your network, or at least how to get to another AS that knows how to get to your network.

Figure C-1 depicts the Internet backbone and the relationship between the ASs, NSPs, and you. For example, assume you purchase Internet connectivity from ISP A. You connect your LAN to the ISP's network through a WAN link. The ISP has configured several ASs, with your networks being represented by AS 1. Your AS advertises your networks to the neighboring ASs using BGP—in this case, AS 22 and AS 56. These systems pass what they learn to their neighbors. In

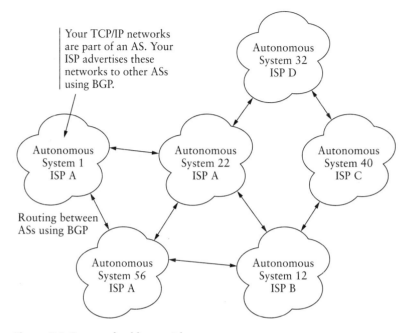

Figure C-1 *Internet backbone with autonomous systems*

the end, each AS knows how to find a route to your networks—and usually more than one.

This representation of the Internet backbone is relatively rudimentary; the actual details are much more complex. Nevertheless, the important points are as follows:

- NSPs route traffic between autonomous systems as peers.
- A provider usually administers more than one autonomous system.

C.2 Domain Name System

The Domain Name System (DNS) is the mechanism by which workstations and systems running TCP/IP **resolve** a name into a unique IP address. Because of DNS, most users never realize that the names they type actually resolve into IP addresses. For instance, if you entered www.awl.com in your web browser, the DNS functions within the

TCP/IP software of your workstation would resolve this name to the IP address 192.207.117.2.

In this book's preface, we noted that you should have some knowledge of DNS. With respect to building an Internet connection, there's really nothing special about DNS. You must, however, ensure that your connection allows appropriate DNS traffic to flow through, just as you would with services such as HTTP and FTP. If you are a one-person show and also have responsibility for configuring e-mail and DNS services, the book *DNS and BIND,* by Paul Albitz and Cricket Liu, may offer some valuable advice.

If you have access to UNIX workstations in your network, and they are configured to use DNS for name resolution, check out the nslookup program. This tool resolves names into IP addresses, and vice versa; it also includes many features for debugging DNS. Another program preferred by many ISPs for testing DNS functions is called dig.

C.3 The Internet Management and Services

Although the construction and operation of the Internet reflects the actions of a loose confederation of ISPs, government agencies, and universities working together toward a common goal, the top-level management is really a centralized body. At the top of the heap is the **Internet Society (ISOC)**, a professional membership organization of Internet experts that comments on policies and practices and oversees a number of other boards and task forces dealing with network policy issues.

The ISOC has chartered the Internet Assigned Numbers Authority (IANA) to manage the assignment of unique values for Internet protocols. This responsibility includes the assignment of IP addresses, domain names, and other things such a port numbers. IANA's web site is http://www.iana.org/.

IANA really doesn't seek direct contact with users, unless absolutely necessary. In fact, it has set up three regional registries that handle the daily requests from ISPs and system administrators (like you and me):

- **American Registry for Internet Numbers (ARIN)**—Assigns IP numbers for networks in North America, South America, the Caribbean, and sub-Saharan Africa. (http://www.arin.net/)

- Réseaux IP Européens—Network Coordination Center (RIPE NCC)—Performs the same task as ARIN for Europe and surrounding countries. (http://www.ripe.net)
- **Asia Pacific—Network Information Center (AP NIC)**—Assigns numbers for networks located in Asia and Pacific Rim countries. (http://www.apnic.net/)

The ISOC also oversees the work of the **Internet Engineering Task Force (IETF)**. The IETF has a slightly different mission than the IANA, concerning itself with standards, and particularly with all things branded TCP/IP. Items that fall into this category include routing protocols and addressing schemes. The IETF is also responsible for the Request for Comments (RFC) process, in which exciting new ideas about Internetworking become real entities. The IETF attempts to ensure that all players in the Internet can intercommunicate so that things run smoothly. The IETF web site (http://www.ietf.org) provides some good information about itself.

Figure C-2 depicts the hierarchy of Internet management.

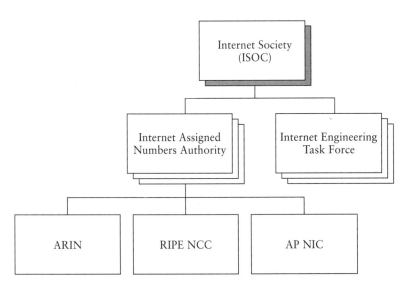

Figure C-2 *Internet management organization*

C.4 Obtaining IP Addresses and Domain Names

Before your LAN can communicate with the Internet, you must take two steps:

1. Obtain a global IP address, or a range of IP addresses, for use in your networks
2. Register a unique domain name for your organization (for example, reallyawesome.org)

Remember, you need to employ global IP addresses for the systems you connect to the Internet, including systems located deep in your LANs. Any system in your network that will exchange packets with the Internet must use a unique IP address. Additionally, you will want to register your chosen domain name for your organization. Domain names, like IP addresses, must be unique.

The path of least resistance in accomplishing these tasks flows through your ISP. With respect to address allocation, the registries follow strict guidelines defined by RFC 2050 (Internet Registry IP Allocation Guidelines) that govern how they allocate IP address ranges. Unless you require a very large address range, it is unlikely that a registry will provide a range directly to you. Instead, it will instruct you to obtain addresses from your ISP.

Several factors explain IANA's strict policy for address allocation. The most important ones relate to address space conservation and routability. In short, the current version of IP used in the Internet (IPv4) does not have enough addresses for everyone, a problem referred to as **address depletion**. With respect to routability, the intention is to keep the IP forwarding tables in the Internet's routers as trim as possible. Allocating a large network range to an ISP enables large numbers of IP addresses to be represented by a single route table entry, a mechanism known as route **aggregation**.

With respect to domain names, your best bet is to leverage your relationship with your ISP and have it register your chosen domain name. The other option is to register your DNS information directly with the **Internet Network Information Center (InterNIC)** at http://www.internic.net/. Unlike IP address allocation, which is delegated by the regional registries, the InterNIC still handles direct requests for DNS registration for the top-level domains, including domains such as .COM, .NET., and .ORG. Outside of the United States, most countries have established a domain administrator that performs similar functions to the InterNIC. You can usually find the address of your country's domain administrator through the regional registry.

Unlike with IP addresses, more flexibility exists with domain names. The RFC 1591 entitled "Domain Name System Structure and Delegation" provides some guidelines on naming conventions. Unlike most RFCs, this one is short—only seven pages!

Obtaining addresses and registering domain names are not fee-free operations. The regional registries now charge fees for the initial registration of address spaces and AS numbers, plus a yearly maintenance fee (which has traditionally been very small). Basically, the registries operate as nonprofit organizations, but they need to pay their employees. Modest fees for their services seem reasonable. Normally, most ISPs "absorb" these costs when you become their customer. In reality, they simply submit your domain name request, as they have already paid to have an IP address pool allocated to them.

C.5 Internet Problems

For the most part, the Internet runs smoothly. There are good days and not-so-good days. In general, the ISPs supporting the backbone and the organizations managing the Internet (such as IANA, registries, and IETF) make a great effort to address issues and problems head on. Nevertheless, we face a few major problems with today's Internet. This section outlines the greatest challenges for you when implementing your connection.

C.5.1 Predicted Growth and Capacity Planning

No doubt you have noticed the Internet is now very, very popular. An autumn 1997 report by International Data Corporation (IDC) estimated the current number of web users and predicted the number in the year 2001, as shown in Table C-1.

Table C-1 Predicted Internet Usage Growth		
	Today	2001
United States	29.2 million	94.2 million
Western Europe	9.9 million	32.1 million
Asia Pacific	8.4 million	36.8 million
Rest of the world	2.7 million	11.4 million

Of course, you should regard these numbers with some caution, especially considering the economic crisis experienced in Asia in 1997 and 1998. The general point is that the growth is not linear, but rather exponential! Some industry analysts and Internet experts have claimed that the collapse of the Internet is imminent. This meltdown hasn't occurred yet, although it does seem possible.

The Internet is feeling some very real growth pains. The ISPs, IETF, and Internet Society face the enormous task of keeping the Internet humming, while at the same time expanding its carrying capacity by a factor of 4. Already ISPs have invested millions of dollars in upgrading their infrastructures. The process will continue to evolve. You should be ready for the days when your users complain, "The Internet is slow today—fix it!"

C.5.2 IP Address Depletion

Another growth pain faced by the Internet today relates to the depletion of available IP addresses. In theory, IPv4 provides 4,294,967,296 unique addresses. In the real-world implementation, however, this number is far smaller. In part, this address depletion reflects the history of how addresses were initially parceled to organizations and companies as either class A, class B, or class C networks. Each class had a fixed number of hosts. Thus, when IBM landed its class A address 9.0.0.0, it won 16 million host addresses. The organizations with class B addresses received 65,536 host addresses.

Seem a bit wasteful? The managers of the Internet thought so, and set out to make life better. Eventually, subnet masking emerged. It allowed address ranges to be doled out from the IANA with greater precision and less waste. Today the IANA advises the regional registries to allocate subnet ranges with a smallest network prefix of /19, which is a mask of 255.255.224.0. Because this prefix provides a large range of networks and hosts, it is typically allocated to ISPs only.

Some disagreement has arisen in the Internet community regarding whether an address space crunch really exists. The policies of the IANA and the efficient management of address pools by ISPs seem to have nipped the problem in the bud. To date, ISPs have not been forced to deny any customer IP addresses. Nevertheless, when you "rent" addresses from an ISP, you will eventually have to give them back. For a small LAN, this process is a pain, but not a crisis. For large organizations, however, it constitutes a major problem. In any event, the days of getting your own IP addresses directly from the IANA are gone.

Today, both NAT and DHCP hold promise for dealing with the apparent lack of IP addresses. In addition, IP version 6 (IPv6) promises to relieve the pressure once it gains widespread acceptance. These topics are covered in greater detail in the other appendices.

Appendix D
Dynamic Host
Configuration Protocol

Dynamic Host Configuration Protocol (DHCP) has made major strides the last few years in helping network administrators deal with the thorny issues of IP management for a diverse user body. DHCP is a protocol that dynamically allocates an IP address to a workstation for some predetermined length of time. This relationship is called a **lease**. During the lease, the DHCP server does not allocate that address to any other workstations on the subnet. Roughly halfway through the lease period, the client will request renewal of the address. If the lease period expires, the client simply reinitiates the process. The whole assignment process takes about four packets.[1] If the client does not ask to renew the address at the end of the lease, the DHCP server places the address back into the available address pool.

This technology relieves the network administrator from the task of statically assigning IP addresses to individual workstations. It has been a great bonus to organizations that support mobile users. A user can simply move his or her workstation between DHCP-enabled subnets and obtain a unique IP address on each network. For instance, a user might begin her day in one facility, move to another facility for the afternoon, and then access the network remotely from home in the evening without reconfiguring her IP address.

DHCP also enables the administrator to use fewer addresses than would be necessary if each workstation had a static address. This strategy capitalizes on the idea that not all users will require IP addresses at exactly the same time.

---

1. When you locate the DHCP server on a different subnet than the hosts, be certain to enable UDP forwarding on the router between the subnets. In particular, the router should listen for BOOTP requests (UDP port 67) and forward them to the IP address of the DHCP server.

In comparison, protocols like IPX/SPX and AppleTalk also dynamically assign addresses to the hosts in a subnet. Instead of using administratively assigned values (that is, the IP address), however, the addresses used in these other protocols consist of the client's MAC address (in IPX/SPX) or a random number (in AppleTalk). In both cases, the host address is assumed to be unique.

Most modern TCP/IP clients now support DHCP. For instance, the Microsoft TCP/IP protocol in Windows 95 and Windows NT supports DHCP. It is supported by the Macintosh operating system version 7.5.2 (and higher) and some of the newer UNIX operating systems, such as Sun Microsystems' Solaris 2.6 and Linux. Interestingly, the UNIX environments have lagged behind the PC and Macintosh environments in terms of available DHCP clients. Many routers now include DHCP servers as software features.

Similarly, support for DHCP server software has grown. For example, Windows NT now offers DHCP server capability. Many of the UNIX environments provide DHCP server functions as well. In addition to the support of the operating system manufacturers, all environments have a smattering of third-party support for DHCP software.

One attractive feature of DHCP is its reduction of IP address management. Instead of visiting desktops to reconfigure addresses, you can manage the address pool on a server without modifying the client. In addition, DHCP allows you to support mobile users who switch subnets several times in a day, as mentioned earlier. It also decreases the number of addresses required to keep your operations rolling. If obtaining globally unique IP addresses is an issue, you may wish to consider implementing DHCP.

Appendix E
Helpful Web Sites

E.1 Firewall/Security Sites

http://www.cert.org—Computer Emergency Response Team (CERT) Coordination Center.

http://www.checkpoint.com—CheckPoint Technology's home page.

http://www.checkpoint.com/products/whitepapers/wpvpn30.pdf— Good description of public-key encryption from CheckPoint Technology's home page.

http://www.clark.net/pub/mjr/pubs/fwfaq—Internet Firewalls Frequently Asked Questions maintained by Marcus J. Ranum. This FAQ site has many good links to other security sites.

http://www.gocsi.com/firewall.htm—CSI's Free Firewall Resource. This site lists about 40 reviewed firewall products.

http://www.greatcircle.com/firewalls/vendors.html—Contains a large list of firewall products categorized by commercial products, freeware, resellers, and so on. Great Circle Associates was founded by D. Brent Chapman, the coauthor of *Building Internet Firewalls.*

http://www.sans.org—SANS Institute. A good source of security information and pointers to other security sites.

http://www.socks.nec.com—SOCKS web page.

E.2 Freeware Sites

http://cws.internet.com—Stroud's freeware web site.

http://www.shareware.com

E.3 Internet Administration Sites

http://www.apnic.net—APNIC.

http://www.arin.net—ARIN.

http://www.ietf.org—IETF.
http://www.iana.org—IANA.
http://www.ripe.net—RIPE.
http://www.rfc-editor.org—Request for Comments (RFC).
http://www.internic.net—The InterNIC web site for DNS administration.

E.4 Internet Service Providers

http://www.thelist.com/—A comprehensive list of Internet service
   providers by geographic region.

Bibiliography

The following references are valuable information sources on connecting your LAN to the Internet.

1. Paul Albitz, Cricket Liu. *DNS and BIND,* 3rd edition. O'Reilly & Associates, Inc., Sebastopol, Calif., 1998.

2. Darryl P. Black. *Managing Switched Local Area Networks: A Practical Guide.* Addison Wesley Longman, Inc., Reading, Mass., 1997.

3. D. Brent Chapman, Elizabeth D. Zwicky. *Building Internet Firewalls.* O'Reilly & Associates, Inc., Sebastopol, Calif., 1995.

4. William R. Cheswick, Steven M. Bellovin. *Firewalls and Internet Security: Repelling the Wily Hacker.* Addison Wesley Longman, Inc., Reading, Mass., 1994.

5. Craig Hunt. *TCP/IP Network Administration,* 2nd edition. O'Reilly & Associates, Inc., Sebastopol, Calif., 1997.

6. Vinay Kumar. *Mbone: Interactive Multimedia on the Internet.* New Riders Publishing, Indianapolis, Ind., 1995.

7. John T. Moy. *OSPF: Anatomy of an Internet Routing Protocol.* Addison Wesley Longman, Inc., Reading, Mass., 1998.

8. Harry Newton. *Newton's Telecom Dictionary,* 14th edition. Flatiron Publishing, Inc., New York, N.Y., 1998.

9. Richard E. Smith. *Internet Cryptography.* Addison Wesley Longman, Inc., Reading, Mass., 1997.

Glossary

ACK See *Acknowledge*.

Acknowledge (ACK) A bit in the TCP/IP header that indicates whether the packet is a response or acknowledgment to a previous packet. The acknowledge bit signifies that the packet is part of a TCP connection between stations.

Address depletion The general reduction of available IP addresses for assignment in the Internet because the current version of IP used in the Internet (IPv4) does not have enough addresses for everyone.

Address lending The practice in which the ISP loans you IP address space while you remain its customer. You must return the addresses to the ISP if you change providers. If you have a large organization and correspondingly large deployment of IP addresses, this transition could be very painful.

Address Resolution Protocol (ARP) A protocol within the TCP/ IP family that resolves an IP address into a 48-bit MAC address. The inverse process—resolving a MAC address into an IP address—is called Reverse ARP (RARP).

ADSL See *Asymmetric Digital Subscriber Line*.

ADSL Transmission Unit (ATU) A device that converts the DSL signal for the terminal. An ATU-R is the customer's device, and the ATU-C is device in the telecom's central office.

Aggregation Allocating a large IP address block to an ISP, which enables the ISP to advertise the addresses by a single route table entry.

Alternate Mark Inversion (AMI) A line coding standard used on T1 circuits in North America. This older standard has since been replaced by B8ZS.

American Registry for Internet Numbers (ARIN) One of the regional registries charged by the Internet Assigned Numbers Authority with distributing and assigning IP numbers for networks in North America, South America, the Caribbean, and sub-Saharan Africa. Also see *Internet Assigned Numbers Authority*.

AMI See *Alternate Mark Inversion.*

APNIC See *Asia Pacific Network Information Center.*

ARIN See *American Registry for Internet Numbers.*

ARP See *Address Resolution Protocol.*

AS See *Autonomous System.*

Asia Pacific Network Information Center (APNIC) One of the regional registries charged by the Internet Assigned Numbers Authority with distributing and assigning IP numbers for networks located in Asia and Pacific Rim countries. Also see *Internet Assigned Numbers Authority.*

Asymmetric Digital Subscriber Line (ADSL) A new generation of digital phone service that can provide data transmission rates approaching 8 Mbps in the downstream direction from the central office and 1.5 Mbps in the upstream direction.

ATU See *ADSL transmission unit.*

Authentication A security process in which only verified users may send and receive packets through your Internet connection. Authentication systems identify the user of the connection.

Autonomous System (AS) A self-contained routing domain defined by the Border Gateway Protocol.

B8ZS See *Binary Eight Zero Substitution.*

Bandwidth The data bit rate throughput in a network or telecommunications circuit. Bandwidth is typically measured in units of bits/second (bps), kilobits/second (Kbps), megabits/second (Mbps), and gigabits/second (Gbps). Note that the measurement is in bits/second, not bytes/second.

Basic Rate Interface (BRI) A type of ISDN circuit consisting of two B channels and one D channel. The standard ISDN service deployed by telecoms to homes and offices, it is sometimes called 2B+D service.

Bastion hosts A security term used to describe hosts and servers that are assumed to be expendable if compromised. Optimally these devices are placed on a separate network apart from your internal network resources.

B channel See *Bearer channel.*

Bearer channel (B channel) The 64 Kbps circuit-switched channel in an ISDN circuit that carries digitized voice or data.

BGP See *Border Gateway Protocol.*

Binary Eight Zero Substitution (B8ZS) A line coding standard used on T1 circuits in North America. It replaces an older standard called AMI.

BOOTP See *Bootstrap Protocol.*

Bootstrap Protocol (BOOTP) A protocol within the TCP/IP family that enables a network device with a MAC address to obtain an IP address during its boot cycle. The administrator must configure a server to provide the same IP address to each network device as it boots.

Border Gateway Protocol (BGP) A TCP/IP protocol used in the Internet to exchange route information between routers. It is the standard routing protocol in the Internet.

BRI See *Basic Rate Interface.*

Broadcast A class of packets that are addressed to all other nodes on a network. Broadcasting is a method of communicating the same data to every node on a network simultaneously.

CA See *Certificate Authority.*

CAP See *Carrierless Amplitude/Phase Modulation.*

Carrierless Amplitude/Phase Modulation (CAP) A proposed standard for the modulation scheme in ADSL. A competing modulation scheme, discrete multi tone (DMT), was the adopted standard.

CBR See *Constant Bit Rate.*

CCITT See *Comité Consultatif International de Telegraphique et Telephonique.*

Central Office (CO) The nearest facility of the telecom.

Certificate Authority (CA) A third party responsible for verifying the integrity of a sender's public key. The CA is an integral part of public-key encryption, which is used today in virtual private networks and secure sockets layer.

Channel Service Unit (CSU) A device that performs control and protective functions on a T- or E-carrier circuit. Specifically, it provides line coding and framing for a data circuit.

CIR See *Committed Information Rate.*

Circuit proxy A device used to implement secure communication between interior network devices and the Internet.

CO See *Central office.*

Comité Consultatif International de Telegraphique et Telephonique (CCITT) Former name of the International Telecommunication Union. The name changed on March 1, 1993.

Committed burst size (Bc) The maximum burst rate that the telecom will support on a Frame Relay circuit.

Committed Information Rate (CIR) The sustained data transmission rate that the telecom will support on a Frame Relay circuit.

Community strings Passwords used by the Simple Network Management Protocol (SNMP). Two types of community strings exist, the "write" and the "read" string.

Connectionless Network technologies for which the delivery of packets is not guaranteed. These devices transmit information without first establishing that the receiver is ready to accept it. Moreover, receiving stations do not acknowledge their receipt of information.

Constant Bit Rate (CBR) Voice and video data that flows at a steady rate with regular time intervals between packets.

Convergence (1) When a neighboring router receives the routing updates, which can consist of many packets, it processes this information and then enters it into its own routing table. After some time, the routing table on each router in the network ceases to change, which means that the routing tables have reached a state of convergence. (2) Digital convergence refers to networking technologies such as ATM that support simultaneous transmission of voice, video, and data.

CPE See *Customer Premises Equipment.*

CSU See *Channel Service Unit.*

Customer premises equipment (CPE) The networking and telecommunications equipment at a customer's site. Equipment such as CSU/DSUs and routers are considered CPE.

D4 A framing standard used on T-carrier circuits. It has been replaced by a newer scheme called ESF.

Datagram A data packet that is transmitted on a network without any regard for sequencing or ordering of packets. The correct order of the packets is reestablished by the receiving station. In TCP/IP, the user datagram protocol (UDP) employs datagram transmission.

Data Link Connection Identifier (DLCI) A header field in a Frame Relay packet that identifies the virtual circuit in which the packet is being transmitted.

Data link layer The second layer of the OSI Reference Model. Functions within the data link layer regulate access to network, providing for communications between devices on the same network (such as NICs). Bridging occurs at this layer.

Data Service Unit (DSU) A device that converts digital data from a router into voltages and encoding for a T- or E-carrier circuit.

D channel See *Delta channel.*

Default action The action that a network access control device should take with a packet that does not meet any previously defined security policies. If the packet filter or firewall has checked the defined policies and still does not know what to do with a packet, the default action specifies whether to forward it (permit) or toss it out (deny). Denying the packet is the recommended action.

Default route The network of last resort in a routing table. Any packet that the router does not match with an entry in its forward table is sent to the gateway listed for the default route. The default route is usually 0.0.0.0 with a mask of 0.0.0.0. This route normally forwards traffic to the ISP.

Default stance The philosophy that defines your security policies. Effectively, only one stance is recommended: All packets are denied except those expressly permitted. This approach would permit services between hosts that have been defined in a policy; all other traffic is denied and dropped.

Delta channel (D channel) The control channel on an ISDN circuit. On a BRI circuit, the D channel is 16 Kbps. On a PRI circuit, it is 64 Kbps.

Demarcation The point in your facility where you connect your equipment to the telecom's network.

Demilitarized Zone (DMZ) The network in between the Internet and your interior networks. Not all Internet connections deploy a DMZ network. The DMZ is also known as the perimeter network. Typically, the servers you share with the Internet reside on the perimeter network.

Denial of Service (DoS) An actual attack in which your Internet connection or some other system in your network is rendered unusable or destroyed. Such attacks are deliberately intended to break systems.

DHCP See *Dynamic Host Configuration Protocol.*

Directory Number (DN) An ISDN term for the "phone number" associated with a piece of ISDN equipment. Usually you are assigned one DN for each B channel within an basic rate interface circuit. This number appears as a normal phone number. When your ISDN equipment dials the ISP's equipment, it dials the DN of the ISP.

Discrete Multitone Modulation (DMT) A standard for the modulation scheme in ADSL. The competing modulation scheme was carrierless amplitude phase (CAP).

DLCI See *Data Link Connection Identifier.*

DMT See *Discrete Multitone Modulation.*

DMZ See *Demilitarized Zone.*

DN See *Directory Number.*

DNS See *Domain Name System.*

Domain Name System (DNS) The modern mechanism for workstations and systems running TCP/IP to resolve a name into a unique IP address. For instance, if you entered http://www.awl.com in your web browser, the DNS functions within the TCP/IP software of your workstation resolve this name to the IP address 192.207.117.2.

DoS See *Denial of Service.*

DSU See *Data Service Unit.*

Dynamic Host Configuration Protocol (DHCP) A protocol that dynamically allocates an IP address to a workstation for some predetermined length of time known as a lease. BOOTP was the predecessor to DHCP.

Dynamic ports A range of ports in TCP. According to the Internet Assigned Numbers Authority, the dynamic and/or private ports are those from 49152 through 65535.

Encryption A process in which data is encrypted into an unreadable format before being transmitted across a network—namely, the Internet.

ESF See *Extended Super Frame.*

Established A TCP connection in which the ACK bit is set to 1 in the packets. You can therefore test a TCP packet to determine if it is part of an established session. The only packet that does not have the ACK bit set in the TCP conversation is the initial packet requesting the setup. Many firewalls implement security policies by applying this test.

Extended Super Frame (ESF) A framing format for T-carrier circuits in North America.

Exterior Networks and objects that reside outside of your interior networks and perimeter network (if applicable). For all practical purposes, the Internet represents the exterior.

Exterior router The router immediately connecting your site to the Internet.

FCS See *Frame Control Sequence.*

File Transfer Protocol (FTP) A client-server protocol that allows a user on one computer to transfer files to and from another computer over a TCP/IP network. Also, the client program that the user executes to transfer files. Anonymous FTP allows users to log in as "anonymous." (Definition from the Free Online Dictionary of Computing found at http://nightflight.com/foldoc.)

FIN See *Finish.*

Finger A program that displays information about a particular user or all users logged onto the system or a remote system. It typically shows the full name, last login time, idle time, terminal line, and terminal location (where applicable). (Definition from the Free Online Dictionary of Computing found at http://nightflight.com/foldoc.)

Finish (FIN) When a TCP session needs to be closed, the station closing the connection sets the "finish" (FIN) bit to 1 in the flags portion of the TCP header. It results in another modified three-way handshake that closes the session.

Firewall A system or group of systems that enforces security policies. Firewall systems may consists of packet filters, circuit proxies, and application gateways. The term also denotes a new generation of products that enable you to implement security.

Flattening The creation of large IP subnets in switched networks without impacting performance via switched packet networks and high-speed uplinks to routers.

Forwarding table A routing table that contains a list of all available networks learned by the router plus any other information added by an administrator.

Fragmentation The break-up of packets into pieces for transmission in various networks. Some technologies, such as FDDI, support much larger packet sizes than others, such as Ethernet. Some fragments can be so small as to be impractical, but are otherwise allowed through a security filter. Attackers can sometimes create peculiar fragment sequences to sneak otherwise disallowed packets past the filter. You should disallow fragmented packets through your firewall.

Frame To actually transmit at the data link layer, a packet must be placed within a frame that includes other information particular to the network technology used (example, Ethernet, FDDI). All frame headers lead with a data link control (DLC) section containing the destination MAC address and source MAC address.

Frame Control Sequence (FCS), Frame Check Sequence The ending portion of a frame following the data payload that contains checksum information on the frame itself.

Frame header The leading portion of a frame, which contains the data link control and sometimes the logical link control (LLC) and subnetwork access protocol (SNAP), depending on the frame type. The data payload follows the frame header.

Frame Relay A packet switching technology commonly used for WAN connections. It is an extension of the venerable X.25 technology, which was slow, but extremely reliable because of its error checking. Unlike a point-to-point circuit, which contains only two endpoints, a Frame Relay network consists of many nodes sharing the same physical network. For this reason, Frame Relay is also known as a point-to-multipoint technology.

Framing The specification of how electronic signaling on a T-1 circuit is divided into 24 DS-0 channels, plus how the communication on the T-1 circuit is controlled. Two options for framing exist: D4 or Extended Superframe Format (ESF). ESF is the standard.

FTP See *File Transfer Protocol*.

G.703 A standard defined by the ITU for transmission facilities running at 2.048 Mbps (E-1) and 64 Kbps. (Definition from the Free Online Dictionary of Computing found at http://nightflight.com/foldoc.)

Gateway (1) In IP networks, a router. See *Router*. (2) The IP address of the first router that can forward a packet toward the destination address.

Generic Routing Encapsulation (GRE) An IP protocol used for tunneling. It is the basis of the point-to-point tunneling protocol used in many virtual private networks.

GRE See *Generic Routing Encapsulation*.

Hop count See *Metric*.

HTTP See *Hypertext Transfer Protocol*.

HTTPS See *Hypertext Transfer Protocol, Secure*.

Hypertext Transfer Protocol (HTTP) The client-server TCP/IP protocol used on the World Wide Web for the exchange of HTML documents. It traditionally uses port 80. (Definition from the Free Online Dictionary of Computing found at http://nightflight.com/foldoc.)

Hypertext Transfer Protocol, Secure (HTTPS) A secure version of HTTP. HTTPS uses Secure Sockets Layer (SSL) to encrypt the data within the HTTP packet to ensure that no one listens to your network conversation. The default HTTPS port number is 443.

IANA See *Internet Assigned Numbers Authority*.

ICMP See *Internet Control Message Protocol*.

IETF See *Internet Engineering Task Force*.

IGRP See *Interior Gateway Routing Protocol*.

IMAP4 See *Internet Message Access Protocol Version 4*.

Information theft A serious hack in which some piece of valuable information is gleaned from your network or its systems. This type of crime is the domain of industrial and governmental espionage.

Initial Sequence Number (ISN) During the setup of a TCP session, which is called a three-way handshake, both stations send one another an initial sequence number. For each packet that follows, the ISN is incremented by 1. By examining the ISN, the receiving station can determine whether the packet was received in the order it was sent.

Integrated Services Digital Network (ISDN) A global telecommunications standard for digital circuit switched voice and data.

Interior The networks and objects that reside inside of your Internet connection. For all practical purposes, the Internet represents the exterior.

Interior Gateway Routing Protocol (IGRP) A proprietary routing protocol developed by Cisco Systems for routing TCP/IP in large networks. IGRP is a distance-vector routing protocol like RIP. Unlike RIP, which uses only one metric (hop count) to find the "best" path to the destination, IGRP provides five metrics. Enhanced IGRP (eIGRP) supports TCP/IP, IPX, and AppleTalk and includes additional features to make it behave more like a link-state routing protocol. Thus eIGRP offers quicker convergence than its predecessor and no broadcasts between routers. When changes occur in the network topology, they are communicated immediately.

Interior router In a network architecture that includes a perimeter network between the Internet and the interior networks, the router connecting the perimeter network to the interior networks. The router connecting the perimeter network to the Internet constitutes the exterior router.

International Standards Organization (ISO) An organization located in Paris, France, that manages the ratification and acceptance of standards for international and national data communications.

International Telecommunications Union (ITU) A global organization that oversees the creation and ratification of telecommunication standards.

Internet Assigned Numbers Authority (IANA) An organization that manages the assignment of unique values for Internet protocols, including IP addresses, domain names, and other things such as port numbers. IANA is assisted by regional registries, which perform the daily tasks of allocating addresses to ISPs and end users.

Internet Control Message Protocol (ICMP) A helper protocol within TCP/IP that provides the following functions: flow control, detection of unreachable destinations, redirection of routes, and checking of remote hosts. ICMP operates at the network layer, which makes sense considering that its function is to control routing.

Internet Engineering Task Force (IETF) An organization that concerns itself with Internet standards, and particularly with all things branded TCP/IP. Items that fall into this category include routing protocols and addressing schemes. The IETF is also responsible for the Request for Comments (RFC) process, in which exciting new ideas about Internetworking become real entities. It attempts to ensure that all players in the Internet can intercommunicate so that things run smoothly.

Internet Exchange Point (IXP) A facility where ISPs connect their networks to those of other ISPs. Also known as a peering location.

Internet Message Access Protocol Version 4 (IMAP4) A protocol allowing a client to access and manipulate electronic mail messages on a server. It permits manipulation of remote message folders (mailboxes) in a way that is functionally equivalent to local mailboxes. (Definition from the Free Online Dictionary of Computing found at http://nightflight.com/foldoc.)

Internet Network Information Center (InterNIC) An organization that is responsible for administering root-level DNS information in the Internet.

Internet Protocol (IP) The network layer protocol that provides Internetworking addressing and routing functions. The current version of IP used in the Internet is version 4 (IPv4).

Internet Service Provider (ISP) An organization that provides Internet connectivity to customers through a private network infrastructure. A handful of large ISPs maintain portions of the Internet backbone and sell connectivity to other ISPs.

Internet Society (ISOC) A professional membership organization of Internet experts that comments on policies and practices and oversees a number of other boards and task forces dealing with network policy issues.

InterNIC See *Internet Network Information Center.*

Inter-Packet Exchange/Sequenced Packet Exchange, (IPX/SPX) The communication protocol developed by Novell Corporation for use with its NetWare operating system.

Intrusion A blanket term describing an event in which an unauthorized party gains access to your network, its components, and resources.

It is commonly called a hack. Intrusion events run the gamut from being relatively benign to really destructive.

IP See *Internet Protocol*.

IP header In a TCP/IP packet, the first portion of the payload. The header contains a number of fields, including the destination and source IP addresses, protocol, and time-to-live.

IPsec See *Secure IP*.

IPX/SPX See *Inter-Packet Exchange/Sequenced Packet Exchange*.

ISDN See *Integrated Services Digital Network*.

ISN See *Initial Sequence Number*.

ISO See *International Standards Organization*.

ISOC See *Internet Society*.

ISP See *Internet Service Provider*.

ITU See *International Telecommunications Union*.

IXP See *Internet Exchange Point*.

LAN See *Local Area Network*.

Latency Describes the travel time of a packet between its source and destination; usually measured in milliseconds (ms).

LDAP See *Lightweight Directory Access Protocol*.

Lease The period during which an IP address is allocated to a client via the Dynamic Host Configuration Protocol.

Lightweight Directory Access Protocol (LDAP) A relatively simple protocol for updating and searching directories running over TCP/IP. (Definition from the Free Online Dictionary of Computing found at http://nightflight.com/foldoc.)

LMI See *Local Management Interface*.

Local Area Network (LAN) A limited-distance, high-speed network that supports many computers (typically ranging from two to several thousand). LANs generally are geographically localized to buildings or floors within buildings. Network speeds within LANs range from 10 Mbps for Ethernet to about 1,000 Mbps for Gigabit Ethernet.

Local Management Interface (LMI) A control protocol found on Frame Relay circuits used by devices to communicate circuit health and status information.

Lookups One of two activities in DNS, in which a client asks a server to resolve a name. It also refers to the process in which a server asks another server to resolve a name.

Loop test A diagnostic typically used on WAN circuits, in which a signal is sent from one device and "reflected" back to the sender from another device. It helps determine where faults lie within a circuit.

During a loop test, the reflecting device is placed in loopback mode. Equipment such as CSU/DSUs have loopback functions.

MAC See *Media Access Control.*

Mail Exchange record (MX record) A component in DNS that helps Internet mail servers send messages to the proper receiving server.

Management Information Base (MIB) A set of parameters that an SNMP management station can query or set in the SNMP agent of a network device (for example, router). (Definition from the Free Online Dictionary of Computing found at http://nightflight.com/foldoc.)

Mask A bit mask used to identify which bits in an IP address correspond to the network address and subnet portions of the address. This mask is often referred to as the subnet mask, because the network portion of the address can be determined by the class inherent in an IP address. The address mask has 1s in positions corresponding to the network and subnet numbers and 0s in the host number positions. (Definition from the Free Online Dictionary of Computing found at http://nightflight.com/foldoc.)

Maximum Transmission Unit (MTU) The largest-size frame that may be transmitted on a network. The MTU for Ethernet is typically 1,518 bytes, while for FDDI it is 4,544 bytes.

MBone See *Multimedia Backbone.*

Media Access Control (MAC) address A 48-bit data link layer address assigned by equipment manufacturers to network interface cards (NICs) in workstations or any other device that communicates on a packet-based network. The MAC address for each device is unique. No two devices (in theory) should have the same MAC address.

Metric The number of routers between the host's network and the destination network. Sometimes called the hop count.

MIB See *Management Information Base.*

MTU See *Maximum Transmission Unit.*

Multicast A classification including packets that are addressed to a predefined group of nodes on a network, but not necessarily to all of the nodes. Multicast is an efficient method of broadcasting packets only to those nodes that are interested in the contents.

Multimedia Backbone (MBone) An experimental IP multicast network that provides real-time transmissions of voice and video. Like cable TV, the MBone provides various multicasts pertaining to a myriad of subjects.

MX record See *Mail Exchange record.*

NAT See *Network Address Translation.*

Network Address Translation (NAT) A technology in which one or more globally unique IP addresses speak for other local IP addresses in your LAN. The global IP sits on the Internet side of the device. When IP hosts in your LANs exchange packets with Internet hosts, the NAT device intercepts these packets and either (1) replaces the source address with its own when the packet is outbound or (2) inserts the local IP address into the packet when it is inbound. Local IP addresses are assigned from a pool of reusable addresses. The recommended practice is to use the private addresses designated by IANA, which include the 10.0.0.0, 172.16.0.0–172.31.255.255, and 192.168.0.0–192.168.255.255 networks.

Network File System (NFS) A protocol developed by Sun Microsystems, which allows a computer to access files over a network as if they were on its local disks. This protocol has been incorporated in products by more than 200 companies, and is now a de facto standard. (Definition from the Free Online Dictionary of Computing found at http://nightflight.com/foldoc.)

Network layer The third layer of the OSI Reference Model. It handles network addressing and routing of data.

Network News Transfer Protocol (NNTP) A protocol for the distribution, inquiry, retrieval, and posting of Usenet news articles over the Internet. It is designed to be used between a news reader client and a news server. (Definition from the Free Online Dictionary of Computing found at http://nightflight.com/foldoc.)

Network Service Provider (NSP) An organization that maintains its own portion of Internet backbone. Typically, NSPs are large companies that maintain global networks and sell Internet service in many countries. They are also called tier one Internet service providers.

Network Termination (NT) A device used to connect ISDN equipment to the telecom's network.

NFS See *Network File System.*

NNTP See *Network News Transfer Protocol.*

NSP See *Network Service Provider.*

NT See *Network Termination.*

Open Shortest Path First (OSPF) A link-state routing protocol used for TCP/IP. OSPF is used within large networks to replace the distance-vector routing protocol RIP. Compared with RIP, OSPF has the advantage of quicker convergence plus significantly reduced broad-

casting between routers. Also, it provides better multipath routing
with the addition of route costing.

Open Systems Interconnect (OSI) Reference Model A seven-layer system
in which each layer has a specific job in supporting network
communications.

OSI See *Open Systems Interconnect.*

OSPF See *Open Shortest Path First.*

Oversubscription When an ISP sells you a connection to its network, it
makes an assumption that you will use only a portion of the leased
circuit capacity at your site. You may have moments of peak traffic,
but on balance your utilization of the WAN circuit will be lower
than its rated capacity. Consequently, ISPs oversell their available
capacity to the Internet.

Packet A (layer 3) unit of data exchanged between network devices.

Packet filtering A network access control technology in which components of the TCP/IP header are compared with a list of rules. If
a packet's header matches a rule, then the action of that rule is
executed, such as forwarding or dropping the packet. If a packet
does not match any rule, the default action is executed.

Passive (PASV) Passive FTP, a variation on the standard FTP. In passive
FTP, the client initiates both the command and data channel to the
server. PASV is a command sent from the client to the server, asking
for the destination port of the data channel on the server.

PASV See *Passive.*

Payload The data portion of a packet or frame.

PDU See *Protocol Data Unit.*

Perimeter network The network found between the Internet and your
interior networks. Not all Internet connections deploy a perimeter
network, which is also known as the demilitarized zone (DMZ).
Typically, the servers you share with the Internet reside on the
perimeter network.

Permanent Virtual Circuit (PVC) The most common type of Frame Relay
circuit.

Physical layer The first layer of the OSI Reference Model. It defines the
electrical characteristics between the network medium and the network device, including wiring and signaling.

Point-of-Presence (POP) A location where a telecom or ISP provides
connectivity to its customers. In the telecommunications arena, a
POP is a location where long-distance vendors connect to local
service providers. In Internet connectivity, a POP is a location

where the customers connect to an ISP's network.

Point-to-Point Protocol (PPP) The Internet standard for transmitting network layer datagrams (for example, IP packets) over serial point-to-point links. PPP can be configured to encapsulate different network layer protocols, such as IP, IPX, or AppleTalk. (Definition from the Free Online Dictionary of Computing found at http://nightflight.com/foldoc.)

Point-to-Point Tunneling Protocol (PPTP) A tunneling protocol commonly used in virtual private networks that provides encryption in the tunnel.

POP See *Point-of-Presence.*

POP3 See *Post Office Protocol Version 3.*

Port A logical channel or channel endpoint in a communications system. The TCP and UDP transport layer protocols use port numbers to distinguish between (demultiplex) different logical channels on the same network interface on the same computer. Each application program has a unique port number associated with it. Some protocols, such as Telnet and HTTP (which is actually a special form of Telnet), have default ports but can use other ports as well. (Definition from the Free Online Dictionary of Computing found at http://nightflight.com/foldoc.)

Port speed The maximum data rate on a Frame Relay circuit.

Post Office Protocol Version 3 (POP3) A protocol that allows a client computer to retrieve electronic mail from a POP3 server via a (temporary) TCP/IP connection. It does not provide for sending mail, which is assumed to be done via SMTP or some other method. (Definition from the Free Online Dictionary of Computing found at http://nightflight.com/foldoc.)

PPP See *Point-to-Point Protocol.*

PPTP See *Point-to-Point Tunneling Protocol.*

Presentation layer The sixth layer of the OSI Reference Model. Technically, it provides standard data presentation routines for cooperating applications to exchange data. In TCP/IP, no functions are defined at this layer.

PRI See *Primary Rate Interface.*

Primary Rate Interface (PRI) A type of ISDN circuit built on a T- or E-carrier circuit. In North America the PRI is 23B+D service, while in Europe it is 30B+D service.

Private key A secret key held by a device taking part in an encrypted communication. Also see *public-key encryption.*

Protocol Data Unit (PDU) A packet of data passed across a network. The term implies a specific layer of the OSI seven-layer model and a specific protocol. (Definition from the Free Online Dictionary of Computing found at http://nightflight.com/foldoc.)

Provisioning In telecommunications the process of placing an order, and installing and testing a WAN circuit.

Public key A shared key held by a device taking part in an encrypted communication. Also see *public-key encryption.*

Public-key encryption A type of encryption in which each node possesses two keys: a public key that it shares with other nodes and a private key that it does not share. The nodes exchange public keys, and then use a third party called a certificate authority (CA) to verify the integrity of the sender's public key. Each node then generates a secret key by combining its private key with the sender's public key. The resultant secret keys are identical, and a third party cannot forge this secret key.

PVC See *Permanent Virtual Circuit.*

QoS See *Quality of Service.*

Quality of Service (QoS) Guaranteed available bandwidth, delay, and transmit priority in shared networks.

RADIUS See *Remote Authentication Dial-In User Service.*

RARP See *Reverse Address Resolution Protocol.*

Registered ports A range of ports in TCP. According to the Internet Assigned Numbers Authority, the registered ports are those from 1024 to 49151.

Remote Authentication Dial-In User Service (RADIUS) A method for authenticating user identities that involves submitting a user name and a digital hash of the password. Usually the user name and password are tested against these values held on a Remote Authentication Dial-In User Service (RADIUS) system, in the operating system, or internally in the firewall.

Remote Monitoring (RMON) A system in which a device (usually called a probe) collects data link layer information from a network much like an analyzer. Typically an RMON probe collects data and then transfers it with a management workstation via SNMP. RMON also describes the contents of an SNMP MIB. An extension called RMON II enables probes to collect network layer information as well.

Remote Procedure Call (RPC) A protocol that allows a program running on one host to cause code to be executed on another host without the programmer explicitly coding for this event. RPC is an easy-to-use and popular paradigm for implementing the client-server model of distributed computing. (Definition from the Free Online Dictionary of Computing found at http://nightflight.com/foldoc.)

Request for Comments (RFC) A forum in which new technologies, methods, and ideas for Internet related items can be discussed online. Typically, RFCs become standards for Internet technologies.

Réseaux IP Européens—Network Coordination Center (RIPE NCC) for Europe One of the regional registries tasked by the Internet Assigned Numbers Authority to distribute and assign IP numbers for networks in Europe and surrounding countries. Also see *Internet Assigned Numbers Authority.*

Reset When a TCP session needs to be closed, a station sets the "finish" (FIN) bit to 1, which results in another modified three-way handshake that closes the session. Another way of shutting down the connection (rather abruptly) is for a station to set the "try again" (RESET) bit to 1, which forces the initiator to reestablish the connection.

Resolve The DNS lookup process in which a client asks a server to resolve a name to an IP address, or an IP address to a name.

Reverse Address Resolution Protocol (RARP) The inverse process of resolving a MAC address into an IP address. ARP is a protocol that resolves an IP address into a 48-bit MAC address.

RFC See *Request for Comments.*

RIP See *Routing Information Protocol.*

RIPE NCC See *Réseaux IP Européens—Network Coordination Center.*

RMON See *Remote Monitoring.*

Router A network device that examines the network layer addresses (IP addresses) within a packet, and then forwards the packet toward the destination based on these values.

Routing The process of guiding (forwarding) a packet through a series of networks based on its network layer address.

Routing Information Protocol (RIP) A network layer protocol used by routers to learn and disseminate information about paths to destination networks and hosts. RIP is commonly used in TCP/IP. This distance-vector routing protocol provides a "best" path to the destination by calculating the minimum number of hop counts. It is standard for each RIP router to broadcast its routing table to other routers every 30 seconds.

Routing table A forwarding table that contains a list of all available networks learned by the router plus any other information added by an administrator.

RPC See *Remote Procedure Call.*

RS232 The most common asynchronous serial line standard. RS232 specifies the gender and pin use of connectors, but not their physical type. (Definition from the Free Online Dictionary of Computing found at http://nightflight.com/foldoc.)

RS449 The Electronics Industry Association's (EIA) recommendation for an interface between the 37 pin and the 9 pin. (Definition from the Free Online Dictionary of Computing found at http://nightflight.com/foldoc.)

Screened subnet A network architecture used for Internet connections in which a perimeter network is placed between the interior networks and the Internet. The perimeter network is the screened subnet.

Screening router A router in the screened host subnet architecture. In this setup, two screening routers filter traffic between your interior networks and the Internet. The router facing the Internet is your exterior router, while the one attached to your interior network is the interior router. The network in between is called the perimeter network or demilitarized zone (DMZ). The servers you share with the outside world reside on the perimeter network. These servers are also named bastion hosts, as they are assumed to be expendable if compromised.

Secret key In public-key encryption, a key generated by combining a node's private key with the sender's public key. The resultant secret keys are identical and cannot be forged by a third party.

Secure IP (IPsec) The standard protocol for encryption in VPNs. It includes a number of features that make it the preferred method of deploying security within VPNs, such as standards for encryption and encapsulation of the entire packet into the tunneled packet. In addition, it authenticates that the sending station is indeed the proper sender.

Secure Sockets Layer (SSL) A protocol designed by Netscape Communications Corporation to provide encrypted communications on the Internet. SSL is layered beneath application protocols such as HTTP, SMTP, Telnet, FTP, Gopher, and NNTP and layered above the connection protocol TCP/IP. It is used by the HTTPS access method. (Definition from the Free Online Dictionary of Computing found at http://nightflight.com/foldoc.)

Sequencing A feature in TCP whereby packets are processed by the receiving application as they were sent. Also see *Initial Sequence Number.*

Service-Level Agreement (SLA) An agreement between two parties in which one party guarantees to the other minimum performance standards for specified services. It is now common for ISPs to offer SLAs to their customers regarding uptime and network accessibility.

Service Profile Identifier (SPID) A key piece of provisioning information that identifies each B channel in an ISDN circuit. These identifiers often appear as telephone numbers with 0000 or 0101 appended to the end. Typically, you configure your ISDN equipment with these values so it can communicate with the ISDN switch in the central office. Failure to configure the SPIDs exactly as indicated by the telecom results in a nonfunctioning ISDN circuit.

Session A conversion in which applications communicate using TCP.

Session layer The sixth layer of the OSI Reference Model. Technically, it manages the connections between cooperating applications. In TCP/IP, no functions are defined at this layer.

Simple Key Management for Internet Protocols A protocol that established session keys to use with IPsec protocol headers. (Definition from *Internet Cryptography* by Richard E. Smith.)

Simple Mail Transfer Protocol (SMTP) A protocol used to transfer electronic mail between computers, usually over a network (such as the Internet). It is a server-to-server protocol, so other protocols are used to access the messages. The SMTP dialog usually takes place in the background under the control of the message transport system (for example, sendmail), but it is possible to interact with an SMTP server using Telnet to connect to the normal SMTP port, 25. (Definition from the Free Online Dictionary of Computing found at http://nightflight.com/foldoc.)

Simple Network Management Protocol (SNMP) The Internet standard developed to manage nodes on an IP network. SNMP is not limited to TCP/IP. Also see *Management information base (MIB).* (Definition from the Free Online Dictionary of Computing found at http://nightflight.com/foldoc.)

SKIP See *Simple Key Management for Internet Protocols.*

SLA *See Service-Level Agreement.*

Small Office and Home Office (SOHO) A market segment characterized by high-volume, commodity products such as NICs, small repeaters, and switches.

SMDS See *Switched Multimegabit Data Service.*

SMTP See *Simple Mail Transfer Protocol.*

SNMP See *Simple Network Management Protocol.*

Socket The Berkeley UNIX mechanism for creating a virtual connection between processes. The socket is associated with a socket address, consisting of a port number and the local host's network address. (Definition from the Free Online Dictionary of Computing found at http://nightflight.com/foldoc.)

SOCKS A client-server architecture for circuit proxies. Originally developed by David Koblas, it is now under the stewardship of NEC. SOCKS software is used to secure Internet connections.

SOHO See *Small Office and Home Office.*

SONET See *Synchronous Optical Network.*

SPID See *Service Profile Identifier.*

Split DNS An architecture in which two copies of a DNS database are maintained; one resolving names for interior users, the other resolving names for Internet users. Typically, the naming information on the exterior server is a subset of the interior server.

SSL See *Secure Sockets Layer.*

Stateful inspection Invented and patented by CheckPoint Technologies, the network access control mechanism used by most firewall products today. In particular, a network access control system using stateful inspection looks for information within the packets indicating the state of communication between hosts. In most cases, this information can be gleaned only by looking deep into a packet's payload and examining all protocol layers (for example, the application layer).

Static route A route added administratively to a router, and not learned from other routers.

Subnet mask See *Mask.*

SVC See *Switched Virtual Circuit.*

Switched Multimegabit Data Service (SMDS) A circuit technology used by telecoms for providing network services to customers. SMDS is also known as Cell Relay. It competes with other circuit technologies, such as Frame Relay.

Switched Virtual Circuit (SVC) A type of Frame Relay circuit in which connectivity between network nodes is built for a session, and then destroyed when no longer needed. The other type of Frame Relay circuit is the permanent virtual circuit (PVC).

SYN See *Synchronize Sequence Numbers*.

Synchronize Sequence Numbers (SYN) During a TCP connection setup (called a three-way handshake), the process in which the initiating station sends a packet to the destination with the SYN bit set to 1 in the header flags.

Synchronous Optical Network (SONET) A transport technology used by telecoms for digital transmission over fiber infrastructures. SONET transmission rates are called *optical carriers (OC-n)*.

SYN flooding A particular type of denial-of-service attack. By flooding packets at a server with the SYN flag set, a hacker will force a server to allocate memory for multiple incoming connections. By not completing the handshake, the server is left with half-open connections. Eventually the server will exhaust its memory pool and either deny any new connections or crash.

TCP See *Transmission Control Protocol*.

Telnet See *Terminal Emulation over a Network*.

Terminal Emulation over a Network (Telnet) A protocol and application used for remote login. The Telnet application uses the protocol and acts as a terminal emulator for the remote login session.

TFTP See *Trivial Transfer File Protocol*.

Three-way handshake The process of setting up a conversation between applications that communicate using TCP. The handshake ensures that a connection exists with the destination station and that the destination station is ready to receive data.

Throughput See *Bandwidth*.

Time-to-Live (TTL) (1) A field in the IP header that prevents packets from circulating indefinitely through an IP network after encountering a routing loop. When an IP packet is forwarded by a router, the router decrements the TTL by 1. (2) A component of a routing table element. The TTL specifies how much longer a particular entry in the routing table will remain valid.

Transmission Control Protocol (TCP) A transport layer protocol that establishes a connection between cooperating applications. TCP is a connection-oriented protocol that provides reliable data delivery.

Transport layer The fourth layer of the OSI Reference Model. In TCP/IP, this layer provides a reliable connection between hosts and programs. It also provides flow control, acknowledgment, sequencing, and checksum functions.

Trivial Transfer File Protocol (TFTP) A TCP/IP file transfer protocol for downloading operational boot code to routers, switches, and diskless workstation. Unlike FTP, this protocol does not include authentication via user name and password. Consequently, it is inherently insecure.

TTL See *Time-to-Live*.

UDP See *User Datagram Protocol*.

Unicast A classification for packets that are addressed to a single destination. Most communication between a host and a server is unicast.

Uniform resource locator (URL) A standard for specifying the location of an object on the Internet, such as a file or a newsgroup. URLs are used extensively on the World Wide Web. In HTML documents, they specify the target of a hyperlink, which is often another HTML document (possibly stored on another computer). (Definition from the Free Online Dictionary of Computing found at http://nightflight.com/foldoc.)

URL See *Uniform Resource Locator*.

User Datagram Protocol (UDP) A transport layer protocol in TCP/IP that does not contain the acknowledgment, handshaking, and sequencing features found in TCP that enable reliable data delivery. Instead, UDP employs source and destination ports and dispenses with the overhead of the connection functions found in TCP.

V.35 The ITU-T standard for data transmission at 48 Kbps over the 60–108KHz group band circuits. It contains the 34-pin V.34 connector specifications normally implemented on a modular RJ-45 connector. (Definition from the Free Online Dictionary of Computing found at http://nightflight.com/foldoc.)

Value-Added Reseller (VAR) An organization that sells services, software, and network equipment to its customers. Unlike a network equipment or software manufacturer, a VAR offers services to assist the customer in the implementation process.

VAR See *Value-Added Reseller*.

Virtual Private Network (VPN) An IP tunnel set up between your site and another on the Internet. It carries network traffic as if it were a dedicated leased-line connection, such as a point-to-point circuit. VPNs take advantage of the Internet as a WAN backbone.

VPN See *Virtual Private Network*.

Well-known ports A range of ports in TCP. According to the Internet
Assigned Numbers Authority, the well-known ports are those from
0 to 1023. (Ports under 1024 can be used only by processes owned
by a server.)

Whois An Internet directory service for looking up names of people on
a remote server. (Definition from the Free Online Dictionary of
Computing found at http://nightflight.com/foldoc.)

X.21 A digital signaling interface recommended by ITU-T that includes
specifications for physical interface elements, alignment of call control characters and error checking, elements of the call control
phase for circuit switched services, data transfer up to 64 Kbps, and
test loops. (Definition from the Free Online Dictionary of
Computing found at http://nightflight.com/foldoc.)

X-Windows system A specification that enables the graphic output of
one device to be redirected to the display of another.

Zone transfer A DNS term that describes the transfer of the name database from a master server to secondary servers.

Index

Addison-Wesley Computer and Engineering Publishing Group

How to Interact with Us

1. Visit our Web site

http://www.awl.com/cseng

When you think you've read enough, there's always more content for you at Addison-Wesley's web site. Our web site contains a directory of complete product information including:

- Chapters
- Exclusive author interviews
- Links to authors' pages
- Tables of contents
- Source code

You can also discover what tradeshows and conferences Addison-Wesley will be attending, read what others are saying about our titles, and find out where and when you can meet our authors and have them sign your book.

2. Subscribe to Our Email Mailing Lists

Subscribe to our electronic mailing lists and be the first to know when new books are publishing. Here's how it works: Sign up for our electronic mailing at **http://www.awl.com/cseng/mailinglists.html**. Just select the subject areas that interest you and you will receive notification via email when we publish a book in that area.

3. Contact Us via Email

cepubprof@awl.com
Ask general questions about our books.
Sign up for our electronic mailing lists.
Submit corrections for our web site.

bexpress@awl.com
Request an Addison-Wesley catalog.
Get answers to questions regarding your order or our products.

innovations@awl.com
Request a current Innovations Newsletter.

webmaster@awl.com
Send comments about our web site.

cepubeditors@awl.com
Submit a book proposal.
Send errata for an Addison-Wesley book.

cepubpublicity@awl.com
Request a review copy for a member of the media interested in reviewing new Addison-Wesley titles.

We encourage you to patronize the many fine retailers who stock Addison-Wesley titles. Visit our online directory to find stores near you or visit our online store: **http://store.awl.com/** or call **800-824-7799**.

Addison Wesley Longman
Computer and Engineering Publishing Group
One Jacob Way, Reading, Massachusetts 01867 USA
TEL 781-944-3700 • FAX 781-942-3076